DEMOCRATISING THE EU FROM BELOW?

Democratising the EU from Below?
Citizenship, Civil Society and the Public Sphere

Edited by

ULRIKE LIEBERT
Jean Monnet Centre for European Studies, University of Bremen

ALEXANDER GATTIG
University of Bremen, Germany

TATJANA EVAS
European University Institute, Florence

ASHGATE

© Ulrike Liebert, Alexander Gattig and Tatjana Evas 2013

All rights reserved. No part of this publication may be reproduced, stored in a retrieval system or transmitted in any form or by any means, electronic, mechanical, photocopying, recording or otherwise without the prior permission of the publisher.

Ulrike Liebert, Alexander Gattig and Tatjana Evas have asserted their right under the Copyright, Designs and Patents Act, 1988, to be identified as the editors of this work.

Published by
Ashgate Publishing Limited
Wey Court East
Union Road
Farnham
Surrey, GU9 7PT
England

Ashgate Publishing Company
110 Cherry Street
Suite 3-1
Burlington, VT 05401-3818
USA

www.ashgate.com

British Library Cataloguing in Publication Data
Democratising the EU from below? : citizenship, civil society and the public sphere.
  1. Deliberative democracy–European Union countries.
  2. Political participation–European Union countries.
  3. Constitutional law–European Union countries. 4. Civil society–European Union countries.
  I. Liebert, Ulrike. II. Gattig, Alexander. III. Evas, Tatjana.
  321.8'094-dc23

The Library of Congress has cataloged the printed edition as follows:
Liebert, Ulrike.
Democratising the EU from below? : citizenship, civil society and the public sphere / by Ulrike Liebert, Alexander Gattig and Tatjana Evas.
   pages cm. – (Politics monographs)
   Includes bibliographical references and index.
   ISBN 978-1-4094-6413-6 (hardback) – ISBN 978-1-4094-6414-3 (ebook) – ISBN 978-1-4724-0830-3 (epub) 1. Political participation–European Union countries. 2. Democratization–European Union countries. 3. Civil society–European Union countries. I. Title.
   JN40.L54 2013
   320.94–dc23

2012047413

ISBN 9781409464136 (hbk)
ISBN 9781409464143 (ebk – PDF)
ISBN 9781472408303 (ebk – ePUB)

Printed in the United Kingdom by Henry Ling Limited, at the Dorset Press, Dorchester, DT1 1HD

Contents

List of Figures		*vii*
List of Graphs		*ix*
List of Tables		*xi*
List of Contributors		*xiii*
Preface		*xvii*
List of Abbreviations		*xix*
1	Democratising the EU from Below? Citizenship, Civil Society and the Public Sphere in Making Europe's Order Ulrike Liebert	1
2	Still 'between Eros and Civilisation'? Citizens, Courts and Constructing European Citizenship Tatjana Evas and Ulrike Liebert	23
3	Disaffected Citizens? Why People Vote in National Referendums about EU Treaty Reform Alexander Gattig and Steffen Blings	61
4	Ignorant Gatekeepers against the EU? v National Political Parties in European Political Communication Kathrin Packham	83
5	Watch-dogs that Cannot Bite? New National Parliamentary Control Mechanisms under the Lisbon Treaty. Aleksandra Maatsch	115
6	A Panacea for Democratic Legitimation? Assessing the Engagement of Civil Society with EU Treaty Reform Politics Petra Guasti	135
7	Still "Second Order?" Re-examining Citizens' Voting Behaviour in European and National Elections 1999–2009 Alexander Gattig, Ewelina Riekens and Ulrike Liebert	165
Index		*195*

List of Figures

2.1	The EU preliminary reference mechanism	33
2.2	Dynamics of European citizenship cases in the ECJ (1994–2011)	35
4.1	Factors explaining the quality of political parties' EU messages	89
4.2	Cube of political parties' European political communication patterns	95
4.3	Model I: strength of political party cues	97
4.4	Model III: revised: clarity of political party cues	101
6.1	Model of viable civic participation in the EU's multilevel polity	140
7.1	European and (preceding) national electoral turnout 2004, EU-27	174
7.2	European and (preceding) national electoral turnout 2009, EU-27	175
7.3	Changes in European and national electoral turnouts 1999–2004–2009 (Czech Republic, Estonia, France, Germany, and Poland)	175
7.4	European/national gaps in party vote share 1999–2004–2009	177
7.5	European/national vote gaps by parties' left-right placement 1999–2004–2009	179
7.6	European/national vote gaps by parties' GAL-TAN position 1999–2004–2009	181

List of Graphs

6.1	Involvement in activities engaging the public, civil society and citizens	154
6.2	Institutions addressed by NGOs regarding the TCE	155
6.3	Institutions addressed by economic organisations regarding the TCE	156

List of Tables

1.1	Four vital elements of public discourse	11
2.1	Main EU law provisions after the Lisbon Treaty, concerning EU citizenship rights and rights of third-country long-term residents	28
2.2	National implementation of EU citizenship directives	30
2.3	Number of citizenship cases and observations by member state	35
2.4	EU Citizenship cases brought to the ECJ, by nationality of referring court	36
2.5	ECJ support for competing models of citizenship in a union of states	49

Chapter 2 Annex

2.1	European Court of Justice judgments on citizenship provisions of the TFEU articles 20 and 21, and directives 2003/86/EC, 2004/38/EC and 2003/109/EC	52
3.1	Actual and reported turnout rates	71
3.2	Distribution of reasons in favour of the TCE across countries	73
3.3	Distribution of reasons for being against the TCE across countries	74

Chapter 3 Annex

3.1	Coding parties into different party families	80
3.2	Multivariate analyses of arguments for the constitution	81
3.3	Multivariate analyses of arguments against the TCE	82
4.1	Ranking order of party performance in communicating EU reform	95

Chapter 4 Annex

4.1	List of political parties included in the analysis	108

4.2	ConstEPS media data set	109
4.3	Empirical operationalisation of causal factors	110
4.4	fsQCA data matrix of outcome and causal variables	112
5.1	List of analyzed plenary debates on the ratification of the Lisbon Treaty	124
6.1	Complex patterns of support towards the EU	144
6.2	CSO visibility in national media coverage of EU treaty ratification, by member states	148
6.3	CSO visibility in media ratification debates, by old and new member states	149

Chapter 7 Annex

7.1	European election turnout in EU-27, 1979–2009	185
7.2	European and national election turnout in six EU member states 1999–2004–2009	186
7.3	Multivariate analyses of turnout determinants in European elections	187
7.4	List of political parties	188

List of Contributors

Steffen Blings is a PhD student in the Department of Government at Cornell University since 2010. His research interests are in the areas of political behavior in advanced industrialised democracies and the intersection of social movements and party politics. He received his BA and MA in political science from the University of Bremen.

Tatjana Evas, Dr iur is a research assistant at the Robert Schuman Centre for Advanced Studies, European University Institute, an assistant professor at the Tallinn Law School and an associate fellow at the Jean Monnet Centre for European Studies, University of Bremen. For her PhD at the University of Bremen she was awarded the '*Bremer Studienpreis*' for the best PhD thesis in social science and humanities in 2011. From 2007 to 2011 she was a researcher with the EU FP6 RECON Project and from 2005–2008 with the project *Citizenship and Constitution: Transformations of the Public Sphere in East- and West-European Integration* (Volkswagen Foundation) at the University of Bremen. In addition to her academic research and teaching on EU law she has served as an expert for the EU Agency for Fundamental Rights, the EU DG Employment, Social Affairs and Inclusion, and the UNHCR. Her most recent publications include the monograph *Judicial Application of European Union Law in Post-communist Countries (*Studies in Modern Law and Policy, Ashgate Publishing 2012); *Multilayered Representation in the European Union: Parliaments, Courts and the Public Sphere* (co-eds with U. Liebert and C. Lord, NOMOS 2012); and *EU Constitutionalization from the Baltic Perspective* (Oslo: RECON Report 2011).

Alexander Gattig, PhD is a senior lecturer in statistical methods at the University of Bremen, Department of Sociology. He received his PhD from the University of Groningen, The Netherlands, and has since collaborated in several national and international research projects including "*Citizenship and Constitution: Transformations of the Public Sphere in East- and West-European Integration*" (Volkswagen Foundation) as well as the EU FP6 Project "Reconstituting Democracy in Europe (RECON)". His research interests and publications include behavioral decision making, political sociology, and electoral behavior. Currently he is interested in comparative welfare state research and the causes and consequences of political polarization.

Petra Guasti, PhD is a senior researcher at the Department of Political Science at the Johannes Gutenberg University of Mainz and a senior researcher at the Department of Political Sociology, Institute of Sociology of the Academy of Sciences of the Czech Republic. She holds an MA in Society and Politics from Lancaster University and a PhD in political sociology from the Charles University in Prague. From 2005 to 2008 she worked at the Jean Monnet Centre for European Studies at the University of Bremen as a researcher in the project "Citizenship and Constitution: Transformations of the Public Sphere in East- and West-European Integration", funded by the Volkswagen Foundation. Her current research focuses on Europeanization in new EU member states, in particular the rule of law and human rights. She is a co-convener of the Standing Group on Central and Eastern European Politics of the European Consortium for Political Research. Her recent publications include the edited volume '*The Nexus between Democracy, Collective Identity Formation and EU Enlargement*' (with J. Hronesova and Z. Mansfeldova, Prague, IS AS CR 2011).

Ulrike Liebert is Professor of Political Science (since 1997), Jean Monnet Chair (*ad personam*) and Head of the Jean Monnet Centre (since 2001) at the University of Bremen. Having received her PhD in Social and Political Sciences at the European University Institute in Florence and her Habilitation at the University of Heidelberg, she has been teaching in Barcelona (UAB) and Cornell University (Government Department) as well as for shorter periods in Moscow (RGGU) and Mexico (Celaya). Her publications include the monograph *Modelle demokratischer Konsolidierung: Italien, Deutschland und Spanien* (1948–1990; Leske+Budrich 1995); *Parliaments and Democratic Consolidation in Southern Europe* (co-eds with M. Cotta, Pinter Publisher 1990); *Gendering Europeanisation* (P.I.E. Peter Lang, 2003); *Europe in Contention: Debating the Constitutional Treaty* (PEPS special issue 2007); *The New Politics of European Civil Society* (co-eds with H.J.Trenz, Routledge 2010), *European Economic and Social Constitutionalism after the Treaty of Lisbon* (co-eds with D.Schiek and H.Schneider, CUP 2011); *Identity and Democracy in the New Europe: The Next Generation Finds its Way* (co-eds with O. Brzezinska, E. Kurucz, R. Sackmann, ARENA Report 2011), and *Multilayered Representation in the European Union: Parliaments, Courts and the Public Sphere* (co-eds with T. Evas and C. Lord, NOMOS 2012). In her current research, she focuses on the state in financial crisis as a problem of democratic institutional decline and innovation.

Aleksandra Maatsch is currently a post-doc researcher at the Institute of Public Goods and Policies (IPP) at the Spanish National Research Council in Madrid (CSIC), Spain. She received her PhD in Political Science at the University of Bremen in 2008, worked there as a researcher at the Jean Monnet Centre for European Studies (2005–8), as well as at the Research Centre for East European Studies (2008–11), and during the period 2008 to 2011 as a researcher in the EU-funded project "Reconstituting Democracy in Europe (RECON)". Since 2008, she has been serving as a consultant with Research voor Beleid (The Netherlands). Among her most recent publications is a book monograph on national citizenship in the European Union: *Ethnic Citizenship Regimes. Europeanisation, Post-War Migration and Redressing Past Wrongs* (Basingstoke: Palgrave Macmillan 2011) as well as book chapters and papers on the role of national parliaments in the European Union.

Kathrin Packham received her PhD in Political Science from the University of Bremen, with a dissertation thesis entitled *Explaining Political Party Performance in European Communication. A Qualitative Comparative Analysis (QCA) of Party Political Cueing in domestic EU Treaty Ratification*. She has been a lecturer in EU studies and comparative politics and researcher at the University of Bremen, among others working for the 6th EU FP-Integrated Project "Reconstituting Democracy in Europe" (RECON, WP5), coordinating a subproject on political party campaigns in the 2009 European elections (2009–10); from 2005–2008 as a PhD Fellow in the research project "Citizenship and Constitutionalisation: Transforming the Public Sphere in East- and West-European Integration" (ConstEPS), funded by the Volkswagen Foundation; and from 2002–3 as a coordinator of the research and training project, "Welche Verfassung für Europa? Vom Konvent zur Regierungskonferenz". Her publications include *Verfassungsexperiment. Europa auf dem Weg zur postnationalen Demokratie?* (co-edited with U. Liebert, J. Falke, D. Allnoch, Vol. 1 "Europäisierung. Beiträge zur transnationalen und transkulturellen Europadebatte", LIT 2003); "From the Contentious Constitution to the Awkward Other ... Social Model. The Constitutional Debate in the British Print Media" (in: Perspectives on European Politics and Society, 8:3/2007); „Interkulturelles und experimentelles Lernen in den European Studies. Eine Simulation der Regierungskonferenz zur Europäischen Verfassung: EuroSim 2004" (CEuS Working Paper 2004/1, with S. Maatsch, T. Schöning and A. Vedder); and others.

Ewelina Riekens is a PhD fellow in the research area "Governance and Regional Development" at the International Graduate School for Global Change in the Marine Realm (GLOMAR), University of Bremen. She received her MA in Political Science at the Department of Political Science in 2010, has been working for several years as a teaching assistant for quantitative and qualitative methods of social sciences, as well as a researcher at the Jean Monnet Centre for European Studies for third party funded projects (in particular ConstEPS and RECON). Her current PhD research focuses on the "EU strategy for the Baltic Sea: Integration of marine and maritime realm".

Preface

The research findings presented in this book originate from "Unity amidst Variety? Intellectual Foundations and Requirements for an Enlarged Europe", a research funding initiative by the Volkswagen Foundation during 2001–2009 which has sponsored the research project "Citizenship and Constitutionalization: Transforming the Public Sphere in East-West European Integration" (ConstEPS, 2005–8), headed by Ulrike Liebert at the University of Bremen, Jean Monnet Centre for European Studies (CEuS). The analyses of the quantitative and qualitative empirical findings assembled by this international and interdisciplinary research team – Tatjana Evas, Alexander Gattig, Petra (Rakusanova) Guasti, Alexandra (Wyrozumska) Maatsch, Kathrin Packham, Ewelina (Pawlak) Riekens – have greatly benefited from a subsequent collaborative project in which the editors and authors of the present book have been involved: "Reconstituting Democracy in Europe" (RECON, funded under the 6th EU FP, 2007–11 and coordinated by Erik O. Eriksen at ARENA, University of Oslo, see http://www.reconproject.eu), and here especially the working groups on "Civil society and the public sphere" (WP5, co-coordinated by Ulrike Liebert and Hans-Jörg Trenz) and "Representation and institutional make-up" (coordinated by Christopher Lord).

We are indebted to many colleagues who have provided invaluable intellectual stimulation and research cooperation along the ways of ConstEPS and RECON, including research workshops and conferences held in Bremen, Prague, Krakow, Oslo and at the EUI. Among these, we want to thank especially Zdenka Mansfeldova (Academy of Sciences, Prague), Zdzislaw Mach (Institute for European Studies, Krakow), Norbert Reich (University of Bremen/Riga Graduate School of Law), Josef Falke (ZERP, University of Bremen), Heiko Pleines (Research Centre on Eastern Europe, Bremen); Philippe C. Schmitter, Bo Strath and Rainer Bauböck (EUI); John Erik Fossum, Erik O. Eriksen and Hans-Jörg Trenz (ARENA/University of Oslo), Ben Crum (Vrije University of Amsterdam), Christoph Meyer (Kings College, London), Kalypso Nicolaidis (St. Anthony's College, Oxford University), and Juan Diez Medrano (Central University, Barcelona).

The co-editors and authors of this collaborative research book are grateful for the funding of this project received from the Volkswagen Foundation and from the European Commission's Sixth Framework Programme for Research. Last but not least, our special thanks for great administrative support and editorial assistance goes to the persons without whom this book could not have materialised, namely to Gisela Lysiak and Jule Holz (CEuS) and Christopher Goddard (Riga Graduate School of Law, Latvia).

Ulrike Liebert, Tatjana Evas, Alexander Gattig. University of Bremen – EUI, Florence, June 2013.

List of Abbreviations

AMO	Association for International Issues (Czech NGO)
CA	Claims-making analysis
CEP	Centre for Economy and Politics (Czech NGO)
CEuS	Jean Monnet Centre for European Studies, University of Bremen
CFSP	Common Foreign and Security Policy
	CIVGOV Organized Civil Society and European Governance
COFAC	Conference of Foreign Affairs Chairs
ComPDA	Comparative Political Discourse Analysis
ConstEPS	"Citizenship and Constitutionalisation: Transforming the Public Sphere in East-West European Integration" (research project, Jean Monnet Centre for European Studies, University of Bremen, 2005–8)
COSAC	Conference of Parliamentary Committees for Union Affairs
CSO	Civil society organization
EB	Eurobarometer
ECJ	European Court of Justice
EE	European Elections
EP	European Parliament
ESDP	European Security and Defence Policy
ETUC	European Trade Union Confederation
EU	European Union
EUI	European University Institute (Florence, Italy)
EWM	Early Warning Mechanism
F-EB	Flash-Eurobarometer
fsQCA	fuzzy set Qualitative Comparative Analysis
MP	Member of the Parliament
MS	Member State
NE	National elections
NGO	Non-governmental organisation
NMS	New EU Member State

PS	Public sphere
QCA	Qualitative Comparative Analysis
TCE	Treaty establishing a Constitution for Europe (signed by EU member governments in December 2004)
TCN	Third Country National
TEU	Treaty of the European Union
TFEU	Treaty on Functioning of the European Union
UK	United Kingdom
UMV	Institute for International Relations (Czech NGO)
US	United States

Chapter 1

Democratising the EU from Below? Citizenship, Civil Society and the Public Sphere in Making Europe's Order

Ulrike Liebert

For the European Union of the 21st century, the search for a more inclusive constitutional settlement entails the challenge of balancing efficient governance – not the least of financial, economic and state debt crises – with popular democratic legitimacy. Arguably, the democratic life of the European Union is a question not only of appropriate supranational institutional design, but also of the quality of democratic institutions and practices of the member states. Construction of such a multilayered regional polity entails the challenge of reconciling the diversity of established – and that is predominantly national – citizenship practices with evolving norms of European constitutionalism. From the EU's 2001 Laeken summit to its 2009 Lisbon Treaty, the relationship of citizenship to the European institutions has become a particularly contested field. Citizens have litigated for European Citizenship rights, thus challenging the Court of Justice to socially embed European constitutionalism; citizens' contestation have troubled national and EU elites during EU treaty reforms, such as in the 2004–5 and 2008–9 ratification referendums. Political parties, civil society organisations, and the mass media – rather than wholeheartedly engaging with the making of the European would-be democratic polity – they have been driving the politicisation of the EU (de Wilde and Zürn 2012). At the same time, by taking issue with the scope, level or exclusiveness of European integration, individual as well as collective acts of participation, litigation and contestation have arguably enhanced the Europeanization of domestic politics and the construction of transnational identities on which the evolving "community of Europeans" relies (Risse 2010).

Yet, the scholarly debate is still inconclusive as to what lessons can be drawn from these challenges for a democratic theory of European constitutionalisation and integration. Are expanding transnational citizenship rights and EU constitutionalisation predicaments or preconditions for European democracy (Bauböck 2004; Crum 2011)? Is a "new citizen politics" (Dalton 2008) the "right or the wrong sort of medicine for the EU" (Hix and Bartolini 2006)? More in particular, are popular participation and public deliberation "misleading ideas" and responsible for the collapse of the European Constitution project (Moravcsik 2006)? Or are European federalists right when making the case for continuous constitutional experimentalism in the EU "in order for democracy not to become an empty shell" (Moravcsik and Mény 2009)? Again, if the EU is a dynamic and contested entity, what kind of order is likely to emerge from the struggles among competing visions for reconstituting European democracy (Eriksen and Fossum 2012: 22–34): An "audit democracy" where member states delegate competences to the Union's regulatory regime but where democracy remains wedded to the nation state? A "federal multinational democracy" based on a supranational democratic constitutional state? Or a "regional-European democracy" based on government without a state? What are the presuppositions for each of these models of reconfiguring democracy regarding, for instance, the role of citizenship, of political parties, of civil society or of the media?

This book submits some of these competing ideas about democratic citizenship in a legitimate European order to social scientific analysis. Bringing together explorations of different societal fields that are involved in the reconstitution of Europe, the chapters included in this book contribute to the study of the European Union from below, or to the political sociology of the EU. They provide comparative accounts of whether, to what extent and how the old EU and the new member states from East Central Europe differ when viewed from the perspective of "democratisation from below". Empirical analyses of democratic practices in the making of a European social and political order result from a larger research programme addressing the questions of "Unity amidst variety? Intellectual foundations and requirements for an enlarged Europe".[1] To answer these questions, we suggest exploring how European citizens, civil society, the media, political parties, parliaments and courts engage with the ongoing reconstitution of democracy in the EU. Our working assumption is that the politicisation of EU constitutional reform in the member states need not necessarily lead to mass popular "constraining dissensus", stalemate, or crisis of the EU. On the opposite, it is a necessary requisite for democratising the EU: Depending on the quality of the democratic linkages provided by their domestic courts, on their EU treaty ratification procedures, the quality of their mass media, of political parties and of civil society organisations, member state democracies will ignore, resist or successfully accommodate the emerging patterns of political conflict about EU polity making.

This introductory chapter is structured as follows: it starts by discussing the state of the art of democratic theory of European integration, or of the empirical democratic theory beyond the state. It then develops the conceptual framework, hypotheses and methodological tools that inform the empirical analyses. Finally, it provides an overview of research findings by way of short chapter synopses.

---

[1] Research funding initiative by the Volkswagen Foundation (2001–9), under which the ConstEPS research project at the University of Bremen, Jean Monnet Centre for European Studies has been funded (2005–8). For partial results see Liebert 2007, Evas 2007, 2012; S. Maatsch 2007, A. Maatsch 2011; Packham 2007, Rakusanova 2007, Wyrozumska 2007.

Democratic Theory beyond the State (of the Art)

This book aims at developing the state of the art of the democratic theory of European integration – and more broadly: political sociological approaches to democratic practices beyond the state – by exploring key episodes of European politics and polity reform. More specifically, we intend to make three original contributions to the developing political sociology of democratic integration beyond the state:

- Taking issue with the reductionism of elitist accounts of EU treaty reform that are out of sync with evolving social and political demands and participatory practices, we complement these by means of a more realistic framework of the EU as a self-constituting political union of states and citizens that is embedded in fields of social practices.
- Conceiving of the self-constitution of the European order as a process of constitutionalisation driven by judicial decisions, on the one hand and treaty reform choices, on the other, we put normative theoretical controversies about the feasibility of different models of democratic constitutionalism in the EU to the test by empirically exploring democratic practices that are involved in making the EU's order.
- Finally, building on the state of the art of empirical analyses of European integration – recent studies of European contestation, political conflict and claims-making – we develop a deliberative-discursive approach, conceiving of the Europeanization of member state democracies as well as the democratisation of the EU as socially embedded complementary processes that are shaped by institutional forms, structured by actors' aims, and framed by public discourses.

In the following, these propositions will be described in more detail and in relation to the evolving state of the art of European constitutional politics and that is, the analyses of democratic integration.

First, our framework of democratic constitutionalism beyond the state aims to correct the conventional elitist focus on EU treaty reform in its two main varieties: liberal intergovernmentalism and the model of delegating national regulatory powers. On the one hand, the intergovernmental focus on treaty negotiation, such as the pioneering study by Thomas König's and Simon Hug's "Policy-making Processes and the European Constitution" (2006), a comparative study of all old and new EU member states in the Intergovernmental Conference of June 2004, explains treaty reforms as an outcome of state and government preferences in constitutional treaty negotiations. Here, the authors deliberately exclude domestic democratic processes as well as transnational dynamics. Thus, due to the restrictions of their methodology they can neither fully account for the ratification crisis or for the subsequent redesign of EU constitutional treaty reform; nor are they capable of assessing the impacts of domestic democratic infrastructures and processes on the EU's crisis, choice and change. On the other hand, Giandomenico Majone's account of the EU as a confederal model of negative self-regulation reaches "beyond intergovernmentalism" to explain the delegation of rulemaking powers to the European institutions by contracts and treaty amendments (Majone 2005: 162; 64). Yet, assuming that "international economic integration, the Nation-State and democracy" to be "an impossible trinity" (Majone 2005: 181), integration and democracy are conceived as a "big trade-off", even a "category mistake", due to federalist bias that allegedly explains the failure of federalist aspirations (Majone 2005: 23ff.; 204; 219). The present book, by contrast, aims to fill the lacunae left by intergovernmentalists while, at the same time, submitting the "big trade-off" claim advanced by confederal models of self-regulation to empirical scrutiny, by exploring fields of democratic practices involved in the EU's multilayered political community "in the making" (see Eriksen 2005; Evas, Liebert, Lord 2012).

Second, our book contributes to understanding the relationship of democracy and European integration by reviewing normative theoretical accounts of democratic constitutionalism in the EU (Eriksen and Fossum 2000; Eriksen 2004; Eriksen 2005; Habermas 2001; Tully 2007; Franzius and Preuss 2011) in light of empirical evidence (Eriksen and Fossum 2012). For this purpose, we conceptualise EU constitutionalism first and foremost as a long-term process that is increasingly relevant not only to experts, political elites, interest groups and public intellectuals, but also to European citizens and the general public at large. In opposition to authors who claim that the EU simply did not need and was not ready to create a Constitution (Grimm 1995; Moravcsik 2006; cf. Eriksen 2009; Liebert 2012b), the authors of this book conceive of the EU's constitutionalisation as an ongoing process of development, including failures, relaunch, and eventual redesign, depending on sustained exchanges between European citizens and political elites. In this context, Bauböck argues that citizenship rights will have to extend beyond nationality and state territory if liberal democracies are to remain true to their own principles of inclusive membership and equal basic rights. To explain the forms and extent of the public's engagement with EU constitutional politics involves issues of democratic quality of domestic politics and, thus, not only of democratically designing the EU. These issues, in turn, require studying the Europeanization of national democratic processes and, specifically, the "politicisation" of domestic EU politics: "[Only] by deliberately politicising the issues involved at the level of Europe as a whole and by gradually building up expectations ... with regard to citizenship, representation, and decision making can one imagine a successful constitutionalisation of the EU" (Schmitter 2000:119; cf. Schmidt 2006; Hix and Bartolini 2006). Thus, for assessing democratic practices involved in EU constitutional politics we use "postfunctional" approaches to European integration that are premised on the assumption of mass public politicisation (Marks and Hooghe 2008). In sum, this approach conceives of democratic constitutionalism in the EU as an ongoing process of conflict and integration, triggered by political spill-over mechanisms and unintended consequences, in particular in terms of politicisation. In response to the post 2008 financial and state debt crisis in the Eurozone some political leaders have called for strengthening the community method for completing EMU from above. Yet, from a bottom-up perspective we would neither expect a fully fledged political federation nor a confederation restricted to market integration. Instead, for the sake of effective problem-solving, EU powers of positive regulation in socially sensitive realms will depend on conventional forms as well as unconventional new modes of generating democratic legitimacy across and beyond state borders. In that respect, a political-sociological approach to European constitutionalism allows empirical testing of claims about the conditions on which the legitimacy of the evolving EU – and its progressive treaty reforms – rely.

Third, as contributions to advancing the political sociology of European integration, we empirically explore the patterns and dynamics of the contentious politics of European constitutional development in the intermediary domains of citizenship, civil society (including interest groups), political parties and the mass public sphere. For this purpose, our analytical framework is informed by conflict approaches to European political sociology, focusing on protest and "contentious politics" (Imig and Tarrow 2001) and on political conflict about European integration and the EU (Marks and Steenbergen 2004; Fligstein 2008; Kriesi et al. 2012). While Imig and Tarrow's conceptual framework focuses the efforts of European citizens to make demands directed towards the supranational level of European government through social movements, protest politics, and contentious political action, Marks and Steenbergen and Kriesi et al. investigated patterns of conflict that are arising at the national and supranational levels of European Union politics, including a range of different actors. Building on this research stream and, specifically, Medrano's analysis of the discursive framing of European integration on the one hand, and of survey data on public support for the EU, on the other (Medrano 2003), the present research, instead of stressing the divergence of "national cultures", also seeks to understand patterns of transnational convergence. For our purposes, we complement existing frameworks for studying protest movements such as "claims making analysis" (CA) by developing the methodology of "comparative political discourse analysis" (ComPDA, see below).[2]

Our book aims to develop these lines of research in two ways. On the one hand, we expand the analyses into further fields of social practices where European citizens can (and did) get involved in the making of the EU's order – in particular by "litigation and adjudication"; "referendum participation in EU politics"; "political party communication"; "national parliamentary ratification"; "civil society participation" and "national and European electoral participation". On the other

---

2 Claims-making analysis (CA) originates in protest event analysis which, in contrast to discursive approaches to media contents analysis, does not study media representations of actors views and arguments about particular events; instead, CA takes the news media as a source for identifying political claims made by social and political actors: "Claims analysis sees reported news as a record of public events, and retrieves information on this aspect" (Statham 2007: 113).

hand, for empirically analyzing political conflict on EU constitutional reform the present analytical framework does not remain restricted to individual or collective preferences and claims-making. The construction of Europe's constitutional order as analysed here is conceived as a discursive battleground between competing ideas, frames, norms and justifications, conducive to "European stories" that are being de- and reconstructed by "intellectual debates on Europe in national contexts" (Lacroix and Nicolaidis 2010). "Making the European Polity" is seen as a process of "reflexive integration in the EU" where deliberation is a key for reflexively organised processes of collective learning (Eriksen 2005). As Eriksen et al. demonstrated, the deliberative dynamics developed by the "Convention on the Future of Europe" has strengthened the differences between the member states; hence, these dynamics did not produce a European culture of consensus and constitutional patriotism (Eriksen et al. 2004). To review this claim in light of post 2004 developments, we comparatively reconstruct political discourses regarding national and European identity, EU constitutionalism, and democratic principles (Dryzek and Berejkian 1993; Triandafyllidou, Wodak and Kryzanowski 2009; Liebert 2012a, 2012b). We argue that, unlike earlier phases of constitutionalisation, constitutional treaty ratification has sparked significant transnational discursive interaction, creating convergence as well as divergence of national political discourses, by contributing to the structuring of political conflict across European member publics (see Evas 2007; Liebert 2007; Maatsch 2007; Packham 2007; Rakusanova 2007; Wyrozumska 2007). As a key proposition we contend that this process has contributed to re-articulating and transforming patterns of conflict that have hitherto shaped political life in Western European along national lines. Yet, these patterns do not easily provide bridges for including the new lines of political conflict that have emerged in the new democracies in East Central Europe.

For further developing our contribution to this evolving research field, the next section will clarify the key concepts, analytical framework, and the methodology that inform the present studies.

Conceptual Clarifications, Methodology and Empirical Evidence

Here, clarifications are in order concerning key concepts, in particular "democratisation from below" and "social fields", the interdisciplinary methodology that we have employed for this study, and databases.

Key Concepts

"*Democratisation from below*" is meant here to indicate a "bottom up" perspective on European integration, conceived as a multi-faceted and multi-sited process. Our explorations of European constitutional politics "from below" concentrate on social and political practices located below both the supranational and the level of national heads of state and government who hold the formal competences for making the EU order. Less visible and more informal agencies include ordinary citizens who may impact social and political struggles about the EU constitutional order, for instance through civil society mobilisation in ratification referendums, or through national and European elections. This de-centred view stands in stark contrast to the traditionally elitist focus of European integration narratives on the ideas and actions of "great men" – and occasionally powerful women – from above, or the power struggles between national and supranational leaders. The bottom-up processes examined by the studies in this book highlight a variety of legal, political and social fields of actors, ranging from individual citizens – national and European voters or litigants –, to judges, parties, media, civil society organisations and members of national parliaments. Despite the diverse spectrum of topics they cover, the studies in this book share a "bottom up" approach or "perspective from below" towards the evolving European order, meaning that they attempt to account for European constitutional politics through the lenses of a political sociology of European integration. Our approach to EU constitutional politics draws on recent advances in the sociology of the European Union (Favell and Guiraudon 2011; Trenz 2011). It aims at exploring conventional and unconventional sources of democratic legitimacy which the EU constitutional order tries to tap – for instance national parliamentary representation and civil society participation. It does so by assessing potentials and limits of participation at supranational and national levels, for instance in the field of elections (where turnout in contemporary democratic states is eroding, too), as well as alternative contestatory practices of "democratisation from below" that involve transformations of power relations. Our approach departs from conventional institutionalist and actor centred perspectives on European integration and constitutionalisation, not by excluding elites and institutions altogether but by putting "fields of social practices" first where political elites and "counter powers" will be struggling about the key "elements of democratic rule", namely "public control with political equality and justification" (Lord 2012: 105).

Regarding the articulation of "*social fields*" of European citizens' political practices, a "social field" is meant here to denote a socially constructed "field of action" which, consisting of institutions and social groups, social practices and cultural conventions, "structures and orientates the individual actions and interpersonal struggles" (Kauppi 2012: 151). In relation to citizens and the EU, we have selected, more specifically, social fields that are involved in the processes of public opinion and political will formation and decision-making about EU constitutional politics. As to where major struggles are to be observed or should be expected about these processes in the making of a European constitutional order, democratic theory provides different guide posts: while liberal democratic theory suggests focusing on the electoral and parliamentary spheres, direct democratic theorists will point to EU referendums, advocates of participatory and of associational democracy will point to the civic sphere of civil society. Finally, proponents of "dual-track democracy" will point to counter-majoritarian court proceedings for protecting minorities against the tyranny of the majority (Pettit

2000; 2006). As a consequence, we select the following six fields of action and interaction for investigation:

- the legal-judicial realm of litigation about EU citizenship;
- EU treaty ratification through popular referendums;
- political party communication with mass publics about EU treaty politics;
- national parliamentary ratification of EU treaty reform;
- citizens' political participation in EU treaty reform through civil society;
- citizen participation in European (and national) elections.

Moreover, to articulate the logic that holds these different social fields together, we have constructed an analytical optic for exploring each of them by appropriate methods while, at the same time, weaving them together into three themes: first, the role of each of the different fields in making the EU order; second, theoretical controversy about the feasibility, preconditions and constraints of citizens' political agency; and third, empirical findings as regards the democratic mechanisms on which accommodation of social and political struggles about EU constitutionalisation relies. While some fields have a formal-legal say in EU constitutional politics (such as the first, second, fourth and sixths fields above) others remain largely informal (third and fifths fields, above). Yet, both types constitute necessary preconditions for the extent to which, and how, citizens' agency can unfold in European politics, policies and polity-making, be it by directly engaging with the EU, or indirectly, via the democratic member states. Whether and to what extent their practices live up to normative democratic expectations is entirely a matter of empirical analysis. The following describes the methodology and empirical data sets we have developed for this purpose.

Interdisciplinary Methodology and Empirical Data Sets

The research methodologies which inform the chapters and the book draw on the evolving political sociology of European integration aimed at an empirical theory of democracy and democratisation. The above overview of the state of the art suggests that developments in this field are driven by a plurality of methodological approaches and empirical methods. For the various East-West European comparative analyses in particular, the present studies develop different conceptual frameworks, coupled with qualitative and/or quantitative methods of analysis. Several contributions use Atlas.ti software for comparative political discourse analysis; one chapter applies "Qualitative Comparative Analysis" (QCA), and two chapters use more conventional methods of descriptive and quantitative statistical analyses. Yet, despite their variety, the contributions to legal, political and sociological analyses as well as to communication studies of European integration share comparative data sets that have been constructed by the research group, albeit using different strategies of comparison: qualitative or quantitative, cross-national or transnational.

The interdisciplinary setup of the research group and contributors to this book makes methodological pluralism a fruitful vantage point for exploring different fields of social practices related to democratic constitutionalism. Each contribution draws on a different methodology or blend of methods. In particular, the chapters also adopt different qualitative and/or quantitative methods of comparative analysis, for instance the method of theoretically informed substantive legal interpretation of ECJ preliminary rulings in litigation about Union citizenship;[3] quantitative statistical analysis of survey data on citizens' motivations for voting for or against EU constitutional treaty reform in national ratification referendums[4] and on European election turnout, by parties;[5] Atlas.ti based analysis of print media coverage of political party communication on EU treaty reform, using the methodology of "Qualitative Comparative Analysis" (QCA);[6] Atlas.ti based comparative discourse analysis of national parliamentary ratification debates on the Lisbon Treaty;[7] mixed qualitative and quantitative methods, including interview data with some 100 civil society organisations for assessing their engagement with citizens and EU treaty reform.[8]

At the same time, and to avoid misunderstandings, it should be made clear that given the limited scope of the present analyses they do not aim at other types of comparative approaches, for instance interregional comparisons.

Methodology of Comparative Political Discourse Analysis

For exploring the discursive dimensions involved in EU politics, we have sought to empirically develop the theoretical framework of "Europe as a Discursive Battleground", proposing discourse analysis for European integration studies (Diez 2001), and analysing "Speaking Europe" as a key component of "the politics of integration discourse" (Diez 1999; Morgan 2005). Departing from

---

3   Evas and Liebert compare three different models of European citizenship against case law justifications; see Chapter 2 in this book.

4   Gattig and Blings compare motives by citizens voting in four national referendums for or against the Constitutional Treaty; see Chapter 3 in this book.

5   Gattig, Liebert and Riekens compare citizen turnout in European elections 1999–2009 to national level turnout in all EU member states, based on aggregate voting data, see Chapter 7, in this book.

6   Packham comparatively assesses how political parties communicate European constitutional treaty reform to mass publics across the different national contexts of six old and new member states; see Chapter 4 in this book.

7   Maatsch comparatively analyses national parliamentary discourses from six member states, by comparative political discourse analysis, using Atlas.ti software, see Chapter 5 in this book.

8   Guasti compares a set of civil society organisations from the same member states as to their perceptions and practices of engaging with the EU Constitutional Treaty, by using network and statistical analysis based on interview and mass survey data; see Chapter 6 in this book.

the postmodern ontology and the micro linguistic features of text analysis to which discursive approaches are often wedded, more recent methodologies have proposed more disciplined text analyses, or structuralist interpretations, such as – drawing on Norman Fairclough's school of "critical discourse analysis" – Ruth Wodak (Wodak and van Dijk 2000; Wodak and Meyer 2009). These frameworks for comparative discourse analysis aim at bridging the gap between the micro level of the text and the political institutional macro level. Yet, as Ole Waever has noted, critical discourse analysis has so far been of little use in European Integration Studies, given two weaknesses: on the one hand, a tendency to resort "to intuitive laundry lists of important questions to ask of a text", and, on the other hand, "limited integration of the different elements" (Waever 2004: 2001).

The methodology of "Comparative Political Discourse Analysis" (ComPDA) that has been developed for the purposes of the present research draws on John Dryzek and Berejikian's work (1993). ComPDA rests on the assumption that neither the interpretative nor pragmatic approaches should be reduced to the other. On the one hand, pragmatic approaches to news media analysis – such as "claims analysis" – are primarily interested in dimensions such as political mobilization and the interaction of collective actors, for instance political parties or social movements, and use the mass media to measure their visibility.[9] They adopt largely quantitative methods focusing on actors, their political claims and strategic interactions. By contrast, interpretive approaches to media analysis in terms of discourse analysis typically adopt exclusively qualitative methods. For instance Critical Discourse Analysis (CDA) asks what language can tell us about society, and looks at a range of different discursive genres, from political speeches to Internet chat (Triandafyllidou, Wodak and Krzyzanowski 2009). Compared to the methods of content analysis of the news media, on the one hand, and interpretive discourse analysis, on the other hand, the ComPDA methodology is premised on the following distinctive assumptions:

- An interest in gaining an understanding of political conflict over European integration that is empirically based on the discursive patterns defined by the salience of topics, direction of arguments and types of justifications.
- The notion of discourse conceived as an independent variable that shapes social and political agency, and where actors/speakers perform as strategic agents to – at best – a very limited degree.
- The role of the mass media defined in terms of agency and not merely platforms.
- The assumption that a combination of qualitative and quantitative methods of comparative discourse analysis must be based on a multi-linguistic research design.

---

9 See Koopmans 2007; Statham 2008; Statham and Trenz (forthcoming).

Before describing these characteristics in more detail, a basic definition of the so-called "vital elements" of "political discourse" is in order. We understand a discourse to be constituted by four elements, the "vital elements of discourse": its ontology or discursive assumptions about the entities that are recognised as existing; the kind and degree of agency that is discursively represented; the motives which are recognised or denied by or to agents, such as self-interests, identities or ideologies; and the types of relationship which are discursively established, for instance hierarchy, opposition, "natural" or "unnatural" (see Table 1.1; Dryzek and Berejikian 1993).

Table 1.1   Four vital elements of public discourse

ONTOLOGY	Construction of entities that are recognised as existing (or not existing).
AGENCY	Varying in degree, from autonomous subjects to objects that are acted upon. Depending on (re-) presentation of "self" and "other".
MOTIVES	Possible types, comprising material self-interests, identities, ideologies, civic virtues etcetera.
RELATIONSHIPS	Described by concepts or metaphors: (unchallenged) hierarchies; opposition between self and other; natural/legitimate vs. unnatural/illegitimate.

Source: Adapted from Dryzek and Berejikian 1993.

Based on this conceptual framework, comparative political discourse analysis can be characterised by the following defining features:

First, for understanding (and thus theorising) political conflict over European integration, ComPDA, when applied to public debates, provides systematically new empirical evidence. That is, it helps construct comparative data sets that allow for testing theoretical claims about the patterns and dynamics of political conflict over European integration. In this framework, public debates about the EU offer a field for examining how different models of political conflict work, each with its different contentious issues, actors and framing strategies, contending justifications and contrasting ideas about the EU's legitimacy. By scrutinising European political discourses at different sites of national public spheres, we explore cross-national patterns of convergence and divergence in the structure of political conflict over Europe. Finally, we can assess the scope and depth of transnational discursive exchanges. More generally, political conflict is defined here as a matter of clashing individual and collective preferences that are shaped by discursively constructed frames through public debate. Thus, ComPDA contributes to yielding new insights into the new mass political patterns and dynamics of political conflict over European integration, across different national contexts. In addition to assessing how different "worlds of Europe" are discursively constructed, it shows what agents with varying degrees of (dis-) empowerment populate these worlds, by what issues and motives they are driven, and how they discursively relate to others, that is what argumentative strategies and modes of justification they use. In this sense, ComPDA functions as a method for identifying discursive patterns of political communication and conflict.

The second underlying assumption of ComPDA is the claim that discourses work as independent variables shaping agency: While political claims-making analysis focuses on the instrumental use of language and ultimately sees discourse as a purposive action (or at least represents it as such), discourse analysis seeks to capture the independent, creative force of language, its ability to convey meaning and representations of the social world. Discourses are analysed according to their ability to structure and coordinate individuals' perceptions of any given social or political field. Individual actors move within discourses, but are only partly able to shape and modify them. A statement that is enacted by and extracted from a media debate is therefore not simply conceived as an individual speech act (as it would be in political claims-making analysis) but is always related to the broader meaning structure from which it originates. Discourse thus unfolds through actors' contributions (speech acts or actions), while these acts are not seen as being necessarily original or intentional, but rather as representing a shared set of concepts, categories and ideas (Dryzek 2005: 1). Discourse shapes agency, in terms of communicative action and, arguably, political agency, too.

Third, in the framework of ComPDA, actors and speakers are not necessarily "rational" in the sense of strategically calculating agents. By contrast, the power of discourses arises from their "ability to structure and coordinate the actions of individual subjects wholly or partly" (Dryzek 2005: 3). Unlike Claims Analysis, PDA builds on the assumption that agency is constituted through communication and language which establishes the "meaning" of action (Dryzek 2005: 3). While political claims-making analyses emphasise the intentional or rational component of speech and action, discourse theory points out the representational nature of discourse, which attributes speech and agency to individual actors. A discourse can, after all, consist of the preferences, positions and arguments of individuals who have no formal relationship to each other and who have no direct interaction (Dryzek 2005: 3).

Fourth, from a political discourse perspective, the media are conceived as agents and not merely as platforms for public debate. Different from the claims-making approach and similar to "media voice impact studies", ComPDA views the role of the media as an active one. In claims-making analysis, the media are mainly perceived as a key arena of political contestation. As such, the media are used by strategically minded political actors for communicating with voters on substantial issues. In this sense, the media are seen as a mirror of political life. For political discourse analysis, the media are not simply a neutral infrastructure for amplifying political events, but also a key player in selecting issues and framing their salience in public debates. As such, the media take an active part in the construction of political reality as represented by media discourse. Differing from mainstream media content analysis, PDA sees media debates as both a reflection of political discussions and as part of social interaction. Journalists are viewed as one type of actor existing alongside others about whom they report, the latter being perceived as speakers with their own voice. Studies on the "media voice" (Trenz et al. 2007) explicitly share the latter view. In sum, ComPDA determines how political elites (such as parties) *and* mass media construct public opinion – and, hence, potentially, how the social constituencies of the emerging European polity conceptualise the EU, its legitimacy, and the roles and competences of member governments, citizens and civil society (Liebert 2007).

Fifth, by combining qualitative and quantitative methods of analysis, the research interest driving ComPDA is to link the insights provided by in-depth qualitative research with empirical validity based on large scale quantitative analysis. Methodologically, this requires incorporating quantitative as well as qualitative elements in the sampling strategy, coding procedures, and in subsequent analysis. This, in turn, mandates a multi-linguistic research design: as a first methodological implication, and following from the two-pronged analytical framework on which it is premised, ComPDA rests on qualitative interpretation aimed at understanding words, sentences and their meanings. Secondly, in order to make political discourse analysis a truly comparative, qualitative interpretative exercise, ComPDA requires a methodology capable of systematically mapping comparable meanings across different discourse worlds and across different languages. Here, the comparative scope of political discourse analysis will vary, depending on the linguistic diversity of the research group and the language proficiencies that its individual members bring to the field of study. It is to be noted that for the sake of inter-subjective reliability, and the validity of comparable interpretive findings, research activities cannot simply be delegated to decentralised units (that is, to researchers in different countries) but must be embedded in a linguistically differentiated, highly interactive and integrated research group.[10]

Empirical Data-sets

The historical episode which the present studies explores in-depth, the process of constitutional crisis, choice and change in the EU, from the Laeken summit in 2001 to the 2009 Lisbon Treaty, has been presented and analysed elsewhere in more detail (see Crum 2011; Fossum and Menéndez 2011). The studies in this book are based on three original data sets that we have collected from different fields involved in this process of European constitutionalization: ConstEPS I "media data set", ConstEPS II "civil society data set", and ConstEPS III "survey data set".[11]

---

10   For further details on the methodology of comparative discourse analysis developed in the ConstEPS project, see Liebert, U. and Trenz, H.J. "Methods of comparative media analysis", in Liebert and Trenz, "*Mediating European democracy: Comparative News Media and EU Treaty Reform in 14 Member States*" (2004–7). RECON research report, ARENA 2008 (pp. 9–27).

11   The ConstEPS comparative data sets cover six EU member states (France, Germany, the UK; the Czech Republic, Estonia, Poland), where ConstEPS data set I has been constructed from national print media coverage of public TCE ratification debates

These data sets have been constructed by a group of researchers[12] collaborating in two international social scientific research projects, the first "Citizenship and Constitutionalisation: Transforming the Public Sphere in East-West European Integration" starting in 2005 and ending in 2008,[13] and the second "Reconstituting democracy in Europe" (RECON), from 2007 to 2011.[14]

The final part of this introduction will give an overview of the chapters in this book and summarise some of their most important findings.

Research Findings

The studies included this book explore different fields of social practices involved in EU constitutional politics, from Laeken to Lisbon. Each contribution aims to advance an empirically informed democratic theory of European integration that helps us to better understand EU constitutional stalemate, crisis and change.

The contributors do so by reviewing more specific debates that have emerged from political sociological studies of European integration dealing with different research fields. They aim to confront critically preconceptions – that is taken for granted ideas from the larger theoretical and political debate – with empirical findings on the democratic practices (or their absence) of European integration. More specifically, each chapter combines theoretical arguments from state of the art discussions with a choice of a distinct mix of qualitative or quantitative methods of analysis and original empirical findings which have not been published elsewhere.[15] In the following, some relevant research findings on controversial issues regarding the reconstitution of democracy in Europe will be highlighted.

2004–5; ConstEPS II is based on structured interviews with 150 intermediary organisations (functional interest groups, organised civil society, and political parties), ConstEPS III contains survey data on citizens' attitudes and political actions regarding the European constitutional project; and ConstEPS IV a collection of the ECJ's preliminary rulings based on Union citizenship norms. For further details, see chapters in this book.

12 The international and multidisciplinary research group consisted of Tatjana Evas, Alexander Gattig, Alexandra (Wyrozumska) Maatsch, Sönke Maatsch, Petra (Rakusanova) Guasti, Kathrin Packham, and Ewelina Rieken; it was directed by Ulrike Liebert, in cooperation and based at the University of Bremen, Jean Monnet Centre for European Studies during the period 2005–11.

13 ConstEPS (2005–8); directed by U. Liebert at Bremen University, and funded by the Volkswagen Foundation (October 2005–September 2008; partially extended until mid-2010). See http://www.monnet-centre.uni-bremen.de/projects/consteps/index.html.

14 RECON (2007–11), coordinated by ARENA, University of Oslo (Erik O. Eriksen), and funded by the EU 6th FP (2007–11), in particular the subproject headed by Ulrike Liebert and Hans-Jörg Trenz "Civil Society and the Public Sphere"see: http://www.monnet-centre.uni-bremen.de/projects/recon/index.htm.

15 See Liebert, Evas, Maatsch, Packham, Rakusanova and Wyrozumski 2007.

In the second chapter entitled *Still "between Eros and civilization"? Citizens, courts and the construction of European citizenship*, Tatjana Evas and Ulrike Liebert explore the legal-judicial realm of litigation about EU citizenship. Their aim is to assess the validity of opposed ideas of European citizenship as being either "an empty shell" constrained by national citizenships; or a "Pandora's box" with ever expanding supranational rights that are in rivalry and superimposed on national ones. For establishing which of the alternative theoretical models of European citizenship is supported by evidence from the evolving judicial constitutionalisation of Union citizenship – court practices triggered frequently by cross-border mobile Union citizens and third country nationals (TCNs) – the chapter presents a systematic interpretation of a comprehensive set of preliminary rulings issued by the ECJ over the past twenty years. The main result the co-authors come up with is that social agency from below in interaction with the national and European judiciary helps advance a new kind of citizenship regime of the EU that reconciles national and supranational provisions on citizenship rights. This regime enables a third way for aliens to turn into members facilitated by commitments to universal rights, principles of non-discrimination and mutual recognition. The authors depict this new type of citizenship as a regime of mutually inclusive citizenships committed to unity amidst diversity.

Alexander Gattig and Steffen Blings, in the third chapter entitled *Disaffected citizens? Why people vote in national referendums about EU treaty reform* scrutinise the highly unpredictable domain of referendums held by member governments on EU issues to better understand why and how people vote. Using statistical analyses they compare the cases of Spain, France, The Netherlands and Luxemburg, that is those four countries where ratification referendums for the TCE were held. As opposed to what the literature suggests, citizen turnout and voting patterns in referendums on EU treaty ratification do not necessarily reflect ignorance and disinterest *vis-à-vis* EU constitutional issues or idiosyncratic features of member state contexts. The authors argue that, independently from the national environments which influence referendum campaigns, citizen voting behaviour can be explained as an effect of cross-country patterns of socio-demographic characteristics, party affiliation and cognitive predispositions of the citizen.

In the fourth chapter, *Ignorant gate-keepers against the EU? National political parties in European political communication,* Kathrin Packham presents a methodologically original QCA study of political party communication with mass publics about EU treaty politics. Assuming that political parties' messages – or "cues" – constitute important factors shaping public attitudes not only on domestic matters but also on issues of European integration and constitutionalisation, she explores how and why political parties' performance in communicating on EU treaty reform politics varies so significantly. The qualitative comparative analysis (following Charles Ragin and Carsten Schneider) draws on data from 40 political parties in six member states to answer the following questions: Which parties succeed and which fail in the competition over cueing the public on contentious

EU issues? What underlying causal factors related to party competition determine the variation in party political cueing performance – ideology? incumbent or opposition status? party system? context? This chapter identifies the conditions under which political parties will perform better or worse, adapting or not reacting to European integration, by comparing their "use" of discourses on Europe in domestic political communication.

In the fifth chapter, *Watch-dogs that cannot bite? New national parliamentary control mechanisms under the Lisbon Treaty* Aleksandra Maatsch studies the field of national parliamentary engagement with EU treaty reforms. Her empirical analysis focuses on reception and evaluation by MPs of the recent reforms concerning national parliaments. By analyzing plenary parliamentary debates on ratification of the Lisbon Treaty she establishes how important or feasible the new competences are from the perspective of citizens' nationally elected representatives who are supposed to implement them: how do they view their functional priorities? Which are their internal and external constraints, which their institutional interests and goals? The research findings suggest that national parliaments clearly prioritised the control function vis-à-vis governments and do not devote much attention to other provisions of the Lisbon Treaty. MP's evaluations of their new role as guardians of the subsidiarity principle and watch-dogs of national governments are mixed: While some MPs confirm that national parliamentary control in the EU has improved, others are profoundly sceptical, perceiving the new parliamentary competences as nothing but an illusion of power.

In her study *A panacea for democratic legitimation? Assessing the engagement of civil society with EU treaty reform politics*, Petra Guasti focuses on the field of civil society engagement with EU treaty reform as an opportunity for generating legitimacy for the EU through citizen participation. For more than a decade, academic and political discussions of the "democratic deficit" have been advocating the formal as well as informal inclusion of organised civil society in policy-making. Yet, despite some progress having been made in the daily functioning of the Union, the democratic deficit appears unresolved. The chapter therefore focuses the potential of civil society organisations (CSO) for contributing to the legitimacy of the EU, by assessing gaps between normative claims and CSO practices. Drawing on the ConstEPS data set II from 100 interviews with CSO, Guasti's analysis finds that official discourses and civil society practices in European constitutional politics diverge in three respects: first, EU official discourses do not match civil society perspectives regarding the proper role of civil society for generating EU legitimacy. Second, empirical analyses of civil society practices in EU constitutional treaty ratification reveal that civil society organisations concentrate on linkages to EU institutions and parties rather than on linkages with citizens and among themselves. Finally, the assessment also shows gaps between official claims and social practices and the kind of legitimacy which organised civil society appears most inclined to provide to the EU polity.

In the final chapter, entitled *Still "second order"? Re-examining citizens' voting behaviour in European and national elections 1999–2009*, Alexander Gattig, Ulrike Liebert and Ewelina Riekens address the field of general European and national elections. It appears a paradox that overall European election turnout has decreased while during the same period the European Parliament has steadily enhanced its powers and symbolic centrality for EU democratic legitimacy. After seven waves of European Parliament elections and European Union enlargement to 27 states, the temporal robustness of the second-order model is therefore being studied more frequently.[16] With the present analysis, the authors rely on aggregate electoral, meso- and individual level survey data analyses for reassessing the patterns and dynamics of national/European election turnout gaps in six new and old EU member states. In particular, the impacts of different political parties are highlighted which have up to now received very little attention in relation to citizens' European electoral participation. The findings demonstrate that although overall European election turnout has dropped, European elections have become less "second order national elections" and more genuine elections. Gaps between national and European levels of electoral participation have diminished, and convergence between old and new member states has increased. The authors' most important finding is that albeit electoral outcomes and party programs are still more in flux in the new than in the old member states they are slowly converging towards party family alliances, with shared characteristics.

In sum, as the overview of findings suggests, we need to revise or even replace a range of prominent but outdated ideas by more differentiated and realistic assumptions, in particular the following: First, the expansion of a new type of European Citizenship has proceeded through cross-border mobile citizens in interaction with the judiciary. Second citizens do hold differentiated motivations for engaging with EU referendums even on exceptionally complex issues such as constitutional treaty ratification. Third, certain kinds of national political parties have turned into agents of European political communication and effectively shape public opinion about the EU. Fourth, many national parliamentarians, although empowered by the Lisbon Treaty, are still sceptical about their capability to perform as effective "watch-dogs" vis-à-vis national government policies of European integration. Fifth, the expectation that civil society will necessarily help legitimise the EU polity may be misleading as long as other requisites – such as NGO's linkages to the citizens – are not taken into account. Finally, sixth, the claim that European elections still perform as "second order" national elections needs qualification, too, in view of cross-national trends towards diminishing turnout gaps between European and national electoral turnout rates and, specifically, a growing number of parties which reverse the gap, attracting more votes in European than in national elections.

---

16 For instance, Hix and Marsh (2011) found that "there are few consistent winners and losers, although socialist parties performed worse in the last three elections than their size and government status would predict" (Hix and Marsh 2011).

Conclusions

A major aim of this book is to discern how the making of Europe's order interacts with democratic practices. This goal requires unpacking the binary of "input" vs. "output" conceptions of legitimacy that dominate current discourses on the EU democratic deficit for the simple reason that social practices involved in "living democracy" in the multilevel context of the European political community cannot be reduced to these terms. Conventional wisdom posits that the EU "democratic deficit" is inevitable if measured by Abraham Lincoln's notions of democratic government (Schmidt 2006). Thus, independently of whether the EU is primarily conceived in terms of "government of the people", "government by the people" or "government for the people", the EU's democratic legitimacy appears to be basically flawed (see Bellamy 2012). For instance, given the EU's lack of a "European demos" or a strong collective identity, the first model of an "EU government of the people" that is based on majority decision-making will not be viable, as it will inescapably suffer from contestations by minorities. Moreover, the second model of democratic legitimacy that focuses on citizens' input into the political process, "EU government by the people" does not appear to work either: even if institutional reforms have repeatedly strengthened the European Parliament, thus creating incentives for citizens' effective engagement with European elections, chronically weak or even declining turnout rates in European elections seem to indicate the contrary. The third and final model of an output oriented form of democratic legitimacy – "technocratic" government "for the people" – seems to be losing out against politicisation and contestation, declining public support, and widespread perceptions that the EU is becoming incapable of effective problem solving. Arguably, EU technocracy has been irrevocably losing its purchase as a source of democratic legitimacy, too. By contrast, the present book is premised on a political sociological approach to the question of democratisation of the Union that is conceived as a matter of political struggles in different fields.

Based on the empirically supported propositions summarised above and developed in more detail in the chapters later we can derive general insights regarding the conditions under which citizens, civil society and public spheres will engage with the making of a European constitutional order. Moreover, these conditions will help us understand the crises, choices and changes that constitutional treaty reform and ratification referendums have triggered between the summits of Laeken and Lisbon as a matter of the democratic practices involved in building the EU from below, from pro-European to openly Eurosceptic perspectives and contestations. The propositions developed here also highlight fundamental agents for mediating political contestation and conflict in democratic ways: not only referendums, elections and parliaments, but also information and communication campaigns by political parties and civil society organisations, as do the mass media and specifically courts and judicial processes.

Given the dual nature of the EU as a Union of states and citizens, different societal fields differ as to how they structure citizens' political agency. In the EU, individuals hold simultaneously citizenship of a state and membership in the Union, each layer providing them with a specific set of rights and opportunities for experiencing and exercising democratic agency. As nationals they are members of a democratic collective represented by a state via the Council (European Council); as Union citizens they enjoy – or are entitled to claim – individual freedoms and fundamental rights, for instance of non-discrimination and equal treatment. Given these complexities of the democratic life of the Union, the principal-agent model of delegation and accountability which is premised on the citizen-agent and on competitive elections will hardly work.

Regarding the democratic mechanisms by which conflict in different political and social fields of action and interaction is articulated and accommodated, the EU is constituted neither as a (multinational) federal state nor merely as an international organisation, but is best understood as a multilevel political community (Franzius and Preuss 2011). In this framework, EU democratic legitimacy is not exclusively a question of the democratic legitimacy of its supranational institutional order, nor is this legitimacy predominantly derived from its democratic member states. Instead, it depends on the interplay and complementary nature of the democratic life of the Union in both supranational institutions and member states. In this context, processes of "democratisation from below" will involve the transformation of power relations, installing mechanisms for "appropriating" power through those who are ruled, for instance by strengthening their powers for exercising oversight, prevention and judgement (Rosanvallon 2008; cf. Schmitter 2012: 30ff.).

Understanding the EU is extremely hard because of the complicated and controversial nature of theoretical and policy debates. The innovative empirical approaches and materials presented by this book will make it an important contribution to understanding EU politics based on sound social scientific empirical findings. We therefore hope the book will fill a gap in academic and public debates linking social scientific analyses of democratic politics with developments of the EU. Alerting readers to the social and political dimensions of EU constitutional crisis, choice and change, readers will engage with these debates by highlighting the emerging democratic nature of European Union development that is all too often obfuscated by technical discourses and expert arguments.

References

Bauböck, R. 1994. *Transnational Citizenship. Membership and Rights in International Migration*. Aldershot: Edward Elgar.

Bellamy, R. 2012. How Democratic is the EU? The Inevitability of a Democratic Deficit, in *Key Controversies in European Integration*, edited by H. Zimmermann and A. Dür. Houndsmill: Palgrave Macmillan.

Crum, B. 2011. *Learning from the EU Constitutional Treaty: Democratic Constitutionalization Beyond the Nation-State*. London/New York: Routledge.

Dalton, R. 2008. *Citizen Politics: Public Opinion and Political Parties in Advanced Industrial Democracies*. Washington: CQ Press.

de Wilde, P. and Zürn, M. 2012. Can the Politicization of European Integration be Reversed? *Journal of Common Market Studies*, 50(1), 137–153.

Diez, T. 2001. Europe as a Discursive Battleground: Discourse Analysis and European Integration Studies. *Cooperation and Conflict*, 36(1), 5–38.

Diez, T. 1999. Speaking "Europe": The Politics of Integration Discourse. *Journal of European Public Policy*, 6(4), 598–613.

Dryzek, J. and Berejikian, J. 1993. Reconstructive Democratic Theory. *American Political Science Review*, 87(1), 48–60.

Dryzek, J. 2005. *Deliberative Global Politics*. Cambridge: Polity.

Eriksen, E.O. 2005. *Making the European Polity. Reflexive Integration in the EU*. London: Routledge.

Eriksen, E.O. et al. 2004. *Developing a Constitution for Europe*. London: Routledge.

Eriksen, E.O. and Fossum, J.E. (eds) 2000. *Democracy in the European Union: Integration through Deliberation?* London: Routledge.

Eriksen, E.O. and Fossum, J.E. (eds) 2012. *Rethinking Democracy and the European Union*. London: Routledge.

Evas, T., Liebert, U. and Lord, C. (eds) 2012. *Multilayered Representation in the European Union. Parliaments, Courts and the Public Sphere*. Baden-Baden: Nomos.

Evas, T. 2012. *Judicial Application of European Union Law in Post-communist Countries* (Studies in Modern Law and Policy). Farnham: Ashgate Publishing.

Evas, T. 2007. Elitist with a Russian Twist: Mass Media Discourses on European Constitutional Ratification in Estonia and Latvia, in *Perspectives on European Politics and Society*, vol. 8, no. 3, 374–413.

Favell, A. and Guiraudon, V. (eds) 2011. *Sociology of the European Union*. Basingstoke: Palgrave Macmillan.

Fligstein, N. 2008. *Euro-clash: The EU, European Identity, and the Future of Europe*. Oxford: Oxford University Press.

Fossum, J.E. and Menéndez, A.J. 2011. *The Constitution's Gift: A Constitutional Theory for a Democratic European Union*. Lanham: Rowman & Littlefield.

Franzius, C and Preuss, U.K. 2011. *Die Zukunft der Europäischen Demokratie*. Berlin: Heinrich Böll Stiftung, 7.

Grimm, D. 1995. Does Europe Need a Constitution? *European Law Journal*, 1(3), 282–302.

Habermas, J. 2001. The Postnational Constellation and the Future of Democracy, in *The Postnational Constellation: Political Essays*, edited by J. Habermas. Cambridge: Polity Press.

Hix, S. and Bartolini, S. 2006. *Notre Europe. Politics: The Right or the Wrong Sort of Medicine for the EU?* Notre Europe.

Hix, S. and Marsh, M. 2011. Second-order Effects Plus Pan-European Political Swings: An Analysis of European Parliament Elections across Time. *Electoral Studies*, 30, 4–15.

Hooghe, L. and Marks, G. 2008. A Postfunctionalist Theory of European Integration: From Permissive Consensus to Constraining Dissensus. *British Journal of Political Science*, 39(1), 1–23.

Imig, D.R. and Tarrow, S.G. 2001. *Contentious Europeans. Protest and Politics in an Integrating Europe*. Lanham: Rowman & Littlefield.
Kauppi, N. 2011. EU Politics. Sociology of the European Union, in *Sociology of the European Union*, edited by A. Favell and V. Guiraudon. London: Palgrave Macmillan, 150–171.
König, T. and Hug, S. (eds) 2006. *Policy-making Processes and the European Constitution: A Comparative Study of Member States and Accession Countries*. London: Routledge.
Kriesi, H. and Grande, E. 2012. *Political Conflict in Western Europe*. Cambridge: University Press.
Lacroix, J. and Nicolaidis, K. (eds) 2010. *European Stories. Intellectual Debates on Europe in National Contexts*. Oxford: Oxford University Press.
Liebert, U. (ed.) 2007. Europe in Contention: Debating the Constitutional Treaty. *Perspectives on European Politics and Society*, 8(3), 235–413.
Liebert, U. 2012a. Civil Society, Public Sphere and Democracy in the EU, in *Rethinking Democracy and the European Union*, edited by E.O. Eriksen and J.E. Fossum. London/New York: Routledge, 112–142.
Liebert, U. 2012b. Rethinking the "No European Demos" Thesis: Transnational Discursive Representation as a Prerequisite of EU Democracy, in *Multilayered Representation in the European Union. Parliaments, Courts and the Public Sphere*, edited by T. Evas, U. Liebert and C. Lord. Baden-Baden: Nomos, 233–254.
Liebert, U. and Trenz, H.J. (eds) 2011. *The New Politics of European Civil Society*. London/New York: Routledge.
Lord, C. 2012. How Democratic is the EU? A Democratic Achievement, not Just a Democratic Deficit, in *Key Controversies in European Integration*, edited by H. Zimmermann and A. Dür. Houndsmills: Palgrave Macmillan, XXX.
Maatsch, A. 2011. *Ethnic Citizenship Regimes. Europeanisation, Post-War Migration and Redressing Past Wrongs*. Basingstoke: Palgrave Macmillan.
Maatsch, S. 2007. The Struggle to Control Meanings: The French Debate on the European Constitution in the Mass Media, in *Perspectives on European Politics and Society*, vol. 8, no. 3, 261–280.
Majone, G. 2005. *Dilemmas of European Integration: The Ambiguities & Pitfalls of Integration by Stealth*. Oxford: Oxford University Press.
Marks, G. and Steenbergen, M.R. (eds) 2004. *European Integration and Political Conflict*. Cambridge: Cambridge University Press.
Medrano, J.D. 2003. *Framing Europe. Attitudes to European Integration in Germany, Spain, and the United Kingdom*. Princeton: Princeton University Press.
Moravcsik, A. 2006. What Can We Learn from the Collapse of the European Constitution Project? *Politische Vierteljahresschrift*, 47(2), 219–41.
Moravcsik, A. and Mény, Y. 2009. A Transatlantic Dialogue about Democracy and its Future, *EUI Review* (Summer), Florence, 19–22.
Morgan, G. 2005. *The Idea of a European Superstate: Public Justification and European Integration*. Princeton: Princeton University Press.

Packham, K. 2007. From the Contenious Cnostitution to the Awkward Other ... Social Model: The Constitutional Debate in the British Print Media, in *Perspectives on European Politics and Society*, vol. 8, no. 3, 281–313.

Pettit, P. 2006. Democracy, National and International. *Monist*, 89, 302–325.

Pettit, P. 2000. Democracy, Electoral and Contestatory. *Nomos*, 42, 105–44.

Rakušanová, P. 2007. The Constitutional Debate: A One Man Show? Vaclav Klaus and the Constitutional Discourse in the Czech Republic, in *Perspectives on European Politics and Society*, vol. 8, no. 3, 342–373.

Risse, T. 2010. *A Community of Europeans? Transnational Identities and Public Spheres*. Ithaca: Cornell University Press.

Rosanvallon, P. 2008. La légitimité démocratique. Paris, Édition du Seuil.

Schmidt, V.A. 2006. *Democracy in Europe: The EU and National Polities*. Oxford: Oxford University Press.

Schmitter, P.C. 2000. *How to Democratize the European Union ... And Why Bother?* Lanham: Rowman & Littlefield.

Schmitter, P.C. 2012. Crisis and Mutation in the Institutions of Representation in "Real-existing" European Democracies: National and Supra-national, in *Multilayered Representation in the European Union. Parliaments, Courts and the Public Sphere*, edited by T. Evas, U. Liebert and C. Lord. Baden-Baden: Nomos, 25–40.

Statham, P. 2007. Political Communication, European Integration and the Transformation of National Public Spheres: A Comparison of Britain and France, in *The European Union and the Public Sphere: A Communicative Space in the Making?* edited by Fossum J. E. and Schlesinger P. London: Routledge.

Trenz, H-J., Conrad, M. and Rosén, G. 2007. The Interpretative Moment of European Journalism. The Impact of Newpaper Opinion Making in the Ratification Process. RECON Online Working Paper 2007/1.

Trenz, H.J. 2011. Social Theory and European Integration, in *Sociology of the European Union*, edited by A. Favell and V. Guiraudon. London: Palgrave Macmillan, 193–214.

Triandafyllidou, A., Wodak, R. and Krzyzanovski, M. 2009. *The European Public Sphere and the Media: Europe in Crisis*. London: Palgrave.

Tully, J. 2007. A New Kind of Europe? Democratic Integration in the European Union, *Critical Review of International Social and Political Philosophy*, 10(1), 71–86.

Waever, O. 2004. Discursive Approaches, in *European Integration Theory*, edited by A. Wiener and T. Diez. Oxford: Oxford University Press, 163–180.

Wodak, R. and Meyer, M. 2009. *Methods for Critical Discourse Analysis*. Sage.

Wodak, R. and van Dijk, T.A. (eds) 2000. *Racism at the Top: Parliamentary Discourses on Ethnic Issues in 6 European States*. Klagenfurt/Celovec: Drava.

Wyrozumska, A. 2007. Who is Willing to Die for the Constitution? The National Debate on the Constitutional Treaty in Poland, in *Perspectives on European Politics and Society*, vol. 8, no. 3, 314–341.

Zimmermann, H. and Dür, A. 2012. *Key Controversies in European Integration*. Houndsmill: Palgrave Macmillan.

Chapter 2
Still 'between Eros and Civilisation'? Citizens, Courts and Constructing European Citizenship

Tatjana Evas and Ulrike Liebert

Introduction

How can a union of states develop a common citizenship, and may this status achieve legitimacy amidst the diversity of the union's component citizenship regimes? For two decades now, the question of how to come to terms with the unprecedented European Union citizenship established by the Maastricht Treaty has been a focus of political science scholarship on citizenship as well as constitutionalist and legal analyses of European integration.[1] The project of Union Citizenship[2] has neither historical antecedent nor does it enjoy historical guarantees (Föllesdal 2001, Keane 2005: 18). Although it grants only a relatively thin layer of rights, European Citizenship is intensely contested on the grounds of national democratic autonomy and state sovereignty on the one hand, and principles of supranational unity and conformity, on the other. *Vis-à-vis* nationally entrenched citizenships, the legally created European citizenship has frequently been seen as a motor of European collective identification but also questioned for tensions between its civic principles and the 'Eros' of national identities (Weiler 1998). However, when looked at through the lenses of a 'more inclusive, multilayered and multicultural conception', Union citizenship has been dubbed a 'prototype for institutional experimentation on citizenship on a global scale' (Kostakopoulou 2007: 623). Normative citizenship theorists have sought to theorise the legitimacy of Union citizenship in accordance with universal, cosmopolitan or post-national norms.[3] Principled critics, by contrast, have challenged these accounts, seeing the European Union as a supranational

---

1 See Bellamy et al. 2006, Eder and Giesen 2001, Meehan 2000, Preuss et al. 2003, Reich 1999; Shaw 2008, Weiler 1998, Wiener 1998.

2 In this article we use the terms 'Union Citizenship', 'European Citizenship' and 'European Union Citizenship' interchangeably as denoting the same phenomenon, if not stated otherwise.

3 See Habermas 1992, 1998, Soysal 1994, Archibugi et al. 1998, Closa 1998a, 1998b; La Torre 1998; Magnette 1999, Delanty 2000, Benhabib 2004; Bellamy et al. 2004; Bellamy et al. 2006; Benhabib 2007; Bauböck 2007; Besson and Utzinger 2007, Liebert 2007; Benhabib 2009.

construction that is frequently in conflict with cosmopolitan norms on the one hand and democratic principles on the other (Balibar 2004, Rousseau 2005).

This chapter takes an interdisciplinary approach to analyse how the citizenship regime of the European Union has evolved from the interplay of two processes: the building of citizenship practices and the negotiation of norms (Jenson 2007). Both respond to problems of globalisation, migration and integration. 'Globalisation' in relation to citizenship refers here to trans-border interactions, including not only the economic and political but also the cultural realm, for instance by diffusing individual human and civic rights (Habermas 1999; Turner 2000; Delanty 2000; Dower and Williams 2002; Benhabib 2009). 'Immigration', on the other hand, refers here to processes of human trans-border mobility that contribute to changing populations and increasing ethnic diversity. Unlike the way in which the citizenship regime of the United States seeks to subsume ethnic diversity into the mainstream culture,[4] European citizenship establishes a more complex and dynamic framework that aims at reconciling principles that are common across the EU with recognition of the diversity of member states' citizenship regimes.

This chapter is premised on the assumption that Union citizenship bridges a diversity of 'modern nation state citizenships' with a 'post-national' approach to supranational citizenship (Eder and Giesen 2001). Yet, in responding to the challenging question how this is achieved, and departing from conventional wisdoms transmitted by citizenship theorists, we explain the development of European citizenship as a result of litigation practices by (transborder mobile but also static) citizens and national courts, on the one hand and, on the other hand, the preliminary rulings issued by the European Court of Justice (ECJ) in response to these cases. In other words, the unfolding transnational judicial dialogue among courts as well as with public and private agents constitutes the core of our argument.

Our position draws on well-established legal theoretical approaches that conceive law as a field of social (societal) practice (that is Joseph Raz 1979, 2005; Luhmann 2004). Following this conception we consider litigation as a form of civil engagement (thus contributing to democratisation from 'below'). While citizens' empowerment is enabled by EU citizenship norms, European judges exercise the authority of interpreting these norms in the context of constitutional pluralism (Maduro 2007) depending on – frequently transborder mobile – citizens who bring their case to the national court where the national judges decide to refer the case to the ECJ (Reich 2005). Thus, without legal action by an individual citizen the 'European Judges' have no power whatsoever (see for example Alter 2000).[5] More

---

4 Robert Putnam noted that changing populations and ethnic diversity continually shape trust, identities, social ties and civic engagement: While 'increased immigration is a strong engine of economic growth and injects creativity and energy into receiving countries and communities, in the short-term, our discomfort with diversity challenges our community bonds and cohesion' (Putnam 2008).

5 Yet, citizens' empowerment through national courts and the European Court of Justice are constrained, too. In her book 'The European Union's Legal System and Domestic

specifically, drawing on MacCormick's institutional theory, democratic law (law enacted by the legislator) that is violated by state organs or other persons becomes alive and meaningful for a concrete person (legal or physical) only through authoritative interpretive decisions of courts and administrative agencies or through individuals' possibility to rely on such authoritative interpretations and to request their enforcement.[6] In that sense, courts and case law are also defining features of the emerging multilevel European polity to the extent to which that polity is based on the rule of law where interpretive acts by courts are key to shaping the relevant legal landscape.[7] Although it is correct that the contestation of legal rules is often initiated by concerned individual citizens, the effects of these judgments are by no means limited to the specific cases presented by these individuals.[8] The judicial decisions can trigger spillover effects – a well-established legal mechanism in both national jurisdictions and at the European level (see, for example, Aalto 2011)

Summarising our argument in a nutshell, we suggest that European citizenship cannot be understood as a legal construction from above, allegedly driven by the ECJ interfering into the autonomy of the member states (cf. Micklitz and De Witte 2012) and single-mindedly pursuing ever more unity and harmonisation between member states (for example Hailbronner 2004; 2007). Instead, European citizenship is clearly driven by agents and processes from below. As a necessary condition, it requires active cross-border mobile citizens, migrant denizens, non-national Union citizens, or

---

Policy: Spillover or Backlash?' Alter extensively discusses the enabling conditions that litigants have to overcome in order to successfully change national practices through litigation at the EU level.

6   MacCormick, N. 2007. *Institutions of Law: An Essay in Legal Theory*. Oxford: Oxford University Press.

7   In this context, Cichowski (2006, 2007) has specifically discussed the role of the national court as an arena for democratic engagement of civil society through litigation related to EU norms, as well as a mechanism conducive to the Europeanization of national societies (2007). On litigation in the European courts as a form of participation in supranational governance see also Alter 2006; Börzel 2006; Cichowski & Stone Sweet, 2003; Conant, 2006. A theoretical discussion on public interest litigation at EU level can be found in Micklitz and Reich (1997). Most recently, Schiek (2010, 2012) has further elaborated on the dual nature of EU litigation and on the role of the European Court of Justice, in particular, assessing it as a forum for representing social values and public interests. In the framework of the EU's multilevel judicial system, Evas and Liebert (2012) have comparatively analysed the constitutive role of national constitutional courts for protecting citizens' political equality at both national and European levels.

8   As an illustration of the far reaching effects single judgments can have, consider the national legislative reaction to the ECJ case in *Zhu and Chen* (C-200/02). As a result of the ECJ judgment the constitution of Ireland was amended to expand grounds for refusal of national citizenship to individuals who did not have an Irish parent. For the so-called 'spillover' effect of legal dicta and reasoning of individual cases on subsequent practice of courts (especially through development of general principles of law), see Takis Tridimas (2007) 'General Principles of EU Law'. On the spillover effects of EU rules on liability for breach of EU law into national public liability laws, see also Alter 2000, Burely and Mattli 1998.

third-country nationals trying to exercise rights that EU law confers on them but that they feel to be deprived of in practice. European citizenship also relies on another set of agents, namely on judges from national courts who are willing to refer conflictive cases to the ECJ whose interpretation of EU norms – the 'preliminary ruling' – they consider sufficiently legitimate to be applied to their domestic context.

This argument is developed in three steps. First, we map the patterns and dynamics of how European citizenship is constructed from below, by ECJ case law deriving from the litigation practices of citizens, non-nationals, migrants, or residents. Then, we review these findings in the light of competing normative citizenship models. In the conclusion, we suggest how to conceptualise the evolving European citizenship.

Constructing European Citizenship from Below: Litigation as Citizenship Practice

The question how a union of states such as the European Union can develop joint regional citizenship, and what precisely this entails for citizenship status and rights (Joppke 2007: 37), is addressed in the following four steps: first, by giving an overview of the legal provisions that constitute European citizenship from the Rome to the Lisbon Treaties; second, by identifying patterns of implementation of European citizenship in member states; third, by exploring litigation as a form of participatory citizenship practice and key to the dynamics of citizenship change in the EU; and fourth, by analysing the interaction of national courts and the ECJ through the 'preliminary reference' procedure.

From 'Free Movement' in the Rome Treaty to European Citizenship after the Lisbon Treaty

For mapping the patterns and dynamics of 'Citizenship of the Union', we make an assumption that in order to assess the inclusiveness vs. exclusiveness of citizenship in the EU context, it is necessary to analyse the legal framework that is shaping and being shaped by evolving policy practices (Wiener 1998; Meehan 2000). The legal framework that now encompasses European citizenship was initiated in the 1957 Rome Treaty on the European Economic Community. Here, the scope of individuals who could enjoy the freedom of movement and non-discrimination was narrowly limited to salaried workers only, thus driven by 'common market' logic. This scope was subsequently expanded to include self-employed persons and service providers as well as family members of eligible citizens.

However, it was not until the early 90s that the right to free movement of persons was extended beyond 'common market' logic to include economically inactive individuals. The 1992 Maastricht Treaty and the subsequently adopted secondary legislation extended the personal scope of the right to free movement to encompass all categories of citizens.⁹ Moreover, it added a substantively new quality to the right of free movement, through introducing the concept of citizenship of the European Union.¹⁰ Interpreting the citizenship provisions of the Maastricht Treaty the ECJ strengthened the essential role of the individual within the Union. Not the economic status of the Union citizen but existence of the citizenship itself became sufficient to trigger protection under EU law. In the 1999 Grzelczyk case the ECJ stated that Union citizenship was 'destined to become the fundamental status of nationals of the Member States'.¹¹ Advocate General Sharpston considers statement of the ECJ in Grzelczyk a far reaching milestone of the case-law, with 'the Court's description of citizenship ... being potentially of similar significance to its seminal statement in Van Gend en Loos'.¹²

The 2009 Lisbon Treaty further expanded the legal framework that regulates European citizenship, by including the 'Democratic Principles' (Articles 9–11), and Part Two 'Non-Discrimination and Citizenship of the Union' (Articles 18 to 25 of the Treaty on the Functioning of the European Union (TFEU), as well as secondary legislation – Directive 2004/38/EC on the right of EU citizens and their family members to move and reside freely within the territory of the Member States (the Citizenship Directive).¹³

---

9   Three directives have been adopted, guaranteeing the right of residence to retired persons, students and inactive people.

10 Now Article 20 TFEU, ex. Article 17 TEC. The Treaty of Amsterdam (1999) further strengthened the rights linked to European citizenship by integrating the Schengen Convention into the Treaty. The Treaty of Nice (2003) introduced qualified majority voting in the field of free movement and residence, which has simplified the legislative process. The extension of the scope of the right to free movement to encompass all categories of citizens was brought about, among other things, by adoption of the three directives, guaranteeing the right of residence to retired persons, students and inactive people.

11 Case C-184/99 *Grzelczyk* [2001] para. 31. This formulation became an established doctrine in case law, see most recently case C-200/02 *Zhu and Chen* [2004] para. 25, case C-135/08 *Rottman* [2010], case C-34/09 *Zambrano* [2011] para. 41, case C-371/08 *Ziebell* [2011] par. 73 (see Annex Table 2.1).

12 C-34/09 *Zambrano* [2011] Opinion of the Advocate General Sharpston, para. 67.

13 The Directive brings together under one legal framework all secondary law provisions associated with exercise of the right of free movement and residence in MS. It replaces all previous EC legislation in this field: Regulation 1612/68 and Directive 64/221/EEC, 68/360/EEC, 72/194/EEC (on the free movement of workers) 73/148/EC, 75/34/EEC, 75/35/EEC (establishment and provision of services); 90/364/EEC (Residence directive); 90/365/EEC and 93/96/EEC (Students). The Directive reconfirms the general right of EU citizens to move and reside in the EU (and thus replaces the 'categorisation' scheme of previous legislative acts); streamlines the conditions and administrative formalities associated with exercise of the right; introduces the right of permanent residence for EU citizens after five years of continuous residence, as well as facilitating movement of family members. Compared to earlier, mostly group-specific, directives, the Citizenship Directive is a legislative attempt to consolidate and further extend the rights of all citizens and their family members associated with exercise of the right of free movement and residence in the EU.

Table 2.1 Main EU law provisions after the Lisbon Treaty, concerning EU citizenship rights and rights of third-country long-term residents[14]

	EU citizens	TCN long-term residents
European Citizenship.	Art. 20 (1), Art. 9	
Right to free movement.	Art. 20 (2) Art. 21 (1) Dir. 2004/38	Dir. 2003/109 Dir. 2004/114
Democratic principles (equality of citizens, right to participate in the democratic life of the Union, citizens' initiative).	Art. 9–11	
Right to vote for and stand as a candidate in municipal elections in the MS of residence.	Art. 20 (2) (b) Art. 22 (1)	
Right to vote for and stand as a candidate in European Parliament elections in the MS of residence.	Art. 20 (2) (b) Art. 22 (2)	
Right to the diplomatic and consular protection of another MS outside the EU.	Art. 20 (2) (c) Art. 23	
Right to petition the European Parliament.	Art. 20 (2) (d)	
Right to complain to the European Ombudsman.	Art. 20 (d)	
Right to address the institutions and advisory bodies of the Union in any of the Treaty languages and to obtain a reply in the same language.	Art. 20 (d)	
Right to family reunification.	Dir. 2003/86/EC	Dir. 2003/86/EC
Prohibition against discrimination based on nationality.	Art. 18	
Right not to be discriminated against on the basis of sex, racial or ethnic origin, religion or belief, disability, age or sexual orientation.	Art. 19 Dir. 2000/43/EC	Art. 13 Dir. 2000/43/EC
Citizens' initiative.	Art. 24	

Source: Authors.
Note: TCN = third country national.

---

14 The table refers to the provisions of the Treaty on the Functioning of the European Union (TFEU) if not stated otherwise. This table does not include asylum seekers and refugees, individuals residing in the EU on the basis of humanitarian status. It also does not include special rights of TCNs from certain countries with which the EU has concluded special agreements, such as EU-Turkey Accession Agreements or Agreements with Mediterranean countries. This table also does not include a whole series of fundamental rights, obligations and principles which follow from the EU Treaties and the case law of the ECJ, such as the right to contact and receive a response from any EU institution in one of the EU official languages, the right to access European Parliament, European Commission, and Council documents under certain conditions, or the right of equal access to the Community civil service.

In addition to primary and secondary legislation directly concerned with the broadening scope of rights conferred on nationals of the EU or their family members, the Lisbon Treaty further extends the right to move and reside freely within the territory of member states to include third-country nationals who are long-term legal residents (Long-Term Residence Directive),[15] and their family members (Family Reunification Directive).[16] Students and researchers from third countries intending to enter an academic institution of the EU member states also benefit from the more specific directives that allow for simplified conditions of admission for this category of individuals.

Table 2.1 (see opposite) summarises the main primary and secondary EU law provisions related to access to citizenship/residence and citizenship rights. In the following analysis, we will concentrate on implementation and litigation related to the central provisions of primary and secondary legislation on European Citizenship that includes Articles 20 to 22 of the TFEU, the Citizenship Directive, Long-term Residence Directive and Family Reunification Directive.[17]

National Implementation of EU Citizenship Directives

The institutionalisation of 'Citizenship of the Union', established by the Maastricht Treaty in 1992,[18] plays an instrumental role in changing the legislative and political environment of national citizenship regimes. It has created opportunities for more inclusive communities, primarily for all citizens of the European Union, but also and increasingly so for third-country nationals. Legislative and conceptual changes introduced by national citizenship policies have not been without contestation (Bauböck et al. 2006). Adoption of the Long-Term Residence, Family Reunification and Citizenship Directives has triggered intensive amendments to national legislation in countries such as Austria, the Czech Republic, Belgium and Hungary. In other countries such as the United Kingdom and Germany, the scope of implementing measures was rather limited, but the application of these Directives has triggered intensive litigation in national courts, leading to a high number of preliminary reference requests to the ECJ.

---

15   Directive 2003/109/EC, which concerns the status of third-country nationals who are long-term residents.

16   Directive 2003/86/EC on the right to family reunification.

17   We define the legal framework regulating EU citizenship as encompassing both EU nationals and long-term residents.

18   The Treaty Establishing the European Community currently in force also includes in Part II 'Citizenship of the Union' in addition to the concept of citizenship of the European Union (Article 17), a catalogue of rights and duties that European citizenship entails (Articles 18–21).

Table 2.2 National implementation of EU citizenship directives

	Dir. 2003/86 (family reunification)		Dir. 2004/38 (right to free movement)		Dir. 2003/109 (long-term residence status)		Art. 20–23 (ex. Art. 17–19 TEC) Union Citizenship
	NM[19]	ECJ	NM	ECJ	NM	ECJ	ECJ[20]
Austria	2		77	1	85		2
Belgium	12		33		41		8
Bulgaria	3		1		2		
Czech Rep.	14		52		53		
Denmark	5		1				
Finland	2		4		9		2
Germany	5		4	4	3	1	20
Estonia	4		5		1		
Ireland	0	1	8	1	0		1
Greece	2		2		2		
Spain	6		8			1	1
France	4		13	1	3		
Italy	2		9		1		2
Cyprus	2		2		2		
Latvia	2		4		4		
Lithuania	8		40		26		
Luxemburg	1	1	2	1	1	1	
Hungary	19		72		40		
Malta	1		5		1		
Netherlands	1		2	5	2		8
Poland	9		7		13		2
Portugal	9		1		4	1	1
Romania	7		9	1	5		1
Slovenia	23		19		27		
Slovakia	3		6		3		
Sweden	3		10		7		2
UK	-		9	3			5
EU27	149	5	405	17	335	5	59

Source: Own compilation on the basis of information provided on the official web page of the European Union, www.eur-lex.eu, under National Implementation Measures for each above-mentioned directive.

---

19 National provisions communicated by MS concerning national execution measures on Council Directive 2003/86/EC of 22 September 2003 on the right to family reunification.

20 This includes cases submitted by national courts through the preliminary reference procedure, where either the national court or the ECJ has relied on Article 17, 18 or 19, and cases brought by the European Commission against MS for failing to fulfil obligations.

Table 2.2 summarises by member state the number of different national measures communicated to the EC, including court cases litigated in the ECJ, that were necessary at national level to give effect to secondary EU legislation on European citizenship. These measures include new acts, or amendments to existing national legal acts, on three main directives, as well as ECJ citizenship litigation on Articles 20–22 of TFEU (ex. Articles 17–19 of TEC).

To understand the full potential of the evolution of European citizenship and its far-reaching implications both for EU citizens and third-country nationals, it is not sufficient to refer only to the EU legislative framework and national implementing measures. It is also necessary to analyse institutional dialogue and interplay among national administrations, governments, national courts, the ECJ, and national as well as non-national citizens and residents. Ultimately, to be fully effective, the body of EU rules must be applied and interpreted by national administrative bodies, and in case of conflict by national courts. Therefore, the conceptualised legal framework of 'Citizenship of the Union' is not only limited to formally binding legal rules but also includes national and ECJ case law. In the following, we will highlight the legal and especially social agency that explains the dynamics of institutionalising European citizenship.

Litigation as European Citizenship Practice

Normative preferences, institutional constraints and established practices at the national level of member states may be slow to accept change, even after formal adoption of EU legal rules and national implementing measures. To challenge the existing boundaries of national legislation or established administrative and/or legal practice, an affected active citizen (resident) with legal standing in a given jurisdiction is necessary. Through national citizenship or residence status an individual has access to various rights that in turn allow for their participation in a given political community. Participation in a political community is conventionally exercised through participation in elections, active citizenship practices such as petitioning and demonstrations, and membership and participation in civic/social movements and NGOs. However, what is less evident is that participation in a given political community may also be exercised through litigation.

Participation through litigation requires an individual's full access to information, including information on national and European legislation and case law, for example. In this context, access to information is a prerequisite for active democratic citizenship practices, from opinion formation to making reasoned decisions and active participation in democratic processes. Access to, and availability of, information may result not only in increased awareness of formal rights, but may also contribute to contestation of obstacles that stand in the way of exercising these rights in practice. Therefore, the right to information not only implies the 'right to know' but also to the 'right to contest'. The right to contest, that is, the right to judicial recourse in a court of law to challenge existing formal rules that mediate an individual's relation to the state or other individuals, helps create a public 'deliberative space'. Consequently, litigation is a legal instrument for contesting legislative boundaries with the aim of either extending or limiting existing legislative regulation.[21] The *Metock* decision is a case in point, where 'collective action'[22] by ten individuals succeeded in reversing a national expulsion decision.[23]

In the context of the EU, the 'deliberative space' that is framed by national and supranational legislation is of a multilayered nature. The link that connects the different layers in the deliberative European court system is defined by the so-called 'preliminary reference procedure' (see below). The key to this decentralised EC legal system can be found in the arrangement that citizens' claims *vis-à-vis* an EU member state regarding application of rights and principles flowing from EC law are adjudicated by national legal forums. Provided that national courts are in doubt on the application of EC law, they can seek assistance from the 'supranational legal forum' of the ECJ through the preliminary reference procedure.[24]

Interaction between National Courts and the European Court of Justice (ECJ)

While the *sui generis* nature of the EU may not illuminate the concept of transnational citizenship in theoretical terms (Olsen 2012), it is essential and central for understanding the exercise of citizenship through the court system.[25] It is typical of political science literature to take a 'top-down' approach to ECJ jurisprudence, whereby the ECJ is assigned the role of gendarme, dictating what member states

---

21 In other words, court cases deal with issues where, at a given time, given boundaries (in substantive or procedural terms) of a given policy or regulation are at stake. They may (but need not) trigger political processes leading to formal legislative codification (regulation) or changes.

22 Different from the US or some national EU MS jurisdictions that allow bringing a case for the 'public good', 'class action' is formally not admitted by the ECJ.

23 In the *Metock* case, a group of third-country nationals and their Union citizen spouses brought a legal action in national courts against refusal by the Minister for Justice, Equality and Law Reform to grant a residence card. To avoid expulsion from Ireland, they relied on the Citizenship Directive to challenge national norms. The High Court submitted to the ECJ a reference for a preliminary ruling concerning interpretation of the Citizenship Directive.

24 In some situations, national courts of final instance have an obligation to submit questions on interpretation of Community law.

25 Specifically, this sui generis nature of the European Community legal order was developed by the ECJ, starting with Case 26/62 van Gend and Loos v Netherlands, where the Court stated that [t]he Community constitutes a new legal order of international law for the benefit of which the states have limited their sovereign rights, albeit within limited fields, and the subjects of which comprise not only member states but also their nationals. Independently of the legislation of member states, community law therefore not only imposes obligations on individuals but is also intended to confer upon them rights which become part of their legal heritage. These rights arise not only where they are expressly granted by the treaty, but also by reason of obligations which the treaty imposes in a clearly defined way upon individuals as well as upon the member states and upon the institutions of the community. (Case 26/62 van Gend and Loos v Netherlands Inland Revenue Administration (1963) ECR I-1).

should do regardless of their will.[26] ECJ judgments are considered only as formal dicta issued at the supranational level by a supranational institution, with national courts and citizens only as the ultimate recipients of EU integration and policy making. However, analysis of the preliminary reference procedure in the field of European Citizenship demonstrates that this is a misleading misconception. The link between the national level and the ECJ is considerably more nuanced and, in particular, works also in the reverse direction, from bottom up (see Figure 2.1 below).

Legal scholarship on ECJ jurisprudence, and the judges themselves, emphasise the dialogical and horizontal nature of the decentralised system of EU law enforcement.[27] In our view, litigation is one of the institutionalised forms of acting out citizenship rights within a given political community. This right is currently limited primarily to national courts, with individuals being generally unable to bring claims directly to the ECJ.[28]

For examining ECJ case law, references by the national courts to the ECJ through the preliminary reference procedure provide an indication of the degree of mutual interaction between the member states and the EU levels (Mancini 2000). In fact, the ECJ may take up a case only if the national court submits a request for a preliminary ruling. Thus, it depends on the national court whether a preliminary

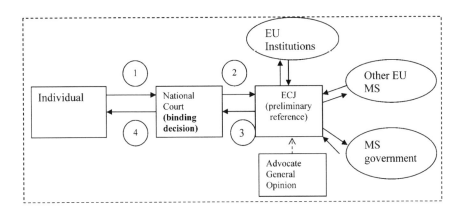

Figure 2.1   The EU preliminary reference mechanism

---

26   The ECJ is a judicial institution, composed of one judge from each MS. It is vested with the authority to adjudicate issues within the competence of the EC Treaty.

27   The ECJ has stated that '[m]oreover, the system of references for a preliminary ruling is based on a dialogue between one court and another, the initiation of which depends entirely on the national court's assessment of whether a reference is appropriate and necessary' (see Case C-2/06 Kempter [2008] ECR I-0000, para. 42).

28   In very limited types of cases, natural and legal persons can bring direct actions to the ECJ. However, as a general rule, this right is limited to the preliminary reference procedure through national courts (see Reich 2001: 4).

reference is submitted or not.²⁹ Any national court – even from the lower levels – has the right to request a preliminary reference ruling. In the ECJ's preparation of a preliminary ruling, member states and other parties have the opportunity to submit their views. The ECJ judgment is then communicated back to national courts. On the basis of the interpretation of EU norms which the ECJ provides, the national court adjudicates the concrete facts of the case under consideration. It is the national court that ultimately issues a legally binding judgment. Legal enforcement of the judgment also occurs at national level.

The Dynamics of European Citizenship Case Law (1994–2010)

Citizenship Rights in the Union are a relatively recent subject of legal analysis (Reich 1999). During the period 1994–2011, the ECJ issued a total of 94 judgments on European citizenship primary law provisions and accompanying secondary legislation. While the number of cases yearly had been very limited up until the year 2000, from 2001 onwards it has increased, reaching a peak in 2008, with fourteen cases. Among the 27 cases submitted to the ECJ in 2008–2009, most cases concern interpretations of the provisions of the Citizenship Directive.

In our analysis we do not concentrate exclusively on litigation cases related to access to legal citizenship status or acquisition of nationality. Informed by the citizenship conception by T.H. Marshall, our focus is considerably broader. As the list of reviewed cases suggests (see Annex Table 2.1) we have included all cases where the status of Union Citizenship is invoked to provide non-nationals with an opportunity to challenge exclusive national practices in a variety of fields (ranging from education and health care to pensions and tax law).

The majority of these cases – a total of 29 – have been brought to the ECJ by German courts, followed by the United Kingdom (16) and Belgium (15 cases).³⁰ Germany, the United Kingdom and The Netherlands have also been among the most active in submitting observations on cases where they were not directly a party. Danish courts have submitted only one reference for a preliminary ruling.³¹ However, the Danish Government submitted 22 observations on ECJ cases concerning European Citizenship brought by other parties. Among the East and Central European member states, the most active were Poland (2 cases; 10 observations), Lithuania (1 case, 2 observation); the Czech Republic and Estonia (6 observations). Only, Slovenia, has not brought a single case or observation.³²

---

29   Although in some cases, an obligation to submit a request for preliminary reference exists.

30   See Table 2.3 and Annex Table 2.1 for a list of all cases.

31   Reference for preliminary ruling from the Vestre Landsret (Denmark) in case C-370/05 *Festersen*.

32   In this section, we refer to all cases from 1994 to 2012: both pending and already decided. Table 2.3 refers only to cases already concluded.

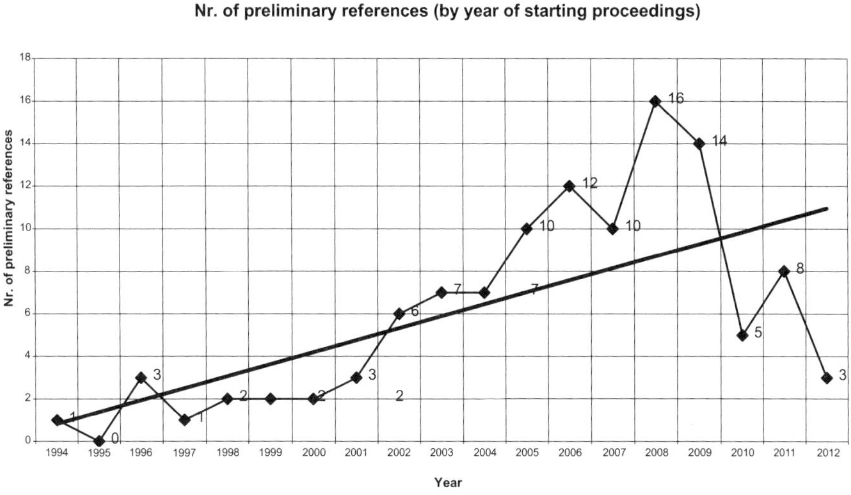

Nr. of preliminary references (by year of starting proceedings)

Figure 2.2   **Dynamics of European citizenship cases in the ECJ (1994–2011)**[33]

Table 2.3   **Number of citizenship cases and observations by member state**

	No. of cases[34]	No. of observations[35]		No. of cases	No. of observations
Austria	6	10	Italy	4	12
Belgium	15	8	Latvia	0	3
Bulgaria	3	0	Lithuania	1	2
Czech	0	6	Malta	0	1
Cyprus	0	2	Netherlands	12	21
Denmark	1	22	Poland	2	10
Estonia	0	6	Portugal	2	6
Finland	3	10	Romania	0	1
France	2	11	Slovakia	0	2
Germany	29	14	Spain	0	7
Greece	1	15	Sweden	1	2
Hungary	0	1	UK	16	23
Ireland	1	8			

---

33 Numbers refer to year of submission; judgments for the year 2010–2011 are indicative – not all pending cases submitted from 2009 have yet been adjudicated by the ECJ.

34 Number of requests for preliminary reference by the nationality of the court submitting a request. Includes all cases (including pending) as of July 2012 that refer to the citizenship provisions of the founding Treaties and the Directive 2004/38.

35 Number of observations submitted to the pending cases (preliminary reference procedure) by the Member States as of July 2012.

Table 2.4   EU citizenship cases brought to the ECJ, by nationality of referring court[36]

	Directive 2003/86[37]	Directive 2004/38	Directive 2003/109	No. of cases, referring to Art. 20–22 EC Treaty (Union Citizenship)
Austria	Dereci	Sahin		6: Dereci, Baumbast; Sahin; Gottwald; Sayn-Wittgenstein; Sahin; Hosse
Belgium		Bressol Zambrano		12: Zambrano, Bressol; Leyman, Eckelkamp et al.; Walloon Govmt; De Cuyper; Comm. v. Belgium; Ioannidis; My; Trojani; Avello,Crzelchik, d'Hoop
Bulgaria		Aladzhov Gaydarov		2: Aladzhov; Gaydarov
Finland				3: Turpeinen; Lindors; Pusa
Germany		Ziolkowski/ Szeja Ziebell Tsakouridis Huber Połat Bekleyen Vatsouras/ Koupatantze Bozkurt P.I.	Derin	27: Schulz-Delzers; Rottmann, Block, Chamier-Glisczinski, Ziebell, Bozkurt, Vatsouras/Koupatantze, Bekleyen, Busley/Cibrian, Comm v Germany, Huber; Zablocka-Weyhermüller; Grunkin and Paul; Comm v. Germany; Habelt, Moser and Wachter; Morgan and Düran; Comm v Germany; Schwarz and Gootjes-Schwarz; ITC; Niebüll; Comm v. Germany; Schempp; Pusa; Orfanopoulos and Oliveri; Gaumain-Cerri, Skanavi, Sala, Uecker
Ireland	Metock	Metock		1: Metock
Spain			F	1: Spain v. UK and Ireland
France		Mayeur		1: Wood
Italy				4: Zanotti, Pignataro; Mariano, Bickel and Franz
Lithuania		Runevič-Vardyn		1: Runevič-Vardyn
Luxemburg	F	F	F	
Netherlands	F	Förster F, F Wolzenberg Sahin		11: Delft, Josemans, Wolzenburg, Förster; F; Eind; Hendrix; Tas Hagen and Tas; N; Eman and Sevinger; Wijsenbeek
Poland				2: Rüffler, Nerkowska
Portugal			F	2: F, Waltraud
Romania		Jipa		1: Jipa
Sweden				2: Comm v. Sweden; Öberg
United Kingdom		Dias McCarthy Lassal Bidar Teixeira Dias Ibrahim		11: Bartlett, McCarthy; Stewart; Teixeira, Bidar; Zhu and Chen; Kaba; Baumbast, Kaba 2, Collins, Kauer
EU				Davis

36 Only concluded cases are included, and MS without any cases on the topic are not included in the table.

37 National provisions communicated by MS concerning national execution measures on Council Directive 2003/86/EC of 22 September 2003 on the right to family reunification.

In view of this contested field of citizenship construction, what are the necessary conditions for institutionalising a common citizenship framework that can achieve stability and legitimacy in the Union, despite the diversity of its member states' citizenship regimes?

Reviewing ECJ Rulings in Light of Alternative EU Citizenship Models

Having mapped the legal developments of European citizenship in the preceding section, in this part we will select a number of recent cases to review the contents of ECJ citizenship rulings in the light of contentious citizenship norms. Citizenship – a status conferring a set of exclusive rights on members who recognise each other as equals in a given political community – necessarily excludes those who do not qualify for inclusion. Although, as a consequence of globalisation, migration and integration, these lines of exclusion/inclusion have become blurred, the question of justification remains an important one. The scholarship on citizenship has put forth competing normative propositions for defending state citizenship, for instance, on grounds of nationality or democracy, or for justifying its transformation towards post-national, regional supranational or cosmopolitan forms of citizenship on grounds such as universal human rights. In the debate about European citizenship, three competing models can be discerned: European citizenship as a secondary complement to national citizenships; as supranational citizenship; and as cosmopolitan (republican) federal citizenship.[38]

I. European citizenship as secondary to nation state citizenship: In this view the nation state should continue to define individual membership in a political community by linking citizenship to nationality. National citizenship regimes (Bellamy 2004: 7ff; Kymlicka 2002) rely on different conceptions: the liberal conception, with a focus on citizenship in terms of individual rights; the communitarian conception, building on the notion of citizenship as belonging to a national community that implies a national identity, a common set of values, and a civic culture; and the republican conception, premised on citizenship as full and equal member participation within the economy and polity. Given Europe's coexisting, but diverging, citizenships, citizenship in a Union of states cannot but be premised on a historically-formed plurality of national citizenship regimes, with differing configurations of rights, meanings and practices.[39] As a consequence, a viable citizenship in the European Union cannot be founded on the Union but only

---

38 For three models of conceptualising the EU polity, see Eriksen and Fossum 2012, among other publications from 'Reconstituting Democracy in Europe' (RECON) Integrated Project in the EU 6th framework research programme, coordinated by ARENA, Oslo (2007–2011).

39 For a study of the different national 'Traditions of Citizenship in the European Union', in the context of five EU Member States – Germany, France, Italy, Belgium and the UK – see Preuss et al. 2003.

on the member states. Only nationals of a member state can be Union citizens. From this position, a statist hold on a Union citizenship is necessary, and Union citizenship must be additional to nationality and cannot replace it.

II. Supranational European Citizenship: From this perspective, European Union citizenship is conceived as part of an elitist project of supranational nation- and state-building (Bellamy 2004: 19, Dobson 2006) that is meant to overcome the excesses of nationalist conflict. Accordingly, 'European citizenship' is defined as an autonomous constitutional category, foundational for the European political community, based on equal rights, and individuals' direct access, de-coupled from the member states. It would not be anchored in past nation state traditions, but rather venture into a new future of Europe.

> What future? No doubt it is as yet difficult to conceive of citizenship, i.e., the status of political subject, in dissociation from nationality. But surely it was equally difficult to imagine, in the eighteenth century, the status of political subject dissociated from the body of the King or from the three orders (Rousseau 2005).

Advocates of this supranational model have criticised EU constitutional reforms for keeping 'citizenship in abeyance',[40] while opponents criticise it because of its emphasis on a thick, homogeneous identity with exclusionary impacts for outsiders (Bhabha 1998, Balibar 2004).

III. Postnational citizenship in the framework of cosmopolitan (republican) federalism. In making the normative case for 'postnational' or 'denationalised citizenship' (see Habermas 1992, 1998, Sassen 2002) Rainer Bauböck has brought transnational minorities centre stage (Bauböck 2000). Departing from the conceptual framework of 'supranational federalism', in *The Rights of Others, Aliens, Residents and Citizens*, Seyla Benhabib has claimed that throughout the EU 'a decoupling of national and cultural origin from the privileges of political membership' has occurred (Benhabib 2004: 155) since European Union citizenship made it 'possible to vote, run for, and hold office in local as well as union-wide elections for all EU citizens'.[41] To describe these evolving practices, the term 'cosmopolitan' suggests that citizenship is premised on cosmopolitan norms, for instance on the European Convention for the Protection of Human Rights and Fundamental Freedoms (CoE 1950). They can

---

40 See, for instance, D. Rousseau who has argued: 'Union citizenship is not made an autonomous legal category, foundational or better, self-foundational. It remains a category without roots in the political space which it designates, rooted in another space – that of the Member States. In fact it remains in dependency, under tutelage, of the nation states. It is linked to the national statist logic and does not inaugurate, at least not in its foundation, a supranational logic' (Rousseau 2005).

41 In particular, Benhabib points out that third-country nationals can participate in local and regional elections in Denmark, Sweden, Finland and the Netherlands, and in Ireland at the local level, and in the UK Commonwealth citizens can vote in national elections, too (Benhabib 2004). For a most comprehensive and recent analysis of this subject, see Shaw (2008).

be defined as republican, to the extent that they conform to a principle of democratic self-governance that includes the 'rights of others', for instance of aliens or residents without a national citizenship. 'Cosmopolitan (republican) federalism' would help reconcile 'the republican ideal of public autonomy, namely, the principle that those who are subject to the law should also be its authors' with 'unity of the demos (...) to be understood not as if it were a harmonious given, but rather as a process of self-constitution, through more or less conscious struggles of inclusion and exclusion' (Benhabib 2004: 216).

These three models of European citizenship have differing implications for the question as to whether and how to justify aliens turning into members. They also diverge regarding the preconditions and limits they establish for granting individual access to rights, membership and participation. In this vein, we will review a number of selected ECJ cases with a focus on the judges' normative justifications for how they reconcile these conflicting normative presuppositions as to what it takes to be a European citizen. Our findings are based on an analysis of the European Union legislative provisions and 1994–2009 jurisprudence on citizenship and residence rights from the ECJ, with a special emphasis on the most recent ECJ cases. Our aim is to identify the normative patterns underlying the constitutionalisation of European citizenship in the Union.

Acknowledging the Primacy of National Citizenship Regimes

The main formal acknowledgement of the diversity of national citizenship regimes and the rights consequent on citizenship comes from the wording of Article 17(1) of the EC Treaty. Article 17(1) states that 'Citizenship of the Union shall complement and not replace national citizenship'. Thus, it is up to every member state to regulate the conditions of naturalisation, and nationals' access to European citizenship. Consequently, setting criteria for determining nationality and naturalisation are within the sovereign competence of the member states.[42] Accordingly, in terms of access to nationality, the ECJ has consistently avoided challenging the fundamental prerogative of the member states to determine nationality laws.[43]

---

42   In 1923, a dispute arose between France and Great Britain as to Nationality Decrees issued in Tunis and Morocco. In this case, the Permanent Court of International Justice (PCIJ) found that at the stage of development of international law, questions of nationality are 'solely within the domestic jurisdiction' (para. 38 PCIJ, *Nationality decrees issues in Tunis and Morocco*, Advisory Opinion, PCIJ Rep. 1923, Ser. B, No.4) of states. Remarkably, 80 years later and in the context of the EU, this finding seemingly remains the leading legal dogma. Interestingly, however, it seems that long before the EU emerged, the PCIJ already anticipated that the exclusive jurisdiction of member states over issues of nationality may be restricted in accordance with the law, if states undertake obligations *vis-à-vis* other states. 'The question whether a certain matter is or is not solely within the jurisdiction of a State is an essentially relative question; it depends upon the development of international relations' (para. 38).

43   See also Case C-192/99 *Kaur*, para. 19; Case C-200/02 *Zhu and Chen*, para. 37.

> Under international law, it is for each Member State, having due regard to community law, to lay down conditions for the acquisition and loss of nationality.
>
> C-369/90, Mario Vicente Micheletti and others v Delegación del Gobierno en Cantabria [1992] ECR I-4239, para. 10.

Secondly, in a situation where exercise of the citizenship right is a matter of 'internal' national situations, the ECJ does not have jurisdiction to adjudicate the case.[44] Thus, in the recent Italian reference *Pigantaro*, the ECJ refused to consider the case in substance on the basis that the factual situation fell within the jurisdiction of national courts.

Ms. Pigantaro, an Italian citizen residing in Italy, was excluded from a list of election candidates for the Sicilian Regional Assembly on the grounds that she did not fulfil the requirement that a candidate resides in the territory of that region at the time of submitting the application. Ms. Pigantaro brought a legal action in the Italian court, arguing that her exclusion from the list of candidates violates *inter alia* Articles 17 and 18 of the EC Treaty. She argued that the free movement of persons of EU citizens should also apply to inter-regional movements. Moreover, she argued that elections in the Regional Assembly are of importance not only to Italian nationals but also to EU nationals. Therefore, the provisions on free movement of persons under EU law should apply to her situation. However, the ECJ did not accept this line of argument.

> Ruling on these provisions, the Court has repeatedly stated that Union citizenship does not aim to extend the scope *ratione materiae* of the Treaty to internal situations with no link with Community law.
>
> C-535/08 *Pigantaro* (order of 26 March 2009), para. 14.

Similarly, in another recent Italian case Ms. Mariano, an Italian citizen, claimed that she had suffered discrimination based on nationality that is prohibited under Articles 12 and 13 of the EC Treaty. In this case, her partner, an Italian national, had had a fatal job accident in Italy. The Italian state denied a widow's pension to her, because they had lived in a non-registered partnership. She argued that if she had lived in cohabitation with a national of any member state other than Italy she

---

44 See also Case C-212/06, *Government of the French Community and Walloon Government*, [2008] ECR. I-1683, paras 38–39, where the ECJ stated that 'Community law clearly cannot be applied to such purely internal situations. It is not possible, […] to raise against that conclusion the principle of citizenship of the Union set out in Article 17 EC, which includes, in particular, according to Article 18 EC, the right of every citizen of the Union to move and reside freely within the territory of the Member States. The Court has on several occasions held that citizenship of the Union is not intended to extend the material scope of the Treaty to internal situations which have no link with Community law'.

would have been entitled to a pension granted in case of an accident, and his child would also have benefited from this annuity. She said that in different member states, the unmarried partner as well as the spouse both benefit from protection. For example, the French and Dutch systems recognise unmarried partners as spouses and their children, with the effect that both benefit from compensation upon the death of the beneficiary. However, the ECJ again declined to consider the case in substance on the basis that the factual situation was a purely internal matter.

> It is important to stress that it is clear from the case that the citizenship of the Union under Article 17 EC, does not seek to extend the scope of the Treaty to internal situations which have no link with Community law (judgments of 5 June 1997, Uecker and Jacquet, C-64/96 and C-65/96, Rec. p. I-3171, paragraph 23; Garcia Avello, paragraph 26, and Schempp, supra, paragraph 20).
>
> *Mariano C-217/08* (order of 17 March 2009), para. 22.

Thirdly, in certain areas of law, member states enjoy a certain autonomy, as for example in the case decided by the ECJ in February 2009, involving double taxation of the inherited assets of Ms. Block, who is resident in Germany. Ms. Block is the sole heir of a person who died in 1999 in Germany, where the deceased was last resident. The estate essentially consisted of capital assets, of which a part was invested in Germany and the remainder with financial institutions in Spain. Ms. Block paid inheritance tax in Spain in respect of the latter assets. The German tax authority fixed the inheritance tax payable by Ms. Block in Germany, without taking into consideration the inheritance tax already paid in Spain. Ms. Block lodged an objection, in which she applied for the inheritance tax paid in Spain to be credited against the inheritance tax to be paid in Germany and, therefore, for the amount in excess of the latter tax to be repaid to her.

> Community law, in the current stage of its development and in a situation such as that in the main proceedings, does not lay down any general criteria for the attribution of areas of competence between the Member States in relation to the elimination of double taxation within the European Community. ... [t]he Member States enjoy a certain autonomy in this area provided they comply with Community law, and are not obliged therefore to adapt their own tax systems to the different systems of tax of the other Member States in order, inter alia, to eliminate the double taxation arising from the exercise in parallel by those Member States of their fiscal sovereignty in consequence thereof, to allow the inheritance tax paid in a Member State other than that in which the heir is resident to be deducted in a case such as that of the main proceedings.
>
> C-67/08, *Margarete Block v. Finanzamt Kaufbeuren*, judgment of 12 February 2009, paras 30–31.

As a result, Ms. Block could not rely on EU law protection to avert payment of double tax on the inheritance.[45]

> [A]ccording to the settled case-law of the Court, the Treaty offers no guarantee to a citizen of the Union that transferring his residence to a Member State other than that in which he previously resided will be neutral as regards taxation. Given the disparities in the tax legislation of the Member States, such a transfer may be to the citizen's advantage or not, according to circumstances.
>
> C-67/08, Margarete Block v. Finanzamt Kaufbeuren, judgment of
12 February 2009, para. 35.

Similarly, member states retain a wide margin of discretion regarding the grant of certain social assistance benefits that are not regulated by secondary Community legislation. In the *Förster* case, involving a young German national who pursued education in The Netherlands and claimed entitlement to maintenance grant, the ECJ considered whether the requirement of five years prior residence established by that member state was justified under Community law. The ECJ observed with reference to its earlier *Bidar* judgement that

> [...] it is permissible for a Member State to ensure that the grant of assistance to cover the maintenance costs of students from other Member States does not become an unreasonable burden which could have consequences for the overall level of assistance which may be granted by that State. [...] it is legitimate for a Member State to grant assistance covering maintenance costs only to students who have demonstrated a certain degree of integration into the society of that State [...] the existence of a certain degree of integration may be regarded as established by a finding that the student in question has resided in the host Member State for a certain length of time.
>
> C 158/07, Jacqueline Förster v Hoofddirectie van de Informatie Beheer Groep,
judgment of 18 November 2008, paras 48–50.

Ms. Förster argued that during three years of residence she was already sufficiently integrated into Dutch society to be able to claim a maintenance grant. However, the ECJ stated that 'a condition of five years' uninterrupted residence is

---

45 See also to that effect, earlier cases: Case C-365/02 *Lindfors* [2004] ECR I-7183, para. 34, where the Court specifically commented on Article 18 in the context of taxation and stated: '(...) It follows that, in principle, any disadvantage, by comparison with the situation in which that citizen carried on activities prior to that transfer, is not contrary to Article 18 EC, provided that the legislation concerned does not place that citizen at a disadvantage as compared with those already subject to such a tax', and Case C-403/03 *Schempp* [2005] ECR I-6421, para. 45.

appropriate for the purpose of guaranteeing that the applicant for the maintenance grant at issue is integrated into the society of the host Member State' (*Förster* case, para. 55). The same criterion of five years residence in a member state is applicable to third-country long-term residents residing in the EU (art. 24(2) of the Directive 2004/38/EC; see also *Förster* case, para. 55).

Finally, regarding limitations on the right of residence of Third Country Nationals (TCN), the ECJ upheld the right of a member state to issue an expulsion order against a TCN on the ground of public policy. Notably, in determining the permissibility of the expulsion order of a Turkish national from the territory of the member state, the ECJ relied on well-established jurisprudence related to the scope of permissible limitations applied to the free movement of workers and services of EU nationals. In the Polat judgment,[46] the Court reviewed the decision taken by a member state to determine the conditions under which the right of residence of a third-country national can be restricted. In this case, an adult child, a Turkish national, who was no longer dependent on his parents, had numerous criminal convictions. The ECJ confirmed that under certain conditions a national expulsion order is in accordance with European Community law.[47]

> The reservations contained in Articles 39 EC and 46 EC permit Member States to adopt, with respect to nationals of other Member States, and in particular on grounds of public policy, measures which they cannot apply to their own nationals, inasmuch as they have no authority to expel the latter from the territory or to deny them access thereto. (…) [Thus, the EEC-Turkey Association Agreement] must be interpreted as not precluding the taking of an expulsion measure against a Turkish national who has been the subject of several criminal convictions, provided that his behaviour constitutes a genuine and sufficiently serious threat to a fundamental interest of society. It is for the national court to determine whether that is the case in the main proceedings.
>
> Case C-349/06, Murat Polat v Stadt Rüsselsheim, paras 38–39.

While in these cases formal national citizenship status was not sufficient for individuals claiming protection by European norms, other cases suggest that formal citizenship is not necessary for aliens to turn into members, at least in areas where the EU seeks to enforce unity.

---

46 The case involved interpretation of the EEC-Turkey Association Agreement. In that sense, it may be argued that TCNs of Turkish nationality receive more preferential treatment than TCNs of states with which the EU does not have Association Agreements.

47 Similarly to provisions on public policy, MS may exercise authority to narrow the scope of Community law rights on the grounds of public security and public health. However, the ECJ has repeatedly explained that restrictions must be interpreted 'narrowly'. Thus, before exercising this authority, a MS must carefully scrutinise the national measure as being based on the personal conduct of the individual, as necessary, and as proportional.

Supranational European Citizenship

The formal 'catalogue of rights' that EU citizens are provided with is certainly rather modest. Moreover, entitlement to European citizenship remains dependent on possession of a national citizenship, where the member states remain the masters of the rules on naturalisation.[48] Yet, for understanding the scope and meaning of European citizenship it is pivotal to consider another strand in the development of ECJ jurisprudence, discussed in this section under the heading of 'unity': European Citizenship not only provides for additional substantive rights such as the right to vote in EU elections, access to information, and others, but also significantly increases the safeguards protecting Union citizens against nationally-biased forms of arbitrary exercise of national rights in the European context through national courts.

Recent ECJ cases increasingly deal with situations that fall within areas where the EU has very limited competences, such as income taxation (*Rüffler*), determination of survivors' benefits (*Zablocka-Weyhermüller*), and issues of double taxation (*Block*), but where a clear link to EU treaty provisions exists.

For instance, as the ECJ acknowledges,

> [i]t is to be noted that, as Community law now stands, a benefit such as that in issue in the main proceedings, which is intended to compensate surviving spouses of victims of war, falls within the competence of the Member States (see, to that effect, Tas-Hagen and Tas, paragraph 21, and Nerkowska, paragraph 23). However, Member States must exercise that competence in accordance with Community law, in particular with the Treaty provisions concerning the freedom accorded to every citizen of the Union to move and reside freely within the territory of the Member States (Tas-Hagen and Tas, paragraph 22, and Nerkowska, point 24).
>
> C-221/07 Krystyna Zablocka-Weyhermüller v Land Baden-Württemberg, 4 December 2008.

The limited competences of the EU do not preclude the ECJ from finding that an exercise of member state competences under certain conditions may be in violation of EU law (*Rüffler, Zablocka-Weyhermüller*). Thus, in the *Zablocka-Weyhermüller* case, a Polish national was able to rely on EU law against the German authorities to protect her right not to be discriminated against in her entitlement to benefits determined solely by national law.

Mrs. Zablocka-Weyhermüller was a Polish national, married to Mr. Weyhermüller, a German national, who received a German pension as a victim of war. The couple resided in Germany. Following the death of Mr. Weyhermüller, Mrs.

---

48 Political science literature on the subject has critically analysed the 'catalogue' and the development of rights provided by EU law (that is recent Kostakopoulou 2001).

Zablocka-Weyhermüller applied for the full surviving dependant's pension as a war widow and indicated that she intended to move her residence to Poland. The German national agency refused to pay full benefits to Mrs Zablocka-Weyhermüller as a surviving spouse of a victim of war, solely for the reason that she moved her domicile to the territory of another member state. Mrs. Zablocka-Weyhermüller challenged this decision.

The ECJ first acknowledged that Zablocka-Weyhermüller as a Polish citizen may rely on the protection provided by the EC treaty, specifically articles 17 and 18 of the EC Treaty. Then the ECJ confirmed that, *per se*, the subject matter of the litigation, survivor pension, falls within the competence of the member states. However, exercise of this right *vis-à-vis* Union citizens is subject to scrutiny under the EU's legislative non-discrimination 'guarantee' on free movement. Thus, although acknowledging the competence of the member states in this area, the ECJ nevertheless stated that

> [n]ational legislation which places certain Community nationals at a disadvantage simply because they have exercised their freedom to move and to reside in another Member State is a restriction on the freedoms conferred by Article 18(1) EC on every citizen of the Union (see, to that effect, Case C-406/04 De Cuyper [2006] ECR I-6947, paragraph 39; Tas-Hagen and Tas, paragraph 31; and Nerkowska, paragraph 32).
>
> C-221/07 Krystyna Zablocka-Weyhermüller v Land Baden-Württemberg, 4 December 2008, para. 35.

In another case, *Rüffler*, concerning the claim of a German citizen against the Polish authorities regarding national law regulating eligible deductibles from income tax, the ECJ similarly found that a German citizen may rely on protection of EU law against national provisions, even though income tax law falls within the scope of national member states.

Mr. Rüffler was a German national, who after retirement in Germany moved with his spouse to Poland. His only income came from two pensions (invalidity and occupational) paid in Germany. The invalidity pension was taxed in Germany, where Mr. Rüffler also paid health insurance contributions. However, the occupational pension was taxed in Poland. According to national Polish law, health insurance contributions are an eligible deductible from the amount of income tax due. Mr. Rüffler applied to the Polish authorities for reduction of income tax by the amount of health insurance contributions paid in Germany, but his application was rejected. In his claim against the negative decision of the Polish authorities, Mr. Rüffler argued that the tax authorities had exhibited selective treatment with regard to Polish tax law and had infringed Community law.

> [I]t would be incompatible with the right to freedom of movement were a citizen to receive, in the host Member State, treatment less favourable than that which

he would enjoy if he had not availed himself of the opportunities offered by the Treaty in relation to freedom of movement (see, by analogy, on treatment in the Member State of which the citizen of the Union is a national, Pusa, paragraph 18; Schwarz and Gootjes-Schwarz, paragraph 88; and Case C-318/05 Commission v Germany [2007] ECR I-6957, paragraph 127).

> C- 544/07, Uwe Rüffler v Dyrektor Izby Skarbowej we Wrocławiu Ośrodek Zamiejscowy w Wałbrzychu, Judgment of the Court (Third Chamber) of 23 April 2009, nyr.

However, not all national rules that potentially affect the free movement of citizens amount to violation of EU law.

Additionally, as discussed above (see *Polat*), member states may also restrict the free movement of persons by relying on the derogations of public security, public health or public policy.

A derogation on the ground of public security was recently addressed in the *Jipa* case. Mr. Jipa, a Romanian citizen, left Romania on September 10th 2006 to travel to Belgium. On account of his 'illegal residence' in Belgium, he was repatriated to Romania on 26 November 2006 under the terms of the Readmission Agreement. On 11 January 2007, the Romanian authorities applied to the Tribunalul Dâmbovița for a measure prohibiting Mr. Jipa from travelling to Belgium for a period of up to three years.

In this regard, the ECJ restated its traditional line of reasoning, stating that although certain derogations from a fundamental freedom or principle are permissible, those derogations must nevertheless be interpreted narrowly and strictly:

> In that respect, the Court has always pointed out that, while Member States essentially retain the freedom to determine the requirements of public policy and public security in accordance with their national needs, which can vary from one Member State to another and from one era to another, the fact still remains that, in the Community context and particularly as justification for a derogation from the fundamental principle of free movement of persons, those requirements must be interpreted strictly, so that their scope cannot be determined unilaterally by each Member State without any control by the Community institutions (see, to that effect, Case 36/75 Rutili [1975] ECR 1219, paragraphs 26 and 27; Case 30/77 Bouchereau [1977] ECR 1999, paragraphs 33 and 34; Case C-54/99 Église de scientologie [2000] ECR I-1335, paragraph 17; and Case C-36/02 Omega [2004] ECR I-9609, paragraphs 30 and 31).

> C-33/07 Ministerul Administrației și Internelor – Direcția Generală de Pașapoarte București v Gheorghe Jipa, Judgment of of 10 July 2008.

Thus, in the case of Mr. Jipa, the Court concluded that

[primary and secondary law] <u>do not preclude national legislation</u> that allows the right of a national of a Member State to travel to another Member State to be restricted, in particular on the ground that he has previously been repatriated from the latter Member State on account of his 'illegal residence' there, provided that the personal conduct of that national constitutes a genuine, present and sufficiently serious threat to one of the fundamental interests of society and that the restrictive measure envisaged is appropriate to ensure the achievement of the objective it pursues and does not go beyond what is necessary to attain it.

> C-33/07 Ministerul Administrației și Internelor – Direcția Generală de Pașapoarte București v Gheorghe Jipa, Judgment of of 10 July 2008.
> (emphasis added)

Furthermore, article 23 of Directive 2004/38/EC of the European Parliament and of the Council of 29 April 2004 on the rights of citizens of the Union and their family members to move and reside freely within the territory of the Member States[49] does not preclude a member state from restricting the right of free movement under certain conditions. In particular, a member state may refuse to allow a national from a non-member state, who is married to a Community national who has not exercised their right to freedom of movement, to rely on Community rules, for instance relating to mutual recognition of diplomas and freedom of establishment.

Yet, European citizenship does not by any means make the EU a fully inclusive homogeneous society of equal citizens. It differentiates between four different categories of individuals: first, citizens of the EU residing in their home country (static EU citizens); second, citizens of the EU residing in one of the EU member states other than their country of nationality (mobile EU citizens); third, citizens of non-EU member states permanently residing on the territory of one of the EU member states (holders of a permanent residence permit); and fourth, citizens of non-EU member states temporarily residing on the territory of one of the EU member states.

In sum, European Citizenship entails a general guarantee. Specifically, this 'guarantee' function of European citizenship makes an exact quantification of the catalogue of rights available to European citizens unimportant. In fact, as it now stands, the so-called catalogue of rights available to a European citizen will depend on national legislation in the host state and in some cases also on that of the home state. EU law provides a guarantee that a particular citizen will not unjustifiably be treated differently either at home or in a host member state. This legal framework rests on the Treaty and has been catalysed by the ECJ. It allows for a plurality of national citizenships, while at the same time ensuring that member states do not

---

49 European Parliament and Council Directive No 2004/38, Art. 23, amending Regulation (EEC) No 1612/68 and repealing Directives 64/221/EEC, 68/360/EEC, 72/194/EEC, 73/148/EEC, 75/34/EEC, 75/35/EEC, 90/364/EEC, 90/365/EEC and 93/96/EEC.

unjustifiably disadvantage citizens of other member states who are exercising their personal right to freedom of movement.

Reconciling Unity and Diversity?

Due to the dependence of litigation cases on particular contexts, the general principles of EU citizenship law need to be reconciled with the recognition of specificities. Therefore EU citizenship is an intrinsically evolving institution. It is neither limited to a catalogue of formal rights, nor does it constitute a legal bond for a given political community. Instead, it establishes a set of guarantees that ensure that the general principles to which member states have committed themselves will be enforced. These guarantees may be at odds with member state practices, and in certain situations these commonly-agreed principles will be violated. For instance, as Lisa Conant has demonstrated in her examination of the Europeanisation of citizenship rights before the courts, the ECJ has been ambitious in pushing the limits of existing legal texts both to enforce and expand European social rights. However, given that 'most European social rights are mere corollaries of economic rights, and because they regulate access to national social rights' she sees them as 'vulnerable to domestic retrenchment' (Conant 2006). Therefore, she concludes that 'the prospects for developing European social solidarity through legal venues remain slim' (Conant 2006). In other fields of litigation, European Citizenship links EU norms and national jurisdictions more productively, driving forward the construction of EU citizenship through the interaction of national and EU institutions. In this process, courts provide a legal-institutional space for public contestation.

From a legal citizenship perspective, the interdependence of levels of citizenship makes it difficult to trace cause/effect relationships between them. This flexibility sits uneasily with existing traditional notions of citizenship. Although EU citizenship does not *de jure* put pressure on existing citizenship regimes (which in principle remain unchanged), the new dimension introduced by the EU may lead to a *de facto* fundamental reshaping of existing institutional practices, especially if the number of EU citizens availing themselves to the free movement provisions expands.[50]

Through its reasoning in the *Zhu and Chen* case, the ECJ has clarified what 'having due regard to community law' means. One of the key questions addressed in *Zhu and Chen* was whether an apparent circumvention of the nationality rules of the UK may lead to the right of the UK not to recognise a duly acquired Irish nationality and thus rights flowing from European citizenship. The ECJ stated that if the legislation of Ireland provides for the *jus soli* principle of acquisition of its nationality, then the UK cannot refuse to recognise Irish nationality, even if an individual has intentionally

---

50 The 'legislation adopting Article 13 [non-discrimination provision] has the potential to take the Union at least one step beyond a concept of citizenship based on nationality, and thus exclusion' (Barnard 1998: 393).

moved from the UK to Ireland and back with the sole purpose of acquiring European citizenship (and consequently the right to reside in the UK).

In sum, discursive analysis shows that ECJ rulings lend support to three different normative models of European citizenship that should be summarised under the labels of 'citizenship diversity'; 'union citizenship' and 'unity in diversity' (see Table 2.5, below).

Table 2.5   ECJ support for competing models of citizenship in a union of states

	I. Citizenship diversity	II. Union citizenship	III. Unity in diversity
(1) Access to Union Citizenship status.	» Statist control of Union citizenship, coupled to nationality of at least one MS. » Exclusive competence of MS to determine conditions and procedures.	» No community regulation of access to citizenship.	» Obligation of MS to recognise the effects of nationality granted by other MS. » Obligation not to restrict the effects of nationality granted by another MS.
(2) Scope of Union Citizenship rights.	» MS, in policy areas of exclusive national competences. » Authority to revoke right of residence of third country nationals.	The EU, in policy areas of EU competences: » Right to free movement and residence within EU territory (Art. 18 (1) EC Treaty), independent from the labour market; » EU catalogue of additional citizenship rights (including political participation in EP elections and local elections in host state; EU Ombudsman).	MS and the EU, in policy areas of shared competences: » *Mutual recognition*: Obligation of MS not to discriminate in the exercise of national citizenship rights of mobile EU citizens legally residing in the host MS (except for national elections); » *Reconciliation of unity and diversity*, subject to derogations provided by legislation and within the scope of Treaty competences.
(3) Enforcement of citizenship rights.	Direct access to national courts.	Indirect access to the ECJ (through national courts).	Preliminary ruling procedure.

Summary and Conclusions

This chapter aimed to research EU Citizenship politics and law as a dynamic institution in the framework of a multilayered European Union. Summarising the findings from sections two and three above, we argue that European Citizenship is characterised by a range of innovative features from an analytical as well as a normative perspective. The social construction of this regime rests on two elements: social agency from below and a normative framework that evolves from a multilayered judicial dialogue. Regarding the analytical pattern that explains the construction – and potential limits – of citizenship of the Union, we advance five arguments:

First, the main 'innovation' brought about by the development of European citizenship lies in its bottom-up dynamics of a multilayered process of construction (Calliess 2007). As demonstrated by the empirical analysis of selected cases of ECJ jurisprudence, the construction of 'Citizenship of the Union' is a 'transnational' process which relies on the cross-border agency of mobile Europeans, be they citizens, denizens (Walker 2008), residents from third countries or transnational minorities (Bauböck 2000).

Second, the construction of European citizenship results from processes of Europeanisation, understood as 'multilayered' interactions in the EU's political and judicial fields, between social, political and judicial actors (Checkel 2001). The interplay between local/regional, national, European and international agents in building the EU's citizenship regime is not hierarchically structured, but one determined by the specificities of situations in which individuals find themselves unlawfully discriminated against.

Third, access to Union citizenship status is conditional on naturalisation procedures that are autonomously regulated by the member states. However, formal citizen status has become less important as a mechanism of inclusion vs. exclusion from rights, as it is counter-balanced by principles such as non-discrimination of non-national in relation to national residents. In the EU legal framework of citizenship, citizenship rights are differentiated, if they depend on member state authority; or they may be unified if they pertain to the scope of EU competences; or they may be shared by both.

Fourth, experiencing and exercising EU citizenship also varies in so far as individuals enjoy differential access to different sets of rights. This depends on the one hand on their status of citizen/non-national/resident/migrant (Vink 2005), and is limited, on the other hand, by structural constraints such as regime competition among the member states (Streeck 1997). In this respect, European Citizenship is most attractive for those individuals who are mobile across national borders – and therefore want to seek the protection of the 'free movement' provision of non-discrimination on the grounds of nationality. Albeit to a more limited degree, European citizenship may also benefit some constituencies among 'static citizens', namely those who stay at home, but can claim protection against discrimination on grounds of gender, ethnicity, language, disability, age, and so on.

Fifth, the multi-layered construction of Union citizenship is evolving rapidly, driven by increasing mobility, migration and catalysed by a growing number of litigation cases taken by individuals to national courts and by national courts to the ECJ, leading to an expanding body of case law.

Normatively speaking, a review of two decades of citizenship litigation in the European courts suggests the emergence of an innovative citizenship discourse and framework. This neither portrays European citizenship as an empty shell at the disposal of sovereign member states nor does it reduce citizens to functional commodities of the single market. Facing the 'wide-open Pandora's Box' (Besson and Utzinger 2007: 573) of evolving European Citizenship jurisprudence, this does not provide an ever-expanding catalogue of supranational citizenship rights, triggering harmonisation across the 27 member states (Closa 1998a, 1998b). In fact, we claim that Union citizenship cannot be grasped by the traditional terms of a supranational rights catalogue, along the lines that T.H. Marshall's framework might suggest. The present analysis contributes to the growing multidisciplinary body of literature assessing European citizenship as a post-traditional case of regional citizenship in a union of states. Synthesising our findings in theoretical terms, the ECJ rulings lend support to three different normative propositions summarised under the labels of 'citizenship diversity'; 'union citizenship' and 'unity in diversity' (see Table 2.4).

Considering the latter, a regional European regime of diverse citizenship framed by cosmopolitan norms, most prominently universal human rights, is not only normatively defendable as an enabling precondition for improving the inclusiveness of democratic self-rule; moreover, as a matter of fact it is also emerging, depending on citizens' 'jurisgenerative' practices of making 'claims across borders' that counteract postdemocratic and technocratic and anonymous forms of global governance (cf. Benhabib 2009: 693; 695f.). Thus, instead of pitting one model of citizenship in Europe against another (EU citizenship as a collection of mutually exclusive national citizenships versus an integrated supranational citizenship), we argue that, in practice, ECJ rulings point towards a third way for aliens to become citizens. The normative signposts that define this way include universal principles such as freedom of movement, mutual recognition and non-discrimination among non-nationals and different categories of nationals. These may not be sufficient for supporting a pan-European identity or social solidarity. Additionally, they involve issues of inverse discrimination, where EU law puts national citizens at a disadvantage compared to mobile citizens. After all, static citizens are in the majority *vis-à-vis* the EC legal framework providing safeguards against the hazards of mobility for still relatively small minorities. Moreover, it is an unresolved issue how this model of a cosmopolitan republican citizenship would ensure political equality as a precondition for curing the so-called 'democratic deficit' of the EU. Will the development of more inclusive forms of regional political community also further political equality and thus the democratic quality of governance in the EU? Arguably, European citizenship and fundamental rights may challenge the nation-state and threaten to escape control by national legislatures, but they also enhance popular democratic sovereignties which technocratic forms of global law undermine (cf. Benhabib 2007; 2009). In this sense, European citizenship constitutes a necessary – albeit not sufficient – condition for a democratically legitimate European order.

Annex

Table 2.1 European Court of Justice judgments on citizenship provisions of the TFEU articles 20 and 21, and directives 2003/86/EC, 2004/38/EC and 2003/109/EC

No. of the case	Year of submission	Year of decision	Name of the case
C-193/94	1994	1996	Skanavi and Chryssanthakopoulos, Criminal proceedings against Sofia Skanavi and Konstantin Chryssanthakopoulos.
C-85/96	1996	1997	Martínez Sala, María Martínez Sala v Freistaat Bayern.
C-64/96	1996	1997	Uecker, Land Nordrhein-Westfalen v Kari Uecker and Vera Jacquet v Land Nordrhein-Westfalen.
C-274/96	1996	1998	Bickel and Franz, Criminal proceedings against Horst Otto Bickel and Ulrich Franz.
C-378/97	1997	1999	Wijsenbeek, Criminal proceedings against Florus Ariël Wijsenbeek.
C-356/98	1998	2000	Kaba, Arben Kaba v Secretary of State for the Home Department.
C-184/99	1998	2001	Grzelczyk, Rudy Grzelczyk v Centre public d'aide sociale d'Ottignies-Louvain-la-Neuve.
C-224/98	1999	2002	d'Hoop, Marie-Nathalie D'Hoop v Office national de l'emploi.
C-413/99	1999	2002	Baumbast, Baumbast and R v Secretary of State for the Home Department.
C-28/00	2000	2002	Kauer, Liselotte Kauer v Pensionsversicherungsanstalt der Angestellten.
C-466/00	2000	2003	Kaba 2, Arben Kaba v Secretary of State for the Home Department.
C-148/02	2001	2003	Avello, Carlos Garcia Avello v Belgian State.
C-482/01	2001	2004	Orfanopoulus, Georgios Orfanopoulos and Others (C-482/01) and Raffaele Oliveri (C-493/01) v Land Baden-Württemberg.
C-387/01	2001	2004	Weigel, Harald Weigel and Ingrid Weigel v Finanzlandesdirektion für Vorarlberg.
C-502/01	2002	2004	Gaumain-Cerri, Silke Gaumain-Cerri v Kaufmännische Krankenkasse – Pflegekasse and Maria Barth v Landesversicherungsanstalt Rheinprovinz.
C-200/02	2002	2004	Zhu and Chen, Kunqian Catherine Zhu and Man Lavette Chen v Secretary of State for the Home Department.
C-456/02	2002	2004	Trojani, Michel Trojani v Centre public d'aide sociale de Bruxelles (CPAS).
C-224/02	2002	2004	Pusa, Heikki Antero Pusa v Osuuspankkien Keskinäinen Vakuutusyhtiö.

No. of the case	Year of submission	Year of decision	Name of the case
C-365/02	2002	2004	*Lindfors*, Marie Lindfors.
C-138/02	2002	2004	*Collins*, Brian Francis Collins v Secretary of State for Work and Pensions.
C-293/03	2003	2004	*My*, Gregorio My v Office national des pensions (ONP).
C-403/03	2003	2005	*Schempp*, Egon Schempp v Finanzamt München V.
C-147/03	2003	2005	*Commission v Austria*, Commission of the European Communities v Republic of Austria.
C-209/03	2003	2005	*Bidar*, The Queen, on the application of Dany Bidar v London Borough of Ealing and Secretary of State for Education and Skills.
C-258/04	2003	2005	*Ioannidis*, Office national de l'emploi v Ioannis Ioannidis.
C-408/03	2003	2006	*Commission v Belgium*, Commission of the European Communities v Kingdom of Belgium.
C-286/03	2004	2006	*Hosse*, Silvia Hosse v Land Salzburg.
C-300/04	2004	2006	*Eman and Sevinger*, M. G. Eman and O. B. Sevinger v College van burgemeester en wethouders van Den Haag.
C-406/04	2004	2006	*De Cuyper*, Gérald De Cuyper v Office national de l'emploi.
C-520/04	2004	2006	*Turpeinen*, Pirkko Marjatta Turpeinen.
C-470/04	2004	2006	*N*, N v Inspecteur van de Belastingdienst Oost/kantoor Almelo.
C-145/04	2004	2006	*Spain v.UK*, Kingdom of Spain v United Kingdom of Great Britain and Northern Ireland.
C-185/04	2004	2006	*Öberg*, Ulf Öberg v Försäkringskassan, länskontoret Stockholm.
C-192/05	2004	2006	*Tas-Hagen*, K. Tas-Hagen and R. A. Tas v Raadskamer WUBO van de Pensioen- en Uitkeringsraad.
C-345/05	2005	2006	*Commission v. Portugal*, Commission of the European Communities v Portuguese Republic.
C-522/04	2005	2007	*Commission v Belgium*, Commission of the European Communities v Kingdom of Belgium.
C-318/05	2005	2007	*Commission v. Germany*, Commission of the European Communities v Federal Republic of Germany.
C-76/05	2005	2007	*Schwarz*, Herbert Schwarz and Marga Gootjes-Schwarz v Finanzamt Bergisch Gladbach.
C-291/05	2005	2007	*Eind*, Minister voor Vreemdelingenzaken en Integratie v R. N. G. Eind.
C-208/05	2005	2007	*ITC*, ITC Innovative Technology Center GmbH v Bundesagentur für Arbeit.
C-392/05	2005	2007	*Alevizos*, Georgios Alevizos v Ypourgos Oikonomikon.
C-287/05	2005	2007	*Hendrix*, D. P. W. Hendrix v Raad van Bestuur van het Uitvoeringsinstituut Werknemersverzekeringen.
C-370/05	2005	2007	*Festersen*, Criminal proceedings against Uwe Kay Festersen.
C-325/05	2005	2007	*Derin*, Ismail Derin v Landkreis Darmstadt-Dieburg.
C-11/06	2005	2007	*Morgan*, Rhiannon Morgan v Bezirksregierung Köln (C-11/06) and Iris Bucher v Landrat des Kreises Düren (C-12/06).

No. of the case	Year of submission	Year of decision	Name of the case
C-50/06	2006	2007	*Comm. vs. NL*, Commission of the European Communities v Kingdom of the Netherlands.
C-104/06	2006	2007	*Commission v Sweden*, Commission of the European Communities v Kingdom of Sweden.
F-54/06	2006	2007	*Davis*, John Davis and Others v Council of the European Union.
C-349/06	2006	2007	*Polat*, Murat Polat v Stadt Rüsselsheim.
C-152/05	2006	2008	*Commission v Germany*, Commission of the European Communities v Federal Republic of Germany.
C-398/06	2006	2008	*Commission vs. NL*, Commission of the European Communities v Kingdom of the Netherlands.
C-524/06	2006	2008	*Huber*, Heinz Huber v Bundesrepublik Deutschland.
C-499/06	2006	2008	*Nerkowska*, Halina Nerkowska v Zakład Ubezpieczeń Społecznych Oddział w Koszalinie.
C-353/06	2006	2008	*Grunkin and Paul*, Stefan Grunkin and Dorothee Regina Paul.
C-212/06	2006	2008	*Walloon Government*, Government of Communauté française and Gouvernement wallon v Gouvernement flamand.
C-158/07	2006	2008	*Förster*, Jacqueline Förster v Hoofddirectie van de Informatie Beheer Groep.
C-33/07	2007	2008	*Jipa*, Ministerul Administrației și Internelor – Direcția Generală de Pașapoarte București v Gheorghe Jipa.
C-221/07	2007	2008	*Zablocka*, Krystyna Zablocka-Weyhermüller v Land Baden-Württemberg.
C-164/07	2007	2008	*Wood*, James Wood v Fonds de garantie des victimes des actes de terrorisme et d'autres infractions.
C-551/07	2007	2008	*Sahin*, Deniz Sahin v Bundesminister für Inneres.
C-11/07	2007	2008	*Eckelkamp*, Hans Eckelkamp and Others v Belgische Staat.
C-229/07	2007	2008	*Mayeur*, Diana Mayeur v Ministère de la Santé et des Solidarités.
C-127/08	2007	2008	*Metock*, Blaise Baheten Metock and Others v Minister for Justice, Equality and Law Reform.
C-544/07	2007	2009	*Rüffler*, Uwe Rüffler v Dyrektor Izby Skarbowej we Wrocławiu Ośrodek Zamiejscowy w Wałbrzychu.
C-67/08	2007	2009	*Block*, Margarete Block v Finanzamt Kaufbeuren.
C-208/07	2007	2009	*Chamier-Glisczinski*, Petra von Chamier-Glisczinski v Deutsche Angestellten-Krankenkasse.
C-269/07	2008	2009	*Commission v Germany*, Commission of the European Communities v Federal Republic of Germany.
C-3/08	2008	2009	*Leyman*, Ketty Leyman v Institut national d'assurance maladie-invalidité (INAMI).
C-123/08	2008	2009	*Dominic Wolzenburg*, Dominic Wolzenburg.
C-35/08	2008	2009	*Busley/Cibrian*, Grundstücksgemeinschaft Busley/Cibrian v Finanzamt Stuttgart-Körperschaften.
C-462/08	2008	2010	*Bekleyen*, Ümit Bekleyen v Land Berlin.
C-480/08	2008	2010	*Teixeira*, Maria Teixeira v London Borough of Lambeth and Secretary of State for the Home Department.

No. of the case	Year of submission	Year of decision	Name of the case
C-22/08	2008	2009	*Vatsouras and Koupatantze*, Athanasios Vatsouras (C-22/08) and Josif Koupatantze (C-23/08) v Arbeitsgemeinschaft (ARGE) Nürnberg 900.
C-242/06	2008	2009	*Sahin*, Minister voor Vreemdelingenzaken en Integratie v T. Sahin.
C-310/08	2008	2010	*Ibrahim*, London Borough of Harrow v Nimco Hassan Ibrahim and Secretary of State for the Home Department.
C-135/08	2008	2010	*Rottmann*, Janko Rottmann v Freistaat Bayern.
C-73/08	2008	2010	Nicolas *Bressol* and Others and Céline Chaverot and Others v Gouvernement de la Communauté française *(Dir. 2004/38/EC) Belgium*.
C-420/08	2008	withdrawn	*Erdil (Dir. 2004/38/EC)*.
C-371/08	2008	2011	*Ziebell*, Nural Ziebell v Land Baden-Württemberg *(Dir. 2004/38/EC), Germany*.
C-276/08	2008	withdrawn	*Rimoumi and Prick (Dir. 2004/38/EC)*.
C-34/09	2009	2011	*Zambrano*, Gerardo Ruiz Zambrano v Office national de l'emploi (ONEm).
C-162/09	2009	2010	*Lassal*, Secretary of State for Work and Pensions v Taous Lassal UK.
C-145/09	2009	2010	*Tsakouridis*, Land Baden-Württemberg v Panagiotis Tsakouridis.
C-208/09	2009	2010	*Sayn-Wittgenstein*, Ilonka Sayn-Wittgenstein v Landeshauptmann von Wien. Austria.
C-325/09	2009	2011	*Dias*, Secretary of State for Work and Pensions v Maria Dias.
C-348/09	2009	pending	*Infusino*.
C-391/09	2009	2011	*Runevič-Vardyn*, Malgožata Runevič-Vardyn and Łukasz Paweł Wardyn v Vilniaus miesto savivaldybės administracija and Others.
C-434/09	2009	2011	*McCarthy (Dir. 2004/38/EC)*.
C-436/09	2009	withdrawn	*Belkiran (Dir. 2004/38/EC)*.
C-503/09	2009	2011	*Stewart*, Lucy Stewart v Secretary of State for Work and Pensions.
C-345/09	2009	2010	*Delft*, J. A. van Delft and Others v College voor zorgverzekeringen.
C-537/09	2009	2011	*Bartlett*, Ralph James Bartlett and Others v Secretary of State for Work and Pensions.
C-56/09	2009	2010	*Zanotti*, Emiliano Zanotti v Agenzia delle Entrate – Ufficio Roma 2.
C-578/10 to C-580/10	2010	pending	Staatssecretaris van Financiën v L. A. C. van Putten, P. Mook and G. Frank.
C-434/10	2010	2011	*Aldzhov*, Petar Aladzhov v Zamestnik director na Stolichna direktsia na vatreshnite raboti kam Ministerstvo na vatreshnite raboti.
C-430/10	2010	2011	*Gaydarov*, Hristo Gaydarov v Director na Glavna direktsia 'Ohranitelna politsia' pri Ministerstvo na vatreshnite raboti.
C-240/10	2010	2011	*Schulz-Delzers*, Cathy Schulz-Delzers and Pascal Schulz v Finanzamt Stuttgart III.
C-424/10 and C-425/10	2010	2011	*Ziolkowski and Szeja*, Tomasz Ziolkowski and Barbara Szeja and Others v Land Berlin *(Dir. 2004/38/EC)*.
C-256/11	2011	2011	*Dereci*, Murat Dereci and Others v Bundesministerium für Inneres.

References

Aalto, P. 2011. *Public Liability in EU Law*. Oxford: Hart Publishing.

Alter, K. 2000. The European Union's legal system and domestic policy: spillover or backlash? *International Organization*, 54(3), 489–518.

Alter, K. 2006. Private litigants and the new international courts, in *Comparative Political Studies*, 39(1), 22–49.

Archibugi, D., Held, D. and Köhler, M. (eds) 1998. *Re-Imagining Political Community: Studies in Cosmopolitan Citizenship*. Stanford: Stanford University Press.

Balibar, E. 2004. *We, the People of Europe? Reflections on Transnational Citizenship*. Princeton: Princeton University Press.

Barnard, C. 1998. Article 13: through the looking glass of union citizenship, in *Legal Issues of the Amsterdam Treaty*, edited by D. O'Keeffe and P. Twomey. Portland/Oregon: Hart Publishing, 375–394.

Bauböck, R. 2007. Why European citizenship? Normative approaches to supranational union. *Theoretical Inquiries in Law*, 8(2), 453–488.

Bauböck, R. 2000. *Political Community beyond the Sovereign State. Supranational Federalism and Transnational Minorities*. IWE Working Paper Series, no. 7, (Austrian Academy of Sciences).

Bauböck, R., Perching, B. and Sievers, W. (eds.) 2006. *Citizenship Policies in the New Europe*. Amsterdam: Amsterdam University Press.

Bellamy, R., Castiglione, D. and Santoro, E. 2004. *Lineages of European Citizenship. Rights, Belonging and Participation in Eleven Nation-States*. Palgrave Macmillan.

Bellamy, R., Castiglione, D. and Shaw, J. (eds.) 2006. *Making European Citizens: Civic Inclusion in a Transnational Context*. Houndmills: Palgrave Macmillan.

Benhabib, S. 2009. Claiming rights across borders: international human rights and democratic sovereignty. *American Political Science Review*, 103(4), 691–704.

Benhabib, S. 2007. Twilight of sovereignty or the emergence of cosmopolitan norms? Rethinking citizenship in volatile times. *Citizenship Studies*, 11(1), 19–36.

Benhabib, S. 2004. *The Rights of Others. Aliens, Residents and Citizens*. Cambridge: Cambridge University Press.

Besson, S. and Utzinger, A. 2007. Introduction: future challenges of European citizenship – facing a wide-open pandora's box. *European Law Journal (ELJ)*, 13(5), 573–590.

Bhabha, J. 1998. Get back to where you once belonged: identity, citizenship, and exclusion in Europe. *Human Rights Quarterly*, 20(3), 592–627.

Burley, A.M. and Mattli, W. 1993. Europe before the court: a political theory of legal integration. *International Organization*, 47(1), 41–76.

Börzel, T. 2006. Empowering citizens in post-decisional politics? *Comparative Political Studies*, 39(1), 128–152.

Cain, B., Dalton, R. and Scarrow, S. 2003. *Democracy Transformed?* Oxford: Oxford University Press.
Calliess, C. 2007. Der Unionsbürger, Status, Dogmatik und Dynamik. *EuR 2007*, 1(2007), 7–42.
Checkel, J. 2001. The Europeanization of citizenship? in *Transforming Europe. Europeanization and Domestic Change*, edited by M. Green Cowles, J. Caporaso and T. Risse. Ithaca: London Cornell University Press, 44–59.
Cichowski, R. and Stone Sweet, A. 2003. Participation, representative democracy and the courts, in *Democracy Transformed?* edited by B. Cain, R. Dalton and S. Scarrow. Oxford: Oxford University Press, 192–220.
Cichowski, R. 2006. Courts, rights and democratic participation. *Comparative Political Studies*, 39(1), 50–75.
Cichowski, R. 2007. *The European Courts and Civil Society. Litigation, Mobilization and Governance*. Cambridge: Cambridge University Press.
Closa, C. 1998a. Some foundations for the normative discussion on supranational citizenship and democracy, in *European Citizenship, Multiculturalism, and the State*, edited by U.K. Preuss, and F. Requejo. Baden-Baden: Nomos, 26–55.
Closa, C. 1998b. Supranational citizenship and democracy: normative and empirical dimensions, in *European Citizenship. An Institutional Challenge*, edited by M. Torre. Dordrecht: Kluwer Law International.
Conant, L. 2006. Individuals, courts, and the development of European social rights. *Comparative Political Studies*, 39(1), 76–100.
Council of Europe 1950. European convention for the protection of human rights and fundamental freedoms. Available at: http://conventions.coe.int/treaty/en/treaties/html/005.htm [accessed: 20 July 2012].
Delanty, G. 2000. *Citizenship in a Global Age. Society, Culture, Politics*. Buckingham: Open University Press.
Dobson, L. 2006. *Supranational Citizenship*. Manchester/New York: Manchester University Press.
Dower, N. and Williams J. (eds) 2002. *Global Citizenship – A Critical Reader*. Edinburgh: Edinburgh University Press.
Eder, K. and Giesen, B. (eds) 2001. *European Citizenship between National Legacies and Postnational Projects*. Oxford: Oxford University Press.
Eriksen, E.O. and Fossum, J.E. (eds) 2012. Europe's challenge: reconstituting Europe or reconfiguring democracy? in *Rethinking Democracy and the European Union*, edited by E.O. Eriksen and J.E. Fossum. London and New York: Routledge, 14–38.
Evas, T. and Liebert, U. (2012). Enhancing democratic legitimacy through constitutional pluralism? The Czech, German and Latvian Lisbon rulings in dialogue, in *Multilayered Representation in the European Union. Parliaments, Courts and the Public Sphere*, edited by T. Evas, U. Liebert and C. Lord. Baden-Baden: Nomos, 107–128.

Föllesdal, A. 2001. Union citizenship: unpacking the beast of burden. *ARENA Working Papers* WP 01/9. Available at http://www.arena.uio.no/publications/working-papers2001/papers/wp01_9.htm [accessed 30 May 2009].
Golding, M.P. and Edmundson, W.A. 2005. *The Blackwell Guide to the Philosophy of Law and Legal Theory*. Oxford: Blackwell Publishing.
Green Cowles, M., Caporaso, J. and Risse, T. (eds) 2001. *Transforming Europe. Europeanization and Domestic Change*. Ithaca: London Cornell University Press.
Habermas, J. 1992. Citizenship and national identity: some reflections on the future of Europe. *Praxis International*, 12(1), 1–19.
Habermas, J. 1998. The European nation-state: on the past and future of sovereignty and citizenship. *Public Culture*, 10(2), 397–416.
Habermas, J. 1999. The European nation-state and the pressures of globalisation. *New Left Review*, 235(1999), 46–59.
Hailbronner, K. 2004. Die Unionsbürgerschaft und das Ende rationaler Jurisprudenz durch den EuGH? *NJW 2004*, 31, 2185–2189.
Hailbronner, K. 2007. Gattousi/Stadt Rüsselsheim – ein neuer Schritt des EuGH zur Entmündigung der Mitgliedstaaten? *NVwZ 2007*, 4, 415–417.
Jenson, J. 2007. The European Union's citizenship regime. Creating norms and building practices. *Comparative European Politics*, 5(1), 53–69.
Joppke, C. 2007. Transformation of citizenship: status, rights, identity. *Citizenship Studies*, 11(1), 37–48.
Keane, J. 2005. *European Citizenship? Historical Foundations, New Departures*. Centre for the Study of Democracy. London/Berlin: WZB.
Kostakopoulou, T. 2007. European Union citizenship: writing the future. *ELJ*, 13(5), 623–646.
Kostakopoulou, T. 2001. *Citizenship, Identity and Immigration in the European Union. Between Past and Future*. Manchester: Manchester University Press.
Kymlicka, W. 2002. *Contemporary Political Philosophy. An Introduction*. Oxford: Oxford University Press.
La Torre, M. (ed.) 1998. *European Citizenship: An institutional Challenge*. The Hague: Kluwer International Law.
Liebert, U. 2007. The European citizenship paradox. Renegotiating equality and diversity in the New Europe, in *Critical Review of International Social and Political Philosophy* (CRISPP), 10(4), 417–442.
Luhmann, N. 2004. *The Law as a Social System* (Ziegert, K.A. translation). Oxford: Oxford University Press.
MacCormick, N. 2007. *Institutions of Law: An Essay in Legal Theory*. Oxford: Oxford University Press.
Maduro, M. 2007. Interpreting European law – judicial adjucation in a context of constitutional pluralism. *European Journal of Legal Studies (EJLS)*, 1(2), 1–21. Available at: http://www.ejls.eu/2/25UK.pdf [accessed: 20 July 2012].
Magnette, P. 1999. *La Citoyenneté européenne. Droits, Politiques, Institutions*. Bruxelles: Editions de l'Université de Bruxelles, Collection 'Etudes européennes'.

Mancini, Judge G.F. 2000. *Democracy and Constitutionalism in the European Union*. Oxford. Portland Oregon: Hart Publishing.
Meehan, E. 2000. Europeanization and citizenship of the European Union, in *Europeanization – Institutions, Identities and Citizenship*, in *Yearbook of European Studies 14*, edited by R. Harmsen and T.M. Wilson. Amsterdam/Atlanta: Rodopi, 157–177.
Micklitz, H.-W. and Reich, N. (eds) 1997. *Public Interest Litigation before European Courts*. Baden-Baden: Nomos.
Micklitz, H.-W. and de Witte, B. (eds) 2012. *The European Court of Justice and the Autonomy of the Member States*. Cambridge: Intersentia.
O'Keeffe, D. and Twomey, P. (eds) 1998. *Legal Issues of the Amsterdam Treaty*. Portland/Oregon: Hart Publishing.
Olsen, E.D.H. 2012. *Transnational Citizenship in the European Union. Past, Present, and Future*. London and New York: Continuum.
Preuss, U.K. and Requejo, F. (eds) 1998. *European Citizenship, Multiculturalism, and the State*. Baden-Baden: Nomos.
Preuss, U.K., Everson, M., König-Archibugi, M. and Lefebvre, E. 2003. Traditions of citizenship in the European Union. *Citizenship Studies*, 7(1), 3–14.
Putnam, R. 2008. *Speech at New York City Commission on Human Rights*. Newsletter 2008, no.1. Available at: http://www.nyc.gov/html/cchr/html/newletter.html [accessed: 28. January 2010].
Raz, J. 1979. *The Authority of Law*. Oxford: Clarendon Press.
Raz, J. 2005. Can there be a theory of law, in *The Blackwell Guide to the Philosophy of Law and Legal Theory*, edited by M.P. Golding and W.A. Edmundson. Oxford: Blackwell Publishing.
Reich, N. 2005. The constitutional relevance of citizenship and free movement in an enlarged Union. *ELJ*, 11(6), 675–698.
Reich, N. 2001. Union citizenship – metaphor or source of rights. *European Law Review*, 7(1), 4–23.
Reich, N. 1999. *Bürgerrechte in der Europäischen Union*. Baden-Baden: NOMOS Verlag.
Rousseau, D. 2005. Citizenship in abeyance. *European Constitutional Law Review*, 1(1), 44–46.
Sassen, S. 2002. Towards post-national and denationalized citizenship, in *Handbook of Citizenship Studies*, edited by F. Isin, Engin and B.S. Turner. London: Sage Publications, 277–291.
Shaw, J. 2008. *The Transformation of Citizenship in the European Union: Electoral Rights and the Restructuring of Political Space*. Cambridge: Cambridge University Press.
Soysal, Y.N. 1994. *Limits of Citizenship – Migrants and Postnational Membership in Europe*. Chicago: The University of Chicago Press.
Streeck, W. 1997. Citizenship under regime competition: the case of the 'European Works Councils'. *MPIfG Working Paper*, 97/3.

Torre, M. (ed.) 1998. *European Citizenship. An Institutional Challenge*. Dordrecht: Kluwer Law International.

Tridimas, T. 2007. *General Principles of EU Law*. Oxford: Oxford University Press.

Turner, B.S. 2000. Review essay: citizenship and political globalization. *Citizenship Studies*, 4(1), 81–86.

Vink, M.P. 2005. *Limits of European Citizenship. European Integration and Domestic Immigration Policies*. Basingstoke: Palgrave MacMillan.

Walker, N. 2008. Denizenship and the deterritorialization in the EU, *EUI Working Papers*, LAW No. 2008/08.

Weiler, J.H.H. 1998: *To be a European Citizen – Eros and Civilization*. CES Working Paper, 1(2). Center for European Studies, Working Paper Series in European Studies, University of Wisconsin. Available at http://aei.pitt.edu/8990/1/weiler.pdf [accessed on 20 July 2012].

Wiener, A. 1998. *'European' Citizenship Practice*. Boulder/Oxford: Westview Press.

Chapter 3

Disaffected Citizens? Why People Vote in National Referendums about EU Treaty Reform

Alexander Gattig and Steffen Blings

Introduction

The failed referendums in France and The Netherlands concerning the Treaty establishing a Constitution for Europe (TCE) came as a huge surprise for European decision makers and marked the preliminary end to a seemingly ever ongoing process of European integration. As a consequence for several years both the idea of further European integration and the idea of further referendums on European matters appeared dead. However, in the light of governing the Euro-crisis both ideas have recently gained popularity again. Moreover since the rejection of the TCE in 2005 two additional successful referendums have been held in Ireland. These divergent results and the potential future importance of referendums on European matters warrant *comparative* research on citizens' voting predispositions in referendums. However, such comparative research up to now is restricted to national accounts of the successful referendum in Spain (Closa 2004), the failed referendums in The Netherlands (Aarts and van der Kolk 2006; Lubbers 2008), in France (Berezin 2006, Brouard and Tiberj 2006, Milner 2006), and comparisons of these two countries (Hooghe and Marks 2006, Qyortrup 2006, Großkopf 2007, Hobolt and Brouard 2011). In addition, Crum (2007) cross-nationally compares party stances on the referendum. He argues that party-voter conflicts on the referendum depend on the political position of the respective party, on whether a party is in government or in opposition, and on the amount of divergence between government and opposition on the TCE. However, up to now – with the exception of Qvortrup (2006) and Gattig and Blings (2012) – there has been no comparative analysis of voter preferences and concerns across different national contexts with positive and negative outcomes. Comparative research has thus been restricted to cases where the outcome has been identical as in France and The Netherlands (rejection of the TCE) and therefore has neglected cases where the outcome was different (acceptance of the TCE, as in Spain and Luxembourg). Consequently, it is not possible to distinguish between solely country-specific reasons for rejecting or supporting the TCE and, if there are, cross-nationally shared patterns of satisfaction and dissatisfaction. The present contribution attempts to fill this gap.

Thus far, political and social scientific analysts (EB-Flash reports 171 and 172) of EU referendums generally treat reasons for failure in country-specific terms (see for example Qyortrup 2006): the French rejected the constitution mainly for social reasons while the Dutch were mostly concerned about a (perceived) loss of sovereignty. At present the field is divided about what the underlying sources of public dissatisfaction with European integration in general and the TCE in particular are: while some argue that the EU could not only rely on output legitimacy and needed to strengthen its democratic institutions (Follesdal and Hix 2002), others claim that we need not worry about the EU democratic deficit or attempt to foster popular acceptance of European treaty reform since citizens would remain most attached to their national (social welfare) states (Moravcsik 2002; 2006). However, the failure of the Irish referendum in 2008 suggests that the lessons learned from the French and Dutch referendums of 2005 were successful only to a very limited extent. This is especially striking since Ireland usually serves as poster child for EU-induced economic success and, hence, output legitimacy. If EU-output orientation had been Irish voters' prime concern, then the reform treaty should have passed by some margin at least. The Irish referendum rejection suggests that voters neither ignore the EU nor are exclusively output oriented. Therefore both, cross-national as well as nationally differentiated, comparative explanations of citizens' voting patterns in EU treaty referendums are necessary.

Without cross-national analyses, it is not possible to say whether the reasons for rejecting or supporting the TCE are solely country-specific or if, in fact, shared underlying patterns of satisfaction and dissatisfaction exist. More specifically, it has not been possible to tell if rejection of the TCE was mainly due to citizens' dissatisfaction with the problem-solving capacity of the EU, that is, the Union's delivery of outputs, or if citizens perceived the EU as highly efficient but pursuing the wrong objectives. In the latter case, improving the output efficiency of the EU may *not* increase the likelihood that treaty reforms will be approved in particular, and might even *lower* popular acceptance in general. In addition, referendums are often considered to be specific kinds of political competition (De Vreese and Semetko 2004) where general patterns of political rivalry do not necessarily apply. More specifically, general party division lines may not hold when specific questions are at stake in a referendum. For example, political parties may be internally divided on a specific question or may form unusual alliances. To the extent to which public debates on the TCE lacked strong and unambiguous party cues (see Packham in this book), referendums on European integration in particular are often shaped by voters' relative ignorance about the issues at stake (Hobolt 2007). This in combination with the apparently simplistic nature of the referendum mechanism – which restricts choice to "yes" or "no" – may make the outcome more dependent on media framing and campaigning than on long-term party allegiances (De Vreese and Semetko 2004). Thus, to date it is unclear to what extent standard explanations of voting behaviour apply to analysis of European referendums, which additionally highlights the necessity for their close cross-national inspection.

In the present contribution, we analyse individual voters' reasons for acceptance and rejection of the TCE in three countries where referendums were held in 2005, that is, France, The Netherlands, and Luxembourg. We supplement this analysis with some brief sketches on Spanish motivations (see below for an explanation concerning the particularity of the Spanish case). In this sense our study extends the scope of previous case-specific research on the failure of the TCE by analysing countries with positive and negative outcomes simultaneously and in more depth than has previously been the case. More specifically, we investigate different motivations in the formation of attitudes towards the TCE, thereby comparing them across countries. Secondly, this study contributes to the literature on referendums as specific arenas for political competition. Thirdly, in political science and especially in research on European integration it is still debated as to which of two major explanatory factors, viz. utilitarian considerations or affective support, exerts the stronger influence on voting behaviour (see Hoohge and Marks 2009; Lubbers 2008). We contribute to this debate by demonstrating how the former are linked to the latter. In other words, we argue that rational considerations as conceptualised by different socio-demographic groups affect motivations for specific preferences concerning the TCE (see also Hooghe, Huo and Marks 2007).

By simultaneously investigating all four countries where referendums on the TCE were held, we also seek to identify factors which may have favoured popular acceptance in one country while leading to rejection in another. We distinguish between preferences and motivations since logically it is perfectly possible for individuals to have identical political preferences (that is, either favouring or opposing the TCE), but for their motivations – or reasons – for these preferences to differ. Likewise, it is possible for citizens to have identical motivations or objectives which translate into different or even opposed political preferences.

Political preferences are shaped by socio-economic rational interests as well as by underlying belief or value systems, such as individual motivations, norms, and identities. Political preferences also depend on public debates which in turn are influenced by the media and political parties (De Vreese and Semetko 2004). In the following we assume that all of these mechanisms play a role in accounting for people's attitudes towards European integration in general and their attitudes towards the TCE in particular. We investigate the effect of the first two explanatory factors (rational interests and value systems) in detail but due to data restrictions we are unable to test here which of them exerts stronger influence.[1] Two of these contributing factors – the mass media and their framing of public debates – are left out of this chapter for two reasons. Firstly, these topics are not that easily investigated by quantitative survey data analysis (but see Hobolt and Brouard 2011 for a linkage of media analysis and survey data) and, secondly, questions pertaining to mass media analysis are examined elsewhere in this book (see chapters by Packham; Guasti). The chapter is structured as follows: first,

---

1 Hooghe and Marks (2004) provide evidence that for European integration in general belief systems are more important than rational considerations.

theoretical arguments for the inclusion of specific variables and the hypothesised effects of these variables are introduced. Then we explain how we created the data for use in the analysis and the methods used to analyse them. We continue with a comparison between our data and actual results on turnout and the yes/no decision. We then present descriptive and statistical analyses of the motivations underlying the respective voting decisions. The final section summarises our findings and lays out some of the implications.

Theory and Hypotheses

In the present analysis, we focus on two major sets of factors contributing to political preference formation: utilitarian rational considerations and motivational or affective support (Gabel 1998, Hooghe and Marks 2004). With respect to rational interests we conceptualise these in terms of socio-demographic groups and argue that these serve as proxies for the gains and losses people can expect from (further) European integration. We distinguish the following socio-demographic factors: profession, age, education, and gender; additionally we also distinguish between countries since the respective effects of these factors may differ between countries, depending on whether, for example, a specific profession in a specific country may gain or lose from additional European integration. We expect interests to differ between these groups along the lines we elaborate in the following paragraphs.

We differentiate professions along the lines of the class schema developed by Erikson and Goldthorpe (Erikson and Goldthorpe 1992). This class conception is widely used both in stratification research as well as in political sociology (see for example Ganzeboom and Treiman 1996; De Graaf, Nieuwbeerta and Heath 1995). It distinguishes between self-employed and employed respondents, the sector the respondents are employed in, and – in the case of employees – between types of labour contract. That is, employees are differentiated by whether they exercise authority at the workplace or not and by whether they are paid per unit they produce or whether they exchange general services. We distinguish the following classes: service class, routine non-manuals, petty bourgeoisie, skilled, workers, unskilled workers, and agricultural workers. It should be noted, however, that this classification excludes all people not in the labour force from statistical analyses.[2] To compensate for this shortcoming, we also used and tested a modified version of this class schema with additional categories for students, homemakers, unemployed people, and pensioners.[3] We modified the original schema because we felt it was

---

2 Some procedures are nevertheless employed to classify these respondents, for example, by assigning them the class of their spouse, by classifying them according to their previous occupation, or by classifying them according to the occupation of their parents. However, due to data restrictions, none of these options was feasible in the context of this research.

3 Such extensions of the Erikson-Goldthorpe schema are common, for example, Brooks, Niuewbeerta and Manza (2006).

especially useful to have a separate category for students since on the one hand this group has been rather supportive of European integration in the past while on the other hand students or organisations more likely associated with them than with others, for example, Attac, have played a major role in opposing the TCE. Standard class conceptions commonly tend to exclude students from analysis on the grounds that they are not (yet) attached to the labour market and hence are not subject to the mechanisms operating via labour contracts. Since the TCE was arguably also contested on economic grounds it appears reasonable to include the unemployed and pensioners as well because these groups have specific economic interests which also potentially diverge from those of the other classes we distinguished.

We argue that more educated citizens have a more favourable attitude towards European integration (H_1) and are hence more likely to accept the TCE (see Gabel 1998). Usually better educated citizens are more mobile and more likely to benefit from increasing integration and market liberalisation since their human capital is more generally usable (see Gabel 1998 for evidence). A related argument refers to professions. Members of the higher classes, for example, the service class and the petty bourgeoisie, should generally be in favour of the TCE, while skilled and unskilled workers should be less supportive. Skilled and unskilled workers especially in Western Europe have (been perceived to) come under severe pressure from competition by Eastern European workers who threaten to replace them for lower wages. For the self-employed and managers on the other hand market liberalisation allows to recruit a cheaper labour force and to outsource production. We compare these groups to the routine non-manuals whose preferences for European integration should be intermediate between the higher and the manual classes (H_2).

Another important group within the EU with sector specific particular interests determining their positions on European integration are farmers and farm workers. This holds despite the fact that they make up a relatively low proportion of the labour force. Since a relatively large proportion of the EU annual budget is allocated to support them, one would expect farmers to be favourable towards integration in general. However, this attitude is heavily dependent on farm size. Although sharing the same profession, their interests are different. While in The Netherlands and France farms are big and have potentially gained from further integration, farmers in Spain mainly own small farms that are endangered by increased competition within the European Single Market. It follows therefore that the latter should be much less in favour of integration in general and market liberalisation in particular (see Klandermands, de Weerd, Sabucedo and Rodriguez 2001 for evidence concerning Spain and The Netherlands). Independent of farmers' country-specific attitudes towards European integration the strong level of dependency on EU politics should result in strong politicisation and explicit and consistent views within this profession (see Imig and Tarrow 2001 for evidence that farmers in fact regularly voice their issues and protest quite often). Since we consider the political preferences of farmers to be country-specific we do not state explicit hypotheses with respect to them but include them as a separate profession that merits closer investigation.

In addition, we assume here that gender effects matter (H_3). Several studies show an increase in the level of interest in politics among women. This, in conjunction with discernibly different political attitudes, has led some researchers to speculate that gender might constitute a new political cleavage (Manza and Brooks 2000, Inglehart and Norris 2000). According to these authors in Western democracies women's political preferences have changed from rather conservative views to more leftist positions (for the EU, see Liebert 1999). Two arguments are given for this transformation. Firstly, the value change of recent generations has resulted in the increasing importance of topics such as equal rights and changing gender roles. These topics are more prominent within leftwing parties and, as a result, women are increasingly favourable towards them. Secondly, women are employed in the welfare sector more often than men and so tend to support political parties that are favourable towards redistribution policies.

A final demographic variable that may determine attitudes towards the TCE is age (H_4). Age potentially influences these attitudes in two ways: first, older cohorts may have a stronger sense of the EU as a means of avoiding violent conflicts, while younger cohorts may take peace for granted. Secondly, older cohorts have had a longer exposure to EU membership and therefore may value the achievements of the EU differently from younger cohorts. The latter argument in turn suggests that age-based attitudes would differ across countries depending on the respective length of EU membership. In the analysis we include age in years as well as a quadratic term for age to control for potential non-linear effects of age. For example, the experience of a war within Europe is limited to the oldest cohorts but is absent for more recent cohorts in most member states (except Slovenia and, from 2013, Croatia).

We also include party affiliation in the set of independent variables but acknowledge that party affiliation is located in between rational considerations and affective support. Party affiliation on the one hand may be based on rational considerations, for example, where the manual classes ally with leftist parties expecting to benefit from redistributive policies. On the other hand people may vote for a party because they feel emotionally close to it, for example if a party is perceived to protect citizens' sense of identity. Parties shape political discourses and debates to a huge extent and provide arguments that are taken up within and form these debates. As regards inclusion of party affiliation, some disagreement exists about the weight that citizens attach to European elections in general and to EU referenda in particular. European elections are generally seen as second-order elections (Van der Eijk and Franklin 1996). In other words, people allegedly place less value on these elections and cast their votes here mainly on the basis of national issues (cf. Gattig et al. in this book). Consequently, Marks and Steenbergen (2002) point out that Europeans' beliefs about European political issues show the same left/right cleavage that structures national politics. This would suggest that the effect of party affiliation is mainly based on the left-right dimension, that is, voters of conservative parties should generally favour additional European integration while leftist voters should be more sceptical about it.[4] It is unclear, however, to what extent additional dimensions, such as the libertarian/authoritarian dimension or the pro-/contra-European integration dimension affect attitudes to the TCE and to what extent these dimensions are reflected within the respective party spectrum in a specific country (see Crum 2007). We therefore include political affiliation here to predict attitudes towards the TCE but do not state specific hypotheses with respect to the effects of party affiliation on the TCE. Nevertheless, we speculate that, depending on specific national debates in any given country, individual members of party families within Europe may have different positions on the TCE. So, for example, the attitude of socialist parties to the TCE differed across countries with, for example, the French socialists being strongly divided while the Spanish socialists acted rather homogeneous in favour of the TCE. We expect this division to be reflected in the respective national electorates. This effect of country-dependency is not restricted to party affiliation as we elaborate in more detail in the following paragraph.

In fact, preferences on the TCE among all of the socio-demographic groups mentioned above may differ because of country effects. First, there are structural factors. The respective groups mentioned above may gain or lose from further European integration depending on the economic prospects of their country. So, for example, employees in Luxembourg may be more favourably inclined towards the TCE than employees in France if in the structural context of their country the former perceive integration as more of an opportunity than a threat. Secondly, European political discourses differ between countries. Political issues are framed by government and party elites who thus shape public preferences. Hence, the way these actors structure a debate may influence the policy positions of the respective profession, age group, or gender. In addition, identical groups within different countries may have more or less to gain from additional European integration. For instance, Hooghe and Marks (2004) argue that political-economic institutions interact with support or opposition to redistribution. They argue that voters in social-democratic welfare states might fear that European integration will dilute their welfare state, while voters in liberal welfare states may benefit from redistribution through the EU. So in social-democratic welfare states we can expect leftwing parties to oppose integration and conservative parties to favour it, while in liberal welfare states the pattern is reversed. This effect additionally leads us to hypothesise that the effect of socio-demographic groups differs from country to country depending on welfare-state institutions. Similarly, Liebert (1999) demonstrates that public support for European integration varies across different welfare regime types, with sizable gender gaps that depend on the degree to which equal rights for men and women have been established in each of them. In member states which take a rather progressive position with regard to women's rights,

---

4   This notion may no longer hold in the light of the current economic crisis where additional political integration has been explicitly favored by left-wing parties in order to overcome the problems of interest rates which strangle sustainable financing of national budgets.

further Europeanisation might endanger the position women have gained over recent decades. For countries where conservative positions and policies prevail, however, European integration can be seen as a means of improving the situation of women. We therefore take into account and specifically test the possibility that these postulated effects of profession, social group and political affiliation differ across countries.

Finally, in addition to rational interests, identities are also an important contributory factor to shaping political preferences regarding Europeanisation in general and opinions on European constitutional treaty reform in particular (Herman, Brewer and Risse 2004). However, most research on the relation between identities, rational considerations, and political preferences is restricted to the question how the two former affect the latter, and whether rational considerations or identities have a stronger influence on political preferences. In this chapter, we first compare the respective motivations and investigate which types of collective identities are linked to acceptance of the TCE and whether the political impact of these identities differs from country to country. For example, one may argue that a strongly European sense of identity leads to more favourable attitudes towards European integration. However, as Gattig and Liebert (2006) pointed out, a sense of European identity has multiple sources, and the precise political impact of such an identity depends on what these specific sources are. To be more specific, an individual who is strongly in favour of "Social Europe" and for whom social values and policies constitute an integral dimension of Europe, might evaluate European integration and the TCE rather differently from an individual who feels European because of Europe's cultural heritage and who holds liberal views on economic matters. But despite this rather fundamental difference, both individuals may state that they have a strong sense of European identity. Accordingly, Gattig and Liebert (2006), using Eurobarometer pre-referendum data up to December 2004 demonstrate these divergent effects of identity in evaluations of the TCE: both a solely European identity and a combination of national and European identity raise acceptance of the TCE. Similarly, identification with the EU rooted in European political integration is associated with a positive evaluation of the TCE, but identification with Europe conceived as a social model results in a negative evaluation.

In addition, we also investigate how rational interests shape motivations, that is, how socio-demographic variables affect the likelihood of mentioning a specific motivation. This is a relatively new stream of research. Our argumentative line in that respect is premised on two assumptions: firstly, people self-select into specific professions or occupations, for example, altruistic individuals should have a greater propensity to work in the care industry than individuals who are mainly interested in maximising financial returns. Secondly, professions themselves shape views and identities, for example, when working abroad or when dealing professionally with European matters. Therefore, we expect a link between socio-demographics and motivations.

Data, Operationalisations, and Measurement

We analysed data from four Flash-Eurobarometer data sets (F-EB 168, F-EB 171, F-EB 172, and F-EB 173). All these surveys were conducted after the respective referendums on the European constitution in Spain (February 2005), France (May 2005), The Netherlands (June 2005), and in Luxembourg (July 2005). The four data sets contain 7030 cases in total (Spain: 2015; France: 2014; The Netherlands: 2000; Luxembourg: 1001). They cover questions of turnout, actual vote in the referendum, socio-demographic characteristics as well as detailed questions concerning the reasons given for participating in the referendum (since in Luxembourg voting in the referendum was mandatory these questions were omitted in that case) and reasons for the specific vote (yes/no) on the TCE. For Spain these questions have been either omitted or re-formulated. We therefore use the other three countries as main tenets for our analyses and supplement them by sketching some results about Spain. These data sets also cover the perceived consequences of the vote.[5]

The original data sets were merged into one data set for our analyses.[6] This enabled us to investigate statistically whether specific influence factors differ between some or all countries. If instead we had analyzed and compared different data sets we could have compared the respective statistical parameters from these analyses but such comparisons would not involve direct statistical tests. The original data sets include a weighting variable using the design weights for the specific countries. This variable ensures that the sample is representative for each individual country. In the merged data set we used this weighting variable in combination with a population weight obtained from the Eurobarometer series.[7] This new weighting variable was used throughout all our analyses. It was necessary to weight the cases because otherwise we would run the risk of considerably overweighting the influence of, for example, Luxembourgian voters.

Operationalisations

As to the different class concepts we wanted to demonstrate empirically whether the additional categories introduced by us result in statistically superior models or whether they only add statistically redundant parameters. As to party preference we reduced and synchronised the complete party spectrum in the respective

---

5   We analysed neither questions concerning the reasons for participation in the referendum nor questions concerning the political consequences of the outcomes of the referenda since these elements go beyond the scope of this chapter.

6   The merged data set is available from the first author upon request.

7   The codebooks which accompany the Standard Eurobarometer data sets specify the population of the respective European countries upon which population weights in the Eurobarometer are in turn based. These population weights remain constant across Eurobarometer data over time and were thus used for our calculations.

countries to allow for meaningful analyses across multiple countries. Since we did not know in advance about how to properly classify political parties, we explored three different alternatives. In the first model we distinguished five major party families (Liberals, Socialists, Conservatives, Greens, rightwing) and relegated smaller parties to the "other" category, resulting in six electoral categories. The second variant had the same categories but in this case small non-extremist parties were transferred from the "other" category into the category which best fitted them (for example, Communists and small left parties were included in the "Socialist" rather than the "other" category) to display a broader left-right antagonism. The final alternative contrasted the extreme left and right with the political centre by splitting party preference into the categories of Communists, Socialists, moderate rightwing, Greens, extreme rightwing, and other. A detailed list with parties and their respective classification is given in the annex.

Methods

For our analysis, we used binary logistic regressions and a variation, viz. the so-called complementary log-log model: since in our data set the respective motivations are sometimes mentioned by only a small minority of voters, we sometimes have a dependent variable (reason mentioned/not mentioned) that is heavily skewed. In these cases the standard logistic regression model results in biased estimators (the same also holds for its variant, the probit model). Since the data are clustered across countries, we adjusted the standard errors according to the Huber/White sandwich estimator (Huber 1967, White 1980).[8]

Before we present the results from our analyses in the following section, we will first compare turnout rates and voting behavior in our data with the real turnout rates and voting behavior to provide an overview concerning the quality of the data and in order to assess the validity of our results. We then turn to the motivations of the respective vote in the referendum. Here, we first provide an overview of reasons for voting for or against the TCE by country in order to give a rough impression of how these reasons differ between countries. Then the question of which social group mentioned what reasons for accepting or rejecting the TCE is investigated in more detail. The final section summarises and draws some conclusions as to the chances for acceptance of a constitution in future referendums.

---

8   Technically, when data are clustered the sample does not consist of random draws from the entire population. In this case standard errors obtained from statistical procedures tend to be distorted, resulting in incorrect estimates concerning the significance levels of these variables. In our study the countries investigated enter the dataset with a fixed number of observations; thus the observations are not a random sample from the combined population of the four countries. The Huber-White estimator controls for this problem by artificially raising standard errors of the estimated parameters.

Results

We begin by comparing our survey data to actual turnout. In Table 3.1, below, columns 3–6 present the actual turnout rates and results from the referendums compared to those in our data. As can be seen, turnout rates in the sample are much higher than actual turnout rates, a common phenomenon in research on voting behaviour. This has a twofold cause: social desirability (there is a norm that one should vote and respondents do not want to announce "in public" that they violate such norms) and measurement error (non-voters are to some extent less likely to be reached by or to participate in surveys). However, the discrepancy between observed and actual behaviour with respect to turnout is quite strong: differences between reported and actual turnout rates range from 15% (France) over 20% (The Netherlands) to 26% (Spain). For Luxembourg the difference is much smaller since voting in the referendum was mandatory there. As to acceptance or rejection of the TCE, it turns out that there are slightly higher acceptance rates in the sample than were actually observed, but overall the differences are small. We therefore consider our estimates concerning the vote cast in the referendum to be valid.

Table 3.1   Actual and reported turnout rates (in %, number of respondents between brackets)

		France	Luxembourg	Netherlands	Spain
Reported turnout	Yes	86.6 (1745)	96.0 (961)	83.5 (1670)	69.12 (1392)
	No	13.4 (270)	4.0 (40)	16.5 (330)	30.88 (622)
Actual turnout	Yes	69.3	86.8	62.8	41.8
	No	30.7	13.2	37.2	58.2
Reported vote	Yes	50.0 (776)	65.2 (612)	41.3 (677)	85.8 (945)
	No	50.0 (776)	34.8 (326)	58.7 (963)	14.2 (156)
Actual vote	Yes	45.32	56.52	38.3	76.7
	No	54.68	43.48	61.7	23.3

Source: Flash-Eurobarometer data sets 168, 171, 172, 173, (turnout rate in Luxembourg based on: http://www.europa-digital.de/aktuell/dossier/verfassung/lux_ja.shtml).

In Search of Valid Classifications

We now turn to the question of which class schema and which party classification are most adequate for explaining attitudes towards the TCE. The categories we added to the standard EG-schema proved to be useful since for both dependent variables the extended version provides a better model fit for the whole sample, though the differences are generally small.[9]

As to party classifications, the one distinguishing Liberals, Socialists, Conservatives, Greens, extreme right and other parties proves to be superior for all countries both in terms of turnout as well as in terms of acceptance/rejection of the TCE. This is a first substantial result since it indicates that Communists do substantially differ from Socialists with respect to turnout and preferences towards the TCE but not from parties which are collapsed into the "other" category.

Different Arguments for Identical Votes? Descriptive Statistics

In the next step, we focus on the relation between motivations and preferences for the TCE. Tables 3.2 and 3.3 compare descriptive statistics for the countries under study. Here, we omit the Spanish data since these questions differed from those asked in the other countries and thus are difficult to compare. We nevertheless sketch some brief results after comparing the other three countries. A specific particularity of the data should be kept in mind: reasons in favour of the TCE were *only* elicited from respondents who stated that they had voted for acceptance. Likewise, respondents who voted against the TCE were only asked for reasons *against* the TCE. It was thus possible to state several reasons for or against the TCE but not for any one respondent to state both sorts of arguments.

As to similarities in attitudes towards the TCE between countries, it appears that the three countries are in fact highly diverse. However in all countries respondents consider the TCE to be important in terms of "European construction" and in all countries this is considered the most important argument for voting in favour of the TCE. In addition, respondents who are in favour of the TCE also state to be in favour of the process of "European construction". This result qualifies the standard interpretation that countries strongly differ in their attitudes towards the TCE. At least for reasons to vote in favour of the Treaty these are strong similarities.

Despite these similarities, some important differences exist between countries. For example, respondents in Luxembourg on average mention *more* arguments in favour of the TCE than in France or in The Netherlands. In addition, in Luxembourg statements such as that the TCE "strengthens the economic situation", "strengthens my country", "contributes to "peace", and is "important for future generations" are highly salient reasons, while they do not hold for the other two countries. Finally, in Luxembourg, respondents strongly consider the TCE to contribute to a social Europe; in The Netherlands this proposition is shared at least to some extent, while in France only a small fraction of respondents mentions this as a reason for voting for the TCE.

---

9   We compared model fit according to the BIC-criterion introduced by Raftery (1995). Here, the model fit based on the log-likelihood is weighted against the number of parameters and the number of respondents to arrive at a parsimonious modelling of the data, that is a model that contains relatively few independent variables. For details see Raftery (1995) as well as Gattig and Blings (2012).

Table 3.2   Distribution of reasons in favour of the TCE across countries (in %, several answers possible)

	France	Luxembourg	Netherlands
Pursue European construction	17.1	24.4	9.9
Integration of new members	1.8	7.0	2.0
Running of EU institutions	3.2	9.2	5.0
Social Europe	2.9	10.6	5.1
Strengthens EU identity	2.9	8.9	1.0
Creates EU identity	1.8	7.0	4.3
Political unification	3.4	8.5	4.2
Strengthens EU towards US	5.0	6.0	3.2
Favours European construction	7.1	10.4	2.7
Strengthens democracy	1.8	6.8	1.9
Supports political parties	2.2	5.3	1.1
Strengthens economic situation	3.4	10.3	5.1
Strengthens my country	5.3	14.6	2.0
Peace	2.9	18.0	1.9
For future generations	4.8	11.8	1.7
Don't see what's negative	1.5	2.3	3.0
Other	11.0	16.1	0.8
DK/NA	0.7	0.9	2.0
Total n	**1745**	**961**	**1670**

Source: Flash-Eurobarometer data sets 171, 172, 173, (no reasons available for Spain).

As to arguments provided by respondents who reported to have voted against the TCE, there are fewer similarities between countries than for people who voted in favour of it. A striking fact is that in Luxembourg the "other" category is most often mentioned. This category is also highly important in France indicating that a considerable proportion of opinions is not adequately reflected in the answering categories and, hence, the data obtained. The differences between France and The Netherlands are striking. While in The Netherlands the most often mentioned reasons are "lack of information" and "loss of national sovereignty", these items only play a very minor role in France – unsurprisingly given the intense debates preceding the referendum there. Hence from these results one might conclude that rejection of the TCE was based on national particularities. Regarding Luxembourg, an interesting result is that "not social enough" was among the most prominent reasons given by those opposing. Apparently the question of whether the TCE adequately constituted a social Europe was highly controversial in Luxembourg since "Social Europe" was not only mentioned as a reason against but also as one of the more important reasons for being in favour of the TCE. This was not the case in the other two Member States.

Table 3.3   Distribution of reasons for being against the TCE across countries (in %, several answers possible)

	France	Luxembourg	Netherlands
Opposes political parties	8.0	2.5	8.2
Not social enough	6.9	7.3	1.3
Draft too liberal	8.4	4.4	2.3
Draft goes too far	1.4	7.0	3.7
Loss of sovereignty	2.2	3.1	10.6
Economic situation too weak	11.4	7.3	3.2
Too technocratic	0.9	3.6	3.1
Lack of information	2.3	6.1	18.9
Too complex	5.4	5.8	3.0
Don't want Turkey in EU	2.8	5.5	2.0
Opposition to enlargement	1.2	4.2	3.6
Not democratic enough	1.2	2.2	3.1
Against European construction	1.8	1.4	4.5
Against political union	0.8	0.8	2.9
Do not see what's positive	1.6	2.3	3.3
Other	9.2	12.7	1.7
DK/NA	1.3	0.2	2.0
Total n	1745	961	1670

Source: Flash-Eurobarometer data sets 171, 172, 173, (no reasons for Spain available).

We supplement these results with some quantitative Eurobarometer-data on Spain. As mentioned above, in Spain question wording differed from the other countries and hence we analyse Spain separately. Here, 76% supported the statement that "[t]he institutions of the EU conjure a good image" and 93% agreed that "Spanish membership in the EU is a good thing" which suggests dissatisfaction neither with the EU institutional setup nor specifically with its outputs. Items relating to EU democratic legitimacy – such as "TCE strengthens democracy in the EU" and "TCE is necessary to pursue European construction" – were evaluated extremely positively, as well (79% and 82.6%). This result is in accordance with frequent mentioning of these aspects in the other three countries thus lending further support to the notion of common European motivations, rooted in a positive perception of European construction. However, in Spain the public was divided as to whether it was provided with sufficient information for the vote in advance (52.9% tended to agree that they had sufficient information while 47.1% tended to reject that statement). Lack of information was mentioned by nearly a fifth of the Dutch as a reason for rejection, while only small minorities shared this motive in France and Luxembourg

Different Arguments for Identical Votes? Results from Statistical Models

Why did people vote for or against the TCE? Is there substantial variation between socio-economic groups, between countries and across party affiliations to justify the notion of nationally diverse motivations or are there common patterns?

Annex Tables 3.2 and 3.3 (see end of chapter) display the results of our analyses in detail. Age and higher education consistently raise the likelihood that all the reasons for the Constitution are mentioned. This result supports the theory of enlightened preferences (for example Anderson, Tilly and Heath 2005) which states that political campaigns generally result in more consistent political views for more highly educated people while for the less educated and the less politically interested, this effect is much weaker. This may be because the more highly educated are more familiar with the debate around the Constitution and are better able to recall the arguments mentioned in this debate. Women are less likely than men to view the constitution as a symbol of Social Europe and as an improvement of the countries' economic situation. As to occupational variables, among the higher classes the petty bourgeoisie is less likely to mention most of the reasons than routine non-manuals, while the service class tends to mention the perceived positive effects of the TCE on political integration more often. This finding suggests that among the white collar professions the service class holds the most strongly politicised views on European integration while the petty bourgeoisie is most disinterested. As to the reasons mentioned, farmers, contrary to expectation, did not differ very much from routine non-manuals. The only differences were a lower propensity to see the advantages of the TCE for European construction and a more positive view of the TCE in terms of European identity. Finally, as to political parties, the Communists, Conservatives, Greens all mention all reasons in favour of the TCE more often than the Socialists/Social Democrats. The question is whether and to what extent this is a result of their differing capacity and willingness to provide their electorates with strong and clear cues on the TCE (see Chapter 4 by Packham, in this book). The only exception from this finding is the perceived effect of the TCE on democracy which is mentioned more often by the Socialists. Unsurprisingly, the extreme rightwing parties hold more negative views on all reasons than all other parties.

It should be kept in mind that these estimates are margin-insensitive. This means that a negative coefficient for a specific reason and a specific group or party affiliation means that this specific group is less likely to mention this argument irrespective of whether the group is likely or unlikely to vote for the constitution. For example, supporters of extreme rightwing parties are less likely to vote for the Constitution than the reference category (in this case: Socialists). Given this lower probability, supporters of extreme rightwing parties who support the TCE are much less likely than Socialists to state that the TCE is essential for European construction.

Finally, there are some common voting patterns across countries: in Luxemburg *all positive* aspects of the TCE are mentioned more often than in France and The Netherlands. That is, even after controlling for political and socio-demographic variables Luxembourgian voters evaluate the TCE more positively than the other two countries and this not due to a single aspect but to a variety of reasons. Interestingly, for most items The Netherlands differ relatively little from France except for the two items "Strengthens European identity" and "Strengthens EU over the US", indicating that symbolic considerations were of little importance in The Netherlands which may have contributed to rejection.

As to reasons against the TCE, an interesting finding is that in The Netherlands "Against European integration" is mentioned most and in Luxemburg least often. Moreover, voters in these two countries were concerned about the loss of national sovereignty and opposed further enlargement. Finally, the Dutch showed little concern for the TCE being too liberal, not including enough social Europe, or have an economic situation that is too weak.

Summary and Conclusions

After many years of increasing economic, legal and institutional integration through successive European Union treaty reforms the failed referendums concerning the Constitutional Treaty in France and The Netherlands have brought this process to a halt. This chapter has investigated the motivations for voting in the four countries where referendums have taken place. Using a broad comparative multivariate approach we find clear evidence that socio-demographic factors as well as party preferences determine the outcome of EU treaty ratification referenda. As to socio-demographics, age and higher education increase the likelihood of being opinionated in favour of Constitutional Treaty ratification, while we find less acceptance of it among the higher classes in comparison to routine non-manual employees. This is striking since social elites have usually been in favour of European integration. The analysis presented in this section also yields some other surprising insights:

First, the reasons Socialist and Communist Party supporters employed to justify their votes were quite different.

Second, the arguments endorsed by supporters of the Greens and the Conservatives for justifying their votes were rather similar, underlining the shared socio-demographic base of these two parties.

Third, although these constituencies appear to be rather similar in their voting profiles across all four referendum countries, the reasons respondents gave for justifying their stances in favour of or against the TCE differed across countries. That is, although preferences for or against the TCE across the different countries were similar for identical socio-demographic groups (Gattig and Blings 2012), the reasons respondents from these groups gave to justify their preferences differed strongly between countries. We take this as evidence for the impact of national – especially media – debates on political preferences.

These findings make it difficult for European party elites to devise common – and that is transnational – European communication strategies for informing and mobilising their mass constituencies to support future treaty reforms. As our analysis of TCE referenda shows, strictly national ratification procedures and campaigns in the different Member States are likely to result in varying motives stated by voters across the countries where referendums are held. In view of these national particularities, we can reasonably speculate that the larger the range of countries adopting national referenda for EU treaty reform grows, the more the reasons motivating voters to support or reject ratification will diverge. Since voters sometimes give different reasons while voting similarly, and similar reasons while voting differently, it would seem that any EU treaty reform will be likely to please some parts of the electorate while inevitably annoying others. Yet, as we have sought to demonstrate in this chapter, beneath the surface of this excessively complex pattern, European citizens' voting behaviour on EU treaty reform is structured across the national context by a limited number of variables, namely socio-demographics and party identification. As a consequence, we should not rule out the possibility that future EU treaty reformers may be able to better respond to – and resonate with – the rational motivations of European constituencies.

References

Aarts, K. and van der Kolk, H. 2006. Understanding the Dutch "no": the euro, the east, and the elite. *PS: Political Science & Politics*, 39(2), 243–246.

Anderson, R., Tilly, J. and Heath, A. 2005. Political knowledge and enlightened preferences: party choice through the electoral cycle. *British Journal of Political Science*, 35(2), 285–302.

Berezin, M. 2006. Appropriating the "no": the French national front, the vote on the constitution, and the "new" April 21. *PS: Political Science & Politics*, 39(2), 269–272.

Brooks, C., Nieuwbeerta, P. and Manza, J. 2006. Cleavage-based voting behaviour in cross-national perspective: evidence from six postwar democracies. *Social Science Research*, 35(2006), 88–128.

Brouard, S. and Tiberij, V. 2006. The not so simple act of saying nay. *PS: Political Science & Politics*, 39(2), 261–268.

Closa, C. 2004. The formation of domestic preferences on the reform of the treaties in Spain. *Comparative European Politics*, 2(3), 320–338.

Crum, B. 2007. Party stances in the referendums on the EU constitution: causes and consequences of competition and collusion. *European Union Politics*, 8(1), 61–82.

De Graaf, N.D., Nieuwbeerta, P. and Heath, A. 1995. Class mobility and political preferences: individual and contextual effects. *American Journal of Sociology*, 100(4), 997–1027.

De Vreese, C. and Semetko, H. 2004. *Political Campaigns in Referendums. Framing the Referendum Issue*. London: Routledge.

Erikson, R. and Goldthorpe, J. 1992. *The Constant Flux: A Study of Class Mobility in Industrial Societies*. Oxford: Clarendon Press.

Follesdal, A. and Hix, S. 2006. Why there is a democratic deficit in the EU: a response to Majone and Moravcsik. *Journal of Common Market Studies*, 44(3), 533–562.

Gabel, M. 1998. *Interests and Integration: Market Liberalization, Public Opinion, and European Union*. Ann Arbor: University of Michigan Press.

Ganzeboom, H. and Treiman, D. 1996. Internationally comparable measures of occupational status for the 1988 international standard classification of occupations. *Social Science Research*, 25(3), 201–239.

Gattig, A. and Blings, S. 2012. Voting on EU constitutional treaty ratification: cross-national patterns of citizens' preferences and motivations. Working Paper, University of Bremen.

Gattig, A. and Liebert, U. 2006. *The European Constitution and the Issue of Identity: Exploring Public Attitudes towards Ratification*, ECPR Joint Sessions of Workshops, Nicosia, Cyprus, 25–30 April 2006.

Großkopf, A. 2007. Why "non" and "nee" to the EU constitution? Reconsidering the shock of the Dutch and the French referenda, EUSA Tenth Biennial International Conference, Montreal, Canada, 17–19 May 2007.

Hermann, R., Brewer, M. and Risse, T. (eds) 2004. *Identities in Europe and the Institutions of the European Union*. Lanham: Rowman & Littlefield.

Hobolt, S.B. 2007. Taking cues on Europe? Voter competence and party endorsements in referendums on European integration. *European Journal of Political Research*, 46(2), 151–182.

Hobolt, S.B. and Brouard, S. 2011. Contesting the Union? Why the Dutch and the French rejected the European constitution. *Political Research Quarterly*, 64(2), 309–322.

Hooghe, L. and Marks, G. 2004. Does identity or economic rationality drive public opinion on European integration? *PS: Political Science and Politics*, 37(3), 415–420.

Hooghe, L. and Marks, G. 2006. Europe's blues: theoretical soul-searching after the rejection of the European constitution. *PS: Political Science and Politics*, 39(2), 247–250.

Hooghe, L. and Marks, G. 2009. A postfunctionalist theory of European integration: from permissive consensus to constraining dissensus. *British Journal of Political Science*, 39(1), 1–23.

Hooghe, L., Huo, J.J. and Marks, G. 2007. Does occupation shape attitudes on Europe? Benchmarking validity and parsimony. *Acta Politica*, 42(2), 329–351.

Huber, J. 1967. *The Behavior of Maximum-Likelihood Estimates under Non-Standard Conditions*. Proceedings of the Fifth Berkeley Symposium on Mathematical Statistics and Probability, (Univ. of Calif. Press), 1(1967), 221–233.

Imig, D. and Tarrow, S. (eds) 2001 *Contentious Europeans. Protest and Politics in an Emerging Polity*. Lanham: Rowman & Littlefield.

Inglehart, R. and Norris, P. 2000. The developmental theory of the gender gap: women's and men's voting behaviour in global perspective. *International Political Science Review*, 21(4), 441–463.

Klandermans, B., de Weerd, M., Sabucedo, J.M. and Rodiriguez, M. 2001. Framing contention: Dutch and Spanish farmers confront the EU, in *Contentious Europeans. Protest and Politics in an Emerging Polity*, edited by D. Imig and S. Tarrow (eds). Lanham: Rowman & Littlefield, 77–96.

Liebert, U. 1999. Gender politics in the European Union: the return of the public. *European Societies*, 1(2), 197–239.

Lubbers, M. 2008. Regarding the Dutch "nee" to the European constitution: a test of the identity, utilitarian and political approaches to voting "no". *European Union Politics*, 9(1), 59–86.

Manza, J. and Brooks, C. 2000. The gender gap in U.S. presidential elections: when? why? implications? *American Journal of Sociology*, 103(5), 1235–1266.

Marks, G. and Steenbergen, M. 2002. Understanding political contestation in the European Union. *Comparative Political Studies*, 35(8), 879–892.

Milner, H. 2006. YES to the Europe I want; NO to this one. Some reflections on France's rejection of the EU constitution. *PS: Political Science & Politics*, 39(2), 257–260.

Moravcsik, A. 2002. In defense of the "democratic deficit": reassessing legitimacy in the European Union. *Journal of Common Market Studies*, 40(4), 603–24.

Moravcsik, A. 2006. What can we learn from the collapse of the European constitutional project? *Politische Vierteljahresschrift*, 47(2), 219–241.

Qvortrup, M. 2006. The three referendums on the European constitution treaty in 2005. *Political Quarterly*, 77(1), 89–97.

Raftery, A.E. 1995. Bayesian model selection in social research. *Sociological Methodology*, 25, 111–163.

Van Der Eijk, C. and Franklin, M. (eds) 1996. *Choosing Europe: The European Electorate and National Politics in the Face of the Union*. Ann Arbor: University of Michigan Press.

White, H. 1980. A heteroscedasticity-consistent covariance matrix estimator and a direct test for heteroscedasticity. *Econometrica*, 48, 817–830.

Annex

Table 3.1 Coding parties into different party families (based on "party proximity", government parties italicised)

	P1	P2 (left/right antagonism)	P3 (communists separated)
Liberals	*UDF* (F); *VVD*, D66 (NL); DP (L)	*UDF* (F); *VVD*, D66 (NL); DP (L); S_9 (S)	*UDF* (F); D66, *VVD* (NL); DP (L);
Socialists	PS (F); PvdA (NL); LSAP (L), *PSOE*, S_6, S_7 (S)	PS, PC, F_1, F_2 (F); PvdA, S (NL); LSAP, Déi Lenk (L), *PSOE*, S_1, S_3, S_4, S_6, S_7 (S)	PS (F); PvdA (NL); LSAP (L), *PSOE*, S_6, S_7 (S)
Conservatives	*UMP* (F); *CDA* (NL); *CSV* (L); PP, S_2, S_4, S_8 (S)	*UMP*, F_3, F_4 (F); *CDA*, CU, NL_1 (NL); *CSV*, L_1 (L); PP, S_2, S_4, S_8 (S)	*UMP* (F); *CDA*, NL_1, CU (NL); *CSV* (L), PP, S_2, S_4, S_8 (S)
Greens	Les Verts (F); GroenLinks (NL); Déi Gréng (L)	Les Verts (F); GroenLinks (NL); Déi Gréng (L)	Les Verts (F); GroenLinks (NL); Déi Gréng (L)
Extreme-right	FN, NMR (F); LPF, Leefbaar Nederland (NL)	FN, NMR (F); LPF, Leefbaar Nederland (NL)	FN, NMR (F); LPF, Leefbaar Nederland (NL)
Other	PC, F_1, F_2, F_3, F_4 (F); S, NL_1, NL_2, CU (NL); Déi Lenk, L_1 (L); S_1, S_3, S_5, S_9 (S)	NL_2 (NL); S_5, S_9 (S)	F_2, F_3, F_4 (F) NL_2 (NL); L_1 (L); S_3, S_5, S_9 (S)
Communists	NA	NA	PC, F_1 (F); SP (NL); Déi Lenk (L); S_1 (S)

Notes:

NL_1: SGP, NL_2: Other

F_1: LCR, F_2: minor left party 2, F_3, F_4: minor right parties

L_1: ADR

S_1: IU, S_2: CiU, S_3: ERC, S_4: PNV, S_5: EA, S_6: CHA, S_7: BNG, S_8: CC S_9: Other

Table 3.2 Multivariate analyses of arguments for the constitution (log-odds, standard errors in brackets)

Independent variables	Essential for Europ. Construction	Essential for the integration of NMS	Essential for smooth running of institutions	Symbol of Social Europe	Strengthens European identity	Symbol for political unification	Strengthens EU over US	Strengthens democracy in Europe	Strengthens my country's economic situation
Constant	-3.92 (.02)***	-4.45 (1.10)***	-6.93 (.056)***	-6.76 (.63)***	-5.90 (.82)***	-8.56 (2.10)	-7.59 (.71)***	-7.21 (3.02)*	-5.4 (.30)***
Age	.037 (.002)***	.03 (.03)	4.3⁻⁴ (4.9⁻⁵)***	.095 (.038)!	.03 (.02)	.14 (.06)*	.12 (.03)***	.006 (.08)	.06 (.004)***
Age finished education	.10 (.005)***	.068 (.027)*	.26 (.029)***	.14 (.008)***	.03 (.006)***	.26 (.09)**	.13 (.019)***	.17 (.07)*	.06 (.02)**
Females	.038 (.002)***	-.22 (.008)***	.14 (.029)	-.34 (.20)!	.31 (.20)	-.08 (.09)	.11 (.12)	-.33 (.28)	-.33 (.02)***
Service class	.14 (.13)	.15 (.03)***	.22 (.12)!	-.04 (.11)	.52 (.37)	.11 (.05)*	.46 (.04)**	1.78 (1.30)	-.25 (.18)
Petty bourgeoisie	-.032 (.005)***	-1.61 (.99)	-1.46 (.76)!	-2.17 (.95)*	-1.51 (1.11)	-.22 (.06)***	-1.35 (1.27)	2.33 (1.72)	.25 (.37)
Skilled m. workers	-.41 (.11)***	-.68 (.26)**	-.84 (.57)	-.51 (.32)	-.60 (.13)***	-1.83 (1.22)	.02 (.02)	.65 (1.11)	-.85 (.24)***
Unskilled m. workers	-1.41 (.088)***	-1.04 (1.06)	-.96 (.76)	-1.03 (.91)	.79 (.64)	.84 (1.0)	-3.97 (1.54)***	1.50 (.33)***	-.84 (1.04)
Farmers/agri. workers	-.70 (.23)**	###	.62 (.43)	-1.37 (1.14)	.86 (.43)*	-1.33 (1.03)	-.88 (1.53)	-2.25 (1.62)	-.62 (.48)
Homemakers	-.28 (.11)*	-1.19 (.85)	.99 (.61)	-1.08 (.60)!	-.046 (.47)	-3.22 (1.46)*	-1.12 (1.12)	2.58 (1.41)!	-1.69 (.77)*
Students (fulltime)	.73 (.076)***	.095 (.04)*	.43 (.09)***	.73 (.42)!	1.27 (.50)**	1.22 (.68)!	.29 (.38)	1.24 (1.32)	.46 (.12)***
Pensioners	.09 (.10)	1.81 (.70)**	1.12 (.36)**	.54 (.20)**	.59 (.18)**	.26 (.02)***	.80 (.10)***	2.41 (1.90)	.15 (.06)**
Unemployed	-.38 (.07)**	-.11 (.37)	-.16 (.26)	.27 (.02)***	.86 (.52)	-.35 (.37)	.29 (.09)**	2.13 (1.42)	-.06 (.02)**
Liberals	.18 (.10)!	.07 (.14)	.03 (.49)	.22 (.08)**	.32 (.03)***	.03 (.33)	.11 (.34)	-.31 (.08)***	.70 (.09)***
Conservatives	.79 (.10)***	.55 (.20)**	.28 (.026)***	.54 (.08)***	.80 (.04)***	.18 (.06)**	.74 (.17)***	-.18 (.008)***	1.47 (.51)**
Greens	.85 (.14)***	.58 (.06)***	.79 (.037)***	.44 (.08)***	.84 (.02)***	.31 (.12)**	1.06 (.18)***	-.61 (.08)***	1.02 (.51)*
Other	-.93 (.036)***	-1.25 (.07)***	-1.17 (.12)**	-1.20 (.22)***	-.90 (.11)***	-1.58 (.63)*	-2.06 (.005)***	-.69 (.11)***	-.94 (.60)
Extreme rightwing	-1.9 (.13)***	-1.31 (1.05)	###	###	###	###	###	-1.07 (1.10)	###
Luxemburg	.37 (.015)***	1.20 (.02)***	1.06 (.08)***	1.22 (.007)***	1.12 (.03)***	.98 (.04)***	.16 (.03)***	1.49 (.02)***	.93 (.001)***
Netherlands	-.84 (.003)***	-.03 (.05)	.44 (.14)**	.39 (.007)***	-1.08 (.04)***	.07 (.02)***	-.55 (.04)***	.13 (.04)**	.07 (.003)***
Pseudo-R²	.082	.066	.087	.057	.063	.084	.090	.062	.076

Note: ! p < .1, * p < .05, ** p < .01, *** p < .001, coding: mentioned 1; not mentioned 0, standard errors adjusted for clustering across countries, ###: no respondents in this category mentioned this reason and hence no parameters could be estimated; source: merged data file from Flash-EB.

Table 3.3 Multivariate analyses of arguments against the TCE (log-odds, standard errors in brackets)

	Not enough social Europe	The draft is too liberal	Draft is advancing too quickly	Loss of national sovereignty	My country is too weak economically	Too technocratic/ juridical	Do not want Turkey in the EU	Opposition to further enlargement	Against European integration
Independent variables									
Constant	-4.27 (.26)***	-4.98 (.17)***	-8.12 (97)***	-5.21 (1.32)***	-3.30 (.11)***	-6.0 (1.64)***	-3.57 (.82)***	-6.72 (3.36)**	-1.86 (.72)*
Age	.082 (.003)***	.09 (.013)***	.15 (.03)***	.09 (.03)*	.08 (.002)***	.04 (.05)	.07 (.03)*.	.13 (.08)!	-.08 (.02)***
Age finshed education	.05 (.008)***	.12 (.001)***	.09 (.004)***	-.04 (.075)	-.14 (.0003)***	.01 (.07)	08 (.009)***	-.14 (.20)	-.05 (.05)
Females	-.33 (.044)***	-.22 (.07)**	-.06 (.22)	-.03 (.10)	.36 (.01)***	-.70 (.60)	-.29 (.14)*	-.16 (.21)	-.17 (.15)
Service class	-.18 (.06)***	.01 (.03)	.06 (.24)	-.74 (.14)***	-.04 (-.006)***	-.04 (.64)	-.54 (.21)*	.23 (.42)	-.15 (.008)***
Petty bourgeoisie	.26 (.004)***	-.081 (.04)*	-.90 (.53)!	-.80 (.90)	-.98 (.93)	-.74 (.16)***	-.32 (.52)	-2.51 (.78)**	-1.14 (1.0)
Skilled m. workers	-.83 (.10)***	-.10 (.13)	.63 (23)**	-.80 (.73)	.19 (.04)***	-.17 (1.22)	.09 (.01)***	.07 (.04)	-.34 (.05)***
Unskilled m. workers	-.75 (.15)***	-.20 (.27)	.54 (.57)	-1.26 (.98)	.24 (.14)!	###	-.73 (.17)***	-1.87 (1.10)!	.93 (.54)!
Farmers/ agri. workers	-2.30 (1.71)	-.28 (.35)	-.78 (.82)	###	-.86 (-.16)***	###	-4.73 (1.67)***	1.15 (.31)***	-1.24 (1.15)
Homemakers	-.77 (.05)***	-.05 (.09)	-1.27 (.24)***	-.73 (1.02)	-.04 (-.14)	.01 (1.70)	-.04 (.68)	-.18 (.70)	-.26 (.25)
Students (fulltime)	.29 (.02)***	.60 (.02)***	1.05 (.55)*	.14 (.55)	.38 (.05)***	.27 (1.17)	-5.99 (1.82)***	.64 (.49)	-.77 (.25)**
Pensioners	.27 (.03)***	-.17 (.05)**	1.27 (50)*	-.56 (.38)	.02 (.04)	-.60 (.80)	.71 (.15)***	-.16 (.22)	-1.34 (.81)
Unemployed	-.53 (.25)*	-.46 (.04)***	.37 (.79)	-.83 (.61)	.36 (.15)*	.12 (.78)	-.41 (.24)!	.19 (.12)	-.24 (.01)***
Liberals	-.53 (.02)***	-.28 (.002)***	-.48 (.16)**	-.44 (-.10)***	.15 (.08)!	-.02 (.90)	-1.49 (1.24)	-.37 (.70)	-.27 (.49)
Conservatives	-1.66 (.10)***	-1.7 (.83)**	-.08 (.21)	-.10 (.37)	-.61 (.08)***	-.11 (.59)	.29 (.19)	-.23 (.33)	.22 (.05)***
Greens	-1.34 (.19)***	-1.40 (.44)***	.37 (.22)!	-.60 (.60)	-.99 (.04)***	-.30 (.30)	.32 (.22)	-.69 (.09)***	-1.94 (1.32)
Other	.90 (.005)***	.83 (.02)***	-.17 (.12)	.34 (.0007)***	.52 (.03)***	.21 (.61)	.03 (.04)	-.56 (.83)	.88 (.13)***
Extreme rightwing	-.20 (-.009)***	-.22 (.34)	-.46 (.69)	.67 (.04)***	.83 (.07)***	1.01 (.69)	.78 (.11)***	.92 (.47)***	1.04 (.14)***
Luxemburg	.97 (.006)***	-.14 (.09)	2.04 (.06)***	.78 (.17)***	.14 (.03)***	1.61 (.11)***	1.0 (.01)***	1.75 (.27)***	-.32 (.07)***
Netherlands	-1.81 (.001)***	-1.25 (.015)***	.96 (.079)***	1.44 (.12)***	-1.57 (.02)***	1.09 (.17)***	-.50 (.02)***	.85 (.14)***	.65 (.05)***
Pseudo-R^2	.119	.105	.051	.075	.92	.056	.066	.068	.072

Note: * $p < .05$, ** $p < .01$, *** $p < .001$, coding: mentioned 1; not mentioned 0, standard errors adjusted for clustering across countries, ###: no respondents in this category mentioned this reason and hence no parameters could be estimated; source: merged data file from Flash-EB.

Chapter 4

Ignorant Gatekeepers against the EU? National Political Parties in European Political Communication

Kathrin Packham

Introduction[1]

In the light of growing public discontent with the mode and pace of executive-driven European integration, the Lisbon Treaty has rediscovered political parties as agents in the emergence of a European public sphere: "Political parties at European level contribute to forming European political awareness and to expressing the will of citizens of the Union" (Treaty of Lisbon, Art. 10(4)). In an attempt to get political parties on board, the European Commission White Paper on a European Communication Policy invoked political parties' "responsibility to use national channels to ensure a robust European debate" (2006: 11).

In academic debate, it is widely acknowledged that political parties are a precondition for democratic legitimacy (Sartori 1976). But it is disputed whether and to what degree they should or could fully assert this role in European Union politics, too. The literature on political parties and EU politics is vast and disparate – and the general tenor rather "desperate": EU-level parties seem both too weak and too remote,[2] and national political parties allegedly act as (somewhat ignorant) gatekeepers against Europeanisation, carefully guarding their domestic predominance and competences.[3] By contrast, empirical findings demonstrate that domestic parties respond differently to the challenges of EU issues that hit home, depending, among

---

1   This chapter summarises the research design and findings from my PhD thesis, presented and defended in September 2009 at the University of Bremen. The author would like to thank Ulrike Liebert, Ben Crum and Arndt Wonka for challenging questions and comments, Carsten Schneider for advice on the application of fsQCA, and CEuS fellows for cooperation and constant exchange, in particular Ewelina Riekens for generous assistance in data analysis. My research has also benefited from the ConstEPS/ESF/EMEDIATE Workshop at the EUI, May 2006, the ConstEPS Workshops at the Institute of Sociology, Academy of Sciences, Prague, June 2007; the ECPR Summer School on European Parties and Party Systems, EUI, Florence, September 2007; and the ConstEPS/RECON conference, Bremen, September 2008.
2   See Day and Shaw 2006, Hanley 2006, Ladrech 2006b, 1999, von Gehlen 2006.
3   See Mair 2000, 2006, Ladrech 2002, 2006a, Deschouwer 2003, 2006.

others, on domestic party competition (cf. Poguntke et al. 2007). But it is still a widely open question as to which parties succeed and which fail in their competition over conveying contentious EU issues to their domestic constituencies.

To explore this research question in more detail, the present chapter adopts a comparative approach to parties in old and new member states. Moreover, it brings together political party research with an analysis of how parties use the mass media for communicating their preferences on salient EU issues (Schmitt 2003, Hooghe and Marks 2007). Recent studies focusing on public mobilisation strategies of political parties have already convincingly demonstrated the added value of combining these two research fields.[4]

The intensity and extension of public ratification debates on the Constitutional Treaty (TCE) in 2004–2005 lend themselves to empirically taking stock of national parties' capabilities in communicating EU issues to wider publics (see Liebert 2007, Packham 2007). They provide opportunities for specifically assessing the Europeanisation of national political parties, with an eye to better understanding why their European political communication performance varies that much. This is an important area of research, as political party messages that the media disseminate to mass audiences contribute to shaping public opinion and citizens' will formation on the pace and direction of European integration (Binzer Hobolt 2006).

The assessment of mass-mediated political party communication draws empirically on an original print mass media data set[5] covering domestic debates on the European Constitution in six East and West European countries, namely the Czech Republic, Estonia, France, Germany, Poland and the United Kingdom. These data on mass-mediatised political party messages will complement the rich theoretical knowledge, the empirical body, and the established data sources of political party research. To anticipate the findings, assessment of national level political party communication on EU Constitutional Treaty reform presents a complex picture: political parties do inform the public on EU issues and, in part, do so in a highly articulate manner, providing strong as well as clear cues on their respective positions. Nevertheless, it stands out that pro-European mainstream parties find it more difficult to convey coherent messages than anti-European parties, thus leaving their constituencies without alternatives and the public susceptible to populism.

To develop and substantiate this argument, the chapter is structured in five parts as follows: the next section draws on the state of the art regarding the communication

---

4 See De Vreese (2006, 2007), Kriesi (2007) and Statham (2008). While media data are certainly not without flaws, neither are other sources of data such as manifesto data, mass or expert surveys (Schmitt 2003, Marks et al. 2007, Volkens 2007, Tsebelis 2005).

5 The data set was collected by an international team of researchers at the University of Bremen in the framework of ConstEPS. See for more information the country case studies in Liebert (2007, PEPS special issue). The ConstEPS media data base consists of 8842 newspaper articles published across 35 different media outlets between October 28, 2004 and October 31, 2005, see Annex Table 4.2.

role of political parties in developing the conceptual framework for empirical analysis (2). Section 3 presents empirical findings on the diversity of mass mediated party communication by 39 national political parties in print media coverage of TCE reform debates in EU member states. Section 4 advances explanations for the empirical diversity of party political communication performance that are developed through fsQCA. The final part draws conclusions about the implications of these findings regarding EU deficits of democratic legitimacy (5).

Parties in European Political Communication: Analytical Framework

The present research rests on the assumption that political elite communication is important because it shapes (at least partially) what the public thinks, but that current research on democracy and European integration has still to come to terms with unresolved conceptual and methodological issues. One of these is conceptualisation of the mass media's role in political communication in major areas of research:

- In public opinion research, the role of the media is generally acknowledged as one component of political communication for explaining formation of individual attitudes.[6] Yet, European public opinion research, thus far, neglects the role of the media when analysing political party communication.[7]
- By contrast, literature on Europeanisation of the public sphere (see Risse 2010) puts the study of mass media content, that is elite discourse, centre stage. However, these studies usually do not acknowledge the *central role of political parties as actors* (or speakers) in the public sphere.[8]
- The literature on political party campaigns addresses linkages between political parties and the electorate. Yet, it focuses too narrowly on political advertising instead of broadening the scope to mass media communication. This applies to EU research, too, for instance research on EP election campaigns that is dominated by the "second-order elections" hypothesis (Reif and Schmitt 1980).
- Last but not least, mainstream party research neglects the role of the mass media in two ways: on the one hand, the liberal-representative paradigm stresses the responsiveness of political parties to citizens' preferences but downplays their top-down communication. On the other hand, contemporary party research has not yet fully incorporated the transformation of political communication through the increasing centrality of *mass media* in modern democracies.

---

6 Besides utilitarian, institutional, socialisation and identity-based explanations (Ray 2007).

7 Political party messages are measured by either expert judgement or manifesto coding estimates; see for example:: Steenbergen et al. (2007), Ray (2003a, 2003b), Hooghe et al. (2004) and Gabel and Hix (2004).

8 Exceptions are Norris (2000), DeVreese (2006) and Statham (2008).

To fill these lacunae, the next part of the chapter develops a conceptual framework and methodological approach for studying political party messages on EU politics and policy-making through the mass media.

The Concept and Quality of Party Political Messages

Political elites – politicians, officials, journalists, experts and sometimes activists – provide information aimed at shaping public opinion or individual attitudes, particularly of those citizens who are expected to be especially attentive towards messages from political parties that they tend to support (Marsh et al. 1996, Hug and Sciarini 2000). To capture elite communication aimed at mass publics, the present framework of analysis draws on the concept of "elite cueing messages" as developed by John R. Zaller.[9]

'Political messages' are conceived as an exogenous, pre-conditional factor and as part of an elite discourse. They comprise two types, "persuasive messages" and "cueing messages":

> Cueing messages (…) consist of "contextual information" about the ideological or partisan implications of a persuasive message. The importance of cueing messages is such that, as suggested by Converse (1964), they enable citizens to perceive relationships between the persuasive messages they receive and their political predispositions, which in turn permits them to respond critically to the persuasive messages (Zaller 1992: 41–42).

Political elite messages gain special importance when elites are divided on an issue. In this case, "members of the public tend to follow the elites sharing their general ideological or partisan predisposition" (Zaller 1992: 9; Gabel and Scheve 2007). When elites are united in their assessment of the situation, the public is likely to follow the lead, accepting and adopting the elite position – the "mainstream pattern" (Zaller 1992: 185). In the context of European integration, this has been coined as "permissive consensus" (Lindberg and Scheingold 1970). Following Zaller (1992), the quality of "party messages" will vary specifically along three dimensions, namely their strength, their direction and their clarity. As a consequence, "(p)olitical parties are most effective when they are united. Internal dissent vitiates the persuasiveness of a partisan message".[10] The strength, direction and clarity of how the media report party political messages therefore constitute the central dimensions for assessing European political communication "from below".

---

9 Yet, for the present purpose, the focus is on the structure and quality of the messages, and does not include the study of the effects that cueing is supposed to have on public opinion (see Zaller 1992).

10 Using data on party positions on European issues from an expert survey, see Ray (2003a quoted after Ray 2007), also De Vreese 2006.

Causal Conditions Shaping the Quality of Party Political Communication

Presumably, the quality of party political communication on Europe is the result of a range of different conditions, and different configurations of these factors will have different explanatory power. Broadly speaking, five spheres in which these factors are located can be expected to matter in this respect: (1) context; (2) ideology; (3) strategy; (4) issue salience and (5) party unity on European integration:

(1) Context matters – Starting with *systemic context factors*, the necessity to act either in a) an environment of public support for, or of public scepticism towards, European integration, or b) a parliamentary ratification process or a referendum campaign, represents opportunities for some parties and challenges for others. Putting Treaty reform to a referendum has strong agenda-setting effects – by and for citizens, parties and the media. Party competition can therefore be expected to increase, and the impact of access to power will be consequently higher.

(2) Ideology matters – Ideological inter-party competition comprises two variables: (a) the position a party family takes on European Integration and, more precisely, (b) the position that party takes on a Constitutional Treaty. Party manifesto and roll call analyses have established that quite some consistency as well as continuity exist in respect to party families' position towards European integration.[11]

(3) Strategy matters – Strategic inter-party competition encompasses three variables which tackle the power dimension of party competition and which have been identified as important factors: (a) a party's position in the domestic party system, for example government and opposition, (b) a party's position in the EU power system, namely its participation in the Constitutional Convention, and (c) the media management a party pursues.

- Central for both the strength and the clarity of cues is the way a party manages its public relations with the mass media – its *media management*, which refers to party activities designed for gaining media attention and providing them with (pseudo-) events (debates, speeches, party and news conferences) or ready-made information via interviews or press releases (McNair 2007).[12] In return, the party enjoys media visibility and control

---

11 The "inverted u-curve" (Hix and Lord 1997; Hooghe et al. 2004; Budge et al. 2001) has been verified across time as well as space – although its reliability in regard to the Central and East European Countries needs some more empirical back-up.

12 McNair disaggregates the concept of party political integration into two main strands: (1) political advertising, and (2) political public relations. The latter further comprises (1) media management or issue management, (2) image-management or marketing, (3) internal communications, and (4) information management. As the prime focus here is on party political communication via the media, it is restricted to media (or issue) management (McNair 2007: 120–131).

over its messages in media coverage.[13]

- A *party's position within the domestic power hierarchy directly affects* its visibility in the media. Governments enjoy privileged access to the media. In line with objectivity and impartiality objectives the media will, however, usually give out information about opposing views (McNair 2007: 65). While governments can act top-down, challengers, among them protest parties, must often take a bottom-up approach involving carefully designed protest activities that create media attention and coverage of their messages (Kriesi 2004: 189ff.).
- Parties that took part in the *Constitutional Convention* are often those in power at the domestic level, so that active participation in drafting Treaty reforms provides them with the additional advantage of assembled expertise and experts, who can act as speakers or commentators in a party's public relations with the media. It is important to remember, too, that the non-member states at that time were effectively excluded from the process (and its outcome) and could therefore be expected to either ignore or oppose ratification.

(4) Issue salience matters: The intra-party competition dimension consists of one major factor: the salience of European integration for a party. If an issue is visibly contested by one party, other political parties are forced to give the issue more attention than perhaps they would have done on their own account. In this way, single protest parties can contribute to an overall increased level of system salience and party competition (Kriesi 2007, Steenbergen and Scott 2004).

(5) Party unity matters: the degree of unity or dissent within a political party on European integration is central for both the visibility and the clarity of its communication. The expectation is that a high level of intra-party unity enables the party to give clear cues to the public. A high level of factionalism has the contrary effect. Generally, it is imperative that high salience comes with high unity. In an environment of a Eurosceptic public, ratification by public vote, and thus increased party competition, might erode this connection.

The following figure "maps" the independent variables that are supposed to capture the main causal factors that shape the quality of party political communication.

---

13 Of course, this is the best case version. Increasingly, this partnership is being eroded as Blumler and Kavanagh (1999) argue. Kriesi puts it figuratively: "Journalists react to attempts of instrumentalisation by declaring war" (Kriesi 2004: 193). As long as this leads to a more critical coverage and not to outright neglect, this war does not affect the media visibility of actors.

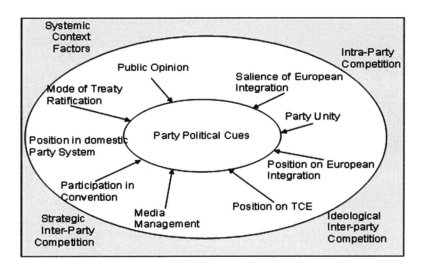

Figure 4.1   Factors explaining the quality of political parties' EU messages[14]
Source: Author.

Methodology of Qualitative Comparative Analysis

For exploring these propositions about the quality of party political messages, QCA as a comparative qualitative methodology has been adopted.[15] Given the relatively "small-n" study – six EU member states with 39 political parties – this allows for maximisation of the number of possible comparisons for testing theoretical propositions. In conceiving each case as a *configuration* of conditions and outcomes, QCA combines the strengths of case-oriented (qualitative) and variable-oriented (quantitative) approaches. In other words, it aims at both qualitative in-depth insights, which case studies can provide, and at the analytical scope of extensive cross-case comparative research (Schneider and Wagemann 2007a: 14). QCA, as an analytical technique, is rather similar to conventional

---

14   For the definition and operationalisation of single variables, please see Annex Table 4.3. Note that – like the independent variables – these causal variables are constructed as sets in which cases have a proportionate membership of either "more in" (>0.5) or "more out" (<0.5). In operation fsQCA evaluates which combinations of cases lead to the defined outcome, that is strong, positive and clear political party cues.

15   The methodology of variable- and case-oriented cross-national qualitative comparative analysis – Fuzzy-set Qualitative Comparative Analysis (fsQCA) – originates in the work of Charles Ragin's "The Comparative Method" (1987; Ragin and Sonnet 2004). It has been developed extensively since (Ragin 2000) including development of specific software tools and textbooks. The software fs/QCA 2.0 and manuals can be downloaded at http://www.u.arizona.edu/~cragin/fsQCA/software.shtml.

quantitative methods (Schneider and Wagemann 2007b: 3) in the sense that patterns in the data are detected with PC support. This approach captures very well not only the complexity of life's reality, and our everyday understanding of it, but also resonates with modern social science theories. These are mostly based on set-theoretical arguments, understanding one social phenomenon as a necessary or sufficient (or both) condition of another phenomenon (Schneider and Wagemann 2007a: 16, 277, Goertz and Starr 2003). QCA can be used for classificatory as well as explanatory purposes and is thus appropriate for analytically approaching the research question outlined above.

Operationalisation and Measurement

This sub-section describes how the quality of political party messages is measured by empirical indicators. "Cases" – that is political parties – will ultimately be attributed values in relation to the characteristics of their communicative performance (see Annex Table 4.4). This measurement method acknowledges the complexity of communication but is parsimonious enough to be replicated and thus tested for its validity. It also is compatible with analyses based on other types of data, for example on party manifestos, public opinion surveys or political discourses. In causal analysis I will, for the matter of this chapter, restrict myself to two characteristics, namely the strength and the clarity of partisan messages.

(1) Strength of Political Party Messages
The strength of a party's messages is operationalised as the party's visibility in the media. This is measured by calculating the number of occurrences (mentions) of *individual political parties and distinguishable party actors* in the press coverage of a specific issue (here: EU Treaty ratification). The "presence" of a party and its actors in print media coverage is thus used as an indicator of the strength of actual party messages.[16] Capturing message strength is to measure the ability of a party to survive in the highly competitive market of media attention.[17]

---

16   This is technically accomplished by computer-assisted semi-automatic coding of media samples structured according to the country. The auto-coding tool was programmed to search for and code all sentences with a party name or synonym. Random sample tests were carried out to ensure coding quality. For each country sample a given set of actors was coded, so that the total number of occurrences per country amounts to 100% of actor occurrences. (The quantitative coding process included approx. 50 other codes.) The visibility of a given party is thus measured as the percentage of its occurrences relative to all coded quotations ('hits') in the country's media coverage.

17   Even though this procedure does acknowledge that media coverage was at very different levels in the cases studied, high variation still occurs across cases. In one country the most visible party has a share of 20% of occurrences (Party A), while in another country the most visible party only reaches 5% (Party B). The obviously very different natures of the domestic ratification debates demand a context-sensitive classification of a party's

(2) Clarity of Political Party Cues

Measurement of the degree of clarity or consistency of a given party's message, as developed for this analysis, departs from others, such as Ray's proposition.[18] The one proposed here further elaborates results obtained by coding party positions in the media. Few parties have been coded as perfectly supportive or completely against the TCE:[19] as a matter of fact, the media actually reflect opposing views within a party that different party actors publicly articulate and report to the media. The question is: to what *degree* is a party able to transcend internal opposition and deliver clear messages? The degree of consistency of a party's position on the TCE is operationalised as the ratio of supportive and negative statements per party. For example, if – out of the statements related to a given party – 35 statements were coded as supportive and 5 as negative, this party's messages can count as much more consistent than those for which the ratio of statements was evenly divided.[20]

Selection of Countries, Parties and Mass Media

For the period of this analysis (October 2004–30 July 2007) a set of 8842 articles from 35 print media outlets from six member states – the Czech Republic, Estonia, France, Germany, Poland, the UK – was selected for study. This includes a diversity of dailies, weeklies, tabloids and quality press as well as sectoral papers.[21] From

---

strength. In other words, we cannot classify Party A as strong and Party B as marginal because both are the most visible parties in their respective domestic public spheres.

18 Ray has prominently pointed out the importance of "having a (coherent) message and staying on message" (De Vreese 2006: 595). Referring to the clarity of political party cues, he has measured this concept using data from an expert survey (2003a). This disregards that political parties will usually go to great lengths to cover up internal conflict and speak with one voice in public. It therefore seems an inappropriate indicator for the clarity of public party messages.

19 Party political statements on the EU which indicate inconclusiveness, disagreement, or speculation are not coded as "neutral" or "divided" but as both positive and negative.

20 In more detail: A party sends clear supportive messages when the ratio is greater than 10, for example 29 positive versus 2 negative statements. It sends a clear negative message when the ratio is between 0.1 and 0, for example 0 positive versus 35 negative statements. Both parties would be assigned the membership value 1, full membership. On the other hand, parties are not members of the set if the ratio of supportive and oppositional statements tends towards 1. This would imply that a party presents itself – or is presented – as completely divided over the issue. The degrees are coded as follows: Clear: $0.1>X>10$; rather clear: $0.1<X<10$; less clear: $0.3<X<4$; not clear at all: $0.725<X<1,4$. Again, the clarity of a message that is not visible in the media cannot be established. In other words, if a message is not visible, it is not clear either and accordingly is not a member of the set of clear messages on the TCE. These cases are also assigned the membership value 0.

21 Two types of search engines were used: Factiva and national search engines (for the remaining newspapers). The key words were "European Treaty"; "European Constitution", "Treaty ratification".

this dataset a qualitative sample of 240 articles was selected for qualitative in-depth coding and discourse analysis (40 articles per country). For the purposes of comparative discourse analysis, a coding scheme was developed and applied using the computer package ATLAS.ti. The following section reports the empirical findings from the comparative print media analysis regarding performance of party political communication on issues of European Constitutional reform.

Empirical Findings: National Political Parties' Mass Media Communication about EU Constitutional Treaty Reform

This section presents the most relevant results from empirical analysis of 39 national political parties' messages in domestic print media debates concerning EU Treaty Ratification in six EU member states (see Annex Tables 4.1 and 4.2).To pave the way for classifying and rank-ordering parties and explaining the findings, a number of preliminary observations are in order regarding their overall variation:

- The yes- and no-camps are about evenly represented across the sample of 31 political parties in the new and old Member States that displayed a position.
- The majority of parties (21 out of 31 cases) are able to transmit at least rather clear cues via the media. Eight of these parties are very successful in this respect. Another eight parties are rather diffuse or vague (less clear) in the message they disseminate. Only two parties represented in the coverage appear completely divided on the issue.
- The analysis shows that highly successful parties (with strong and clear messages) are likely to be mainstream parties with governmental aspirations: those in the pro-camp are incumbent; those in the no-camp are the largest opposition parties.
- Interestingly, the strong no-camp consists exclusively of liberal-conservative parties, while the strong pro-camp includes different political colours (social-democratic, liberal, conservative). This suggests a possible impact of the incumbency status on a supportive position on the TCE.
- However, other parties with governmental aspirations are likely to be strongly represented in the media, but without a clear message. Strong but diffuse messages, be they in favour of or against the Treaty, seem to be a common characteristic of these parties, and especially social-democratic parties and Christian-democrats, that is parties said to be generally belonging to a pro-European core.
- Some small radical and opposition parties do make it into the mass media, if only barely. They often display a very clear position for or against the Treaty. Is this the reason for their visibility?
- The following additional observations can be made in regard to country specific patterns:
- Parties from different party alliances differ in their support for or opposition

to the EU constitution in their domestic arenas. While opposition did to some extent exist in Germany and France, the pro-TCE alliance of parties was considerably stronger. In Estonia, a permissive consensus was at work. The most difficult position was occupied by the Polish SLD as the only pro-TCE party with all other parties opposing the Treaty. The heaviest conflict, however, in terms of party communication through the media, could be expected in CZ and the UK, where both camps are about the same size and weight. At first sight it seems that the latter party systems perform better than the other in terms of offering alternatives to citizens.

- This impression fades when one looks more closely at the degree of clarity displayed by these alliances. In the UK, in particular, the conflict was rather subdued because neither the pro- nor the anti-TCE camp could unambiguously and consistently present its message, presumably because of internal disagreements.
- No referendum was planned in Germany. Nevertheless, it is an interesting case and an example *par excellence* of a loose or broken cartel. While the governing coalition parties SPD and Bündnis 90/Grüne were loyal to the elite consensus, EU support from the main opposition parties appears rather half-hearted. It is the CSU (which is a likely candidate – not very liberal, but national conservative) that breaks the consensus with a growing number of MPs publicly opposing the TCE in the *Bundestag*.[22] Internally, this rubs off on its larger sister, the CDU, which found its own dissenters. Since the CDU is a strong first-time supporter of European integration, the situation is not only uncomfortable but seriously damaging for its strategic position at the domestic, but also at the European, level.
- Classifying political parties' media communication about the EU:
- We find three sets of overlapping parties: (1) those with strongly visible party messages, (2) those with positive party messages on the TCE, and (3) those with clear party messages. For visualising their performance, we have allocated each of the parties – according to its performance in all three dimensions – to one of the corners of a three dimensional property space – a cube. Figure 4.2 shows a high diversity of patterns across the 39 cases, since every corner – every combinatorial type of party message characteristics – is populated by several parties.
- Within the limits of this chapter it is not possible to discuss these patterns in their entirety. I will therefore highlight some of the most important findings here:
- The upper right corner (SPC) includes five parties that succeeded in sending strong, positive and clear messages to newspaper readers. At first glance, this group seems rather heterogeneous. It is made up of conservative parties, the Estonian Res Publica, the French UMP and the Czech Christian

---

22 See Wolff (2008) on the position and behaviour of the Bavarian CSU government in the Convention process.

Democrats (KDU-CSL), as well as left parties, the German SPD and Polish SLD. The commonality: all of these are incumbent parties.[23]

- The three parties just below (SpC) were equally successful in visibly and unambiguously *opposing* the TCE. All of them are (liberal) conservative parties, the Czech ODS, the British Conservatives and the Polish PiS. This no-camp is made up entirely of the largest opposition parties in the respective countries.
- Visible, but not very clear in their message, were those five parties which assemble in corner SPc. They took a positive stance toward the TCE, but failed to do so consistently. This is – again – a mixed group, with the German Christian Democrats (CDU) and Estonian liberal KESK, and the United Kingdom, Czech, and French social democratic parties, Labour, CSSD, and PS.
- In the lower left corner (spc) we find a group of eight parties which were not able to send strong messages and thus were barely or not at all visible in the media – the challengers in party competition. Most of them are small regional or radical parties. (These cases were excluded from parts of the further analysis)
- While they had a rather small share of coverage, four parties in corner sPC were able to clearly transmit their support for the TCE to the media. This was a heterogeneous group, too, consisting of the United Kingdom and Estonian liberal parties (LibDems, ER), the French UDF, and Die Grünen from Germany.
- The set of nine parties that assemble in corner spC is the largest. These are parties which were visible, if not very much so, in domestic ratification coverage. However, their decidedly critical stance towards the European constitution became very clear. Of these, only the Polish Peasants' Party (PSL) was a partner in a coalition government at that time. Other Polish political parties represented here are the Selfdefence (S) and the League of Polish Families (LPR). Three French parties can be found here, two of which are located on the (extreme) right: the Front National (FN) and the MPF, and one on the left margin, the PCF. Two very different parties in the United Kingdom share the same pattern: the Eurosceptic UKIP and the Green Party. The socialist party DIE LINKE is the only party speaking out *clearly* against the Treaty in Germany.

---

23 References to incumbent or opposition status of political parties refer to the period under investigation between Autumn 2004 and Autumn 2005.

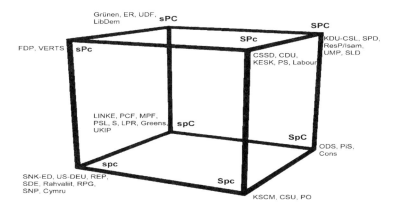

Figure 4.2   Cube of political parties' European political communication patterns[24]

Source: Author.

Ranking Mediated Political Party Communication on EU Reform

Summarising the previously reported results, political parties can be ranked by four broader categories according to their performance in communicating EU Treaty issues to mass public audiences. The categories are in bold letters and cases are clustered on the left and right according to the parties' respective positions on the TCE.

Table 4.1   Ranking order of party performance in communicating EU reform

In favour of TCE (16)	Political party cues	Against TCE (17)	No. of cases
KDU-CSL, SPD, ResP/Isamaa, UMP, SLD	Strong and clear message	PiS, ODS, Cons	8
LibDem, UDF, ER, Grünen	Weak, but clear message	LINKE, MPF, FN, PCF, PSL, S, LPR, Greens, UKIP	13
CSSD, CDU, KESK, PS, Labour	Strong, but diffuse message	KSCM, CSU, PO	8
VERTS, FDP	Weak and diffuse message	US-DEU, SDE	4

Source: Author.

---

24   Explanatory note: The capital letters – S, P, and C – stand for Strong, Positive and Clear. The small letters – s, p, c – stand for Not Strong (that is weak), Not Positive (that is opposed to the TCE), and Not Clear (that is confused).

It is not self-evident why a weak but clear message should be superior to a strong but diffuse message. From a theoretical point of view, party competition serves to structure the policy space along different policy alternatives (as represented by individual political parties). We know from the theory on party cartelisation (Katz and Mair 1995, Blyth and Katz 2005) that the main parties in search of the support of the mean voter tend to develop a mainstream policy cartel. The essential function of presenting clear policy alternatives falls, therefore, to anti-cartel parties. Even if access to the public arena is often restricted for these parties (so that they are only weakly visible in the media), the opposition also forces cartel parties to sharpen their positions. In short, weak but clear cues perform a more important function in informing citizens than do strong but diffuse messages. Those parties whose messages are neither very visible nor clear must be counted as clear communication failures.

The finding of striking diversity not across the member states but across the 39 parties included in our sample here leads to the question of what factors are at work for explaining their performance in communicating EU issues to citizens (readers). The next section will explore the causal effect of possible explanatory factors (see Figure 4.2, previously), such as the party family, manifesto commitment, the status of the party within the domestic system of party competition, and the degree of agreement on EU integration within the party. Furthermore, the influence of context factors such as public opinion on the EU, and the respective mode of ratification (by referendum or in the parliament), will be measured.

Explaining the Europeanisation of Party Messages in the Mass Media

What factors determine the heterogeneous quality of partisan messages on EU reform? To answer this question, various types of data, such as expert judgements, manifesto data, mass surveys, and interviews, were used for analysis (see Annex Table 4.3). In the course of analysis, the empirical examination will challenge some of the claims derived from the literature in party and media studies.

"Top Dogs" or Challengers? Explaining the Strength of Partisan Media Messages

There is no simple cause immediately discernible for explaining the greatly differing visibility – or strength – of party messages in domestic mass media. Possible determinants of the strength of political party cues in the media include three factors (see Model I, Figure 4.3): active media management (and absence thereof) stands at the core of the explanation; similarly, the salience of European integration, that is the degree to which a party considers European integration important or not, is a crucial element; finally, a referendum context often serves to enhance party visibility.

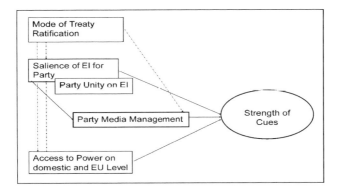

Figure 4.3   Model I: strength of political party cues
Source: Author.

These explanations apply to a range of different party types, as the following examples illustrate:

- The first type of party delivering strong messages on the EU comprises *opposition parties which take a strong and united stance towards European integration*.[25] These would be liberal, social-democratic and Christian-democratic opposition parties – as long as they are unified on their position. Empirical examples include: the German Christian-democratic parties CDU and CSU, and the Polish PO. These are large, mainstream opposition parties rather than small or protest parties, suggesting that the status of would-be government parties can be considered crucial for the visibility of partisan cues.
- The second type includes *unified parties which have been part of the Convention*.[26] This includes government as well as (mostly mainstream) opposition parties, because often the broad setup of the Convention enabled representatives of the opposition to take part, too. If a party has a stake in constitution making at the EU level, this certainly reflects, but also promotes, its standing in the domestic arena. Parties meeting this configuration of variables are the Czech parties CSSD and KDU-CSL, the German SPD and GRÜNE, and the Polish SLD. *In cases where parties find the issue of EU integration salient and are additionally united on their respective position, it is irrelevant whether ratification takes place through a parliamentary or a popular vote*. Parties will not hesitate to promote this position publicly, pursuing active media management.

---

25 In the language of QCA, this first causal path is defined as SALIENCE*UNITY*power*MEDIAPR (raw coverage 0.515625).

26 Causal path: SALIENCE*UNITY*MEDIAPR*CONVENT (raw coverage 0.515625).

- The third type of party for which strong EU messages has been found[27] presents another quite interesting finding: in the context of a EU referendum the effect of "unity" can be reversed. *As hypothesised, the level of unity or disunity on the issue of EU integration becomes meaningless in a situation where all parties are challenged to campaign (and compete) publicly on the issue.* Still, the one characteristic that such parties have in common is that they find European integration generally important, and thus pursue active media management. The following parties meet this condition: the Czech ODS, the French PS and UMP and the British Conservatives.
- The fourth type of party is the most complex but empirically the least important.[28] Using challengers' bottom-up communication strategies (Kriesi 2004), the referendum context provides an opportunity for these parties to express their general anti-system opposition, and for trying to utilise or sway public opinion on European integration. These characteristics fit mainly with small protest parties on the left and right margins of party competition. An empirical example is the Polish PiS.

The findings confirm that usually internal party unity is a key to explaining strong messages. But internal unity on European integration issues becomes rather irrelevant for the strength of party cues in a referendum context; here all parties – regardless of their internal unity – have to participate in the debate. In a parliamentary ratification, however, parties that are internally divided try to avoid divisive issues.

Other expectations could not be confirmed. Notably, access to power is not influential in the way it is commonly hypothesised. Only in the United Kingdom did the incumbent Labour Party gain considerably more attention than the opposition.

"Friendly Dissenters": Explaining the Clarity of Mediated Party Messages

Even though most parties displayed preferences in favour of or against the Treaty, the degree of certainty with which they communicated their stances to the public differed substantially. While some parties were very firm, others were rather hesitant, to say the least. The best example of the latter is the French Socialist Party, which had actually decided on its position on the TCE through an internal referendum, only to be torn between the now officially affirmed positive position and the vocal no-campaign led by influential party actors afterwards.

However, more parties than not (21 out of 31 cases) are able to at least transmit rather clear messages via the media, and eight parties are very successful in this respect. The same number of eight parties, by contrast, is rather vague (less clear) in the messages they disseminate. Only two parties represented in the coverage are

---

27 Causal path: SALIENCE*MEDIAPR*CONVENT*REFERENDUM (raw coverage 0.562500).

28 Causal path: salience*unity*power*MEDIAPR*convent*REFERENDUM (raw coverage 0.265625).

completely divided on the issue, namely the PS and the CSU. This distribution is surprisingly even across the competing camps: clarity and confusion nicely spread among supportive as well as opposing political parties (see Table 4.1). Still, it seems to be more difficult to present the pro-constitutional position in a clear fashion – or to find agreement on this within a party in the first place. No other obvious patterns – in regard to party size, family or incumbency – were discernible.

One could have hypothesised that public opinion would affect the clarity of party messages, when it was in opposition to a party's stance on the TCE. However, empirical evidence shows again that public opinion does not play a major role in shaping the parties' public communication. Thus, the explanation is complex, but by looking into individual cases it appears plausible. Five causal paths may explain an outcome of CLEAR CUES, which will be summarised in the following:

(1) Opposition and Protest Parties:
- The empirically most relevant explanation is about the almost ideal-typical marginal protest parties, which oppose both European integration and the TCE, and in an environment of a referendum are likely to protest very clearly, even though they do not even consider European integration as particularly important.[29] Internal party unity is here of no relevance. A number of parties in the sample meet these characteristics, mostly right, partly radical right, parties: in France the MPF and the FN, in Poland S, PiS and LPR, and the UKIP in the United Kingdom.
- Even if parties are not unified but consider the EU as important, in a referendum context their rejection of both European integration and the TCE is strong enough to send clear oppositional cues. These parties are opposition parties, too, but they differ from the previous party type in that they consider European integration important.[30] This moves them closer to the strategic power centre. Typical cases in this party category comprise the British Conservatives or the Czech ODS, that is parties that are aware of the importance of the EU for executives. Moreover, opposition left parties are also to be subsumed here – as for example the Parti Communiste Francais (PCF). They, too, are more prone to acknowledge the EU's salience than right-wing nationalist parties are.
- Another category of parties perceives European integration as important and has developed a common position on this issue, which enables it to transmit clear messages, even if it is located rather on the margins of domestic power play, and even when ratification takes place through a parliamentary ballot.[31] An example of this would be the German leftist

---

29 Path CP1: Core*constitution*salience*power*MEDIAPR*convent*REFERENDUM+ (raw coverage 0.263636).

30 Path CP2: Core*constitution*SALIENCE*unity*power*MEDIAPR*REFERENDUM+ (raw coverage 0.154545).

31 Path CP3: ore*CONSTITUTION*SALIENCE*UNITY*power*MEDIAPR*convent*referendum (raw coverage 0.081818):

party DIE LINKE. This is actually a very equivocal case, which illustrates the merits of opposition and the risks of incumbency in regard to the clarity of cues. While the party succeeds in manufacturing clear oppositional cues, the media data show the rise of internal tensions due to the increased involvement of some party actors in executive tasks. While DIE LINKE is only barely represented in the Bundestag, it is a junior coalition partner to the SPD in the government of Land Mecklenburg-Vorpommern. As the party on the ground had decided firmly against the Treaty, the more positively inclined ministers had no choice but to insist upon Prime Minister Ringstorff's (SPD) abstention from voting in the Bundesrat vote.

(2) Parties in Power at Both the National and the EU Level
In this group of parties more commonalities exist in their awareness of the salience of the EU, their high level of media activity, and their positive position on the TCE.

- For this group of parties, even in a referendum context, party dissent is no hindrance to clear messages. If a governmental party has called for a referendum, it is naturally in favour of the Treaty in whose negotiation it took part, even if it does not belong to a core pro-European party family.[32] The French UMP is an example of this configuration.
- The second party configuration comes close to the ideal-typical *governmental type of party*, being strongly and consistently in favour of both the EU and TCE.[33] Unsurprisingly, this type of party is found where a strong elite consensus is still valid, for example in Germany. Both coalition partners, the SPD and Bündnis 90/DIE GRÜNEN qualify as such.

Summarising the relevance of these findings for party and media literature, the following revisions to our original causal model are suggested (see Model III):

First, the most likely explanation for clear party messages to the public on EU Treaty reform is that these can be found predominantly among protest parties, who rally against EU Treaty reform in referendum campaigns. By contrast, to be in favour of the TCE seems to predispose a party to confused cues. In this case, the more a party had a solid unified position on EU politics, the more it would be expected to send clear messages to the public – and vice versa. In the light of our evidence, the lack of such an impact is an interesting finding.

Second, the explanatory link appears to be more complex, and the respective influence of party unity to depend on the context and type of party. Internal unity is most important for parties in the parliamentary ratification debate. Parties in a referendum context can often send clear cues despite being rather divided on the

---

32   CP4: core*CONSTITUTION*SALIENCE*unity*POWER*MEDIAPR*CONVENT* REFERENDUM+ (raw coverage 0.145455).

33   CP5: ORE*CONSTITUTION*SALIENCE*UNITY*POWER*MEDIAPR*CONVENT*referendum (raw coverage 0.236364).

issue of European integration. For the most successful parties, however, the degree of unity is irrelevant, with many parties failing to send clear cues even when they are rated as rather united on the issue by experts.[34]

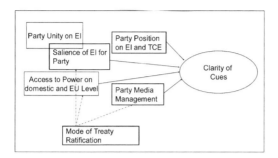

Figure 4.4   Model III revised: clarity of political party cues
Source: Author.

Summary and Conclusion

The research question formulated at the outset as the rationale driving the present analysis has been "How and why do mass media communication patterns of political parties on contentious issues of EU Treaty reform vary?" The answers – based on a qualitative comparative analysis using data from over 8000 articles and 35 domestic print(ed) media outlets in the Czech Republic, Estonia, France, Germany, Poland and the United Kingdom – are summarised by the following propositions:

1. Systematically compiled comparative media data are necessary to provide information on a) the visibility (strength) of political party communication in the public sphere, b) the position (direction) parties take on issues of EU Treaty reform, and c) how clearly this position is presented to mass audiences. The most successful type of party is the one that succeeds in sending strong and clear cues on its positions via the media. Based on these three characteristics of political party cues, eight different patterns of party communication were visualised by a cube-shaped "European public

---

   34   This finding puts in question the use of expert judgement data for measurement of party messages. In several studies on the impact of cueing on public opinion formation, expert judgements on the internal unity of political parties are used in order to measure the cohesion of cues (Ray 2003, Gabel and Scheve 2007). The present analysis shows that this practice is rather questionable because, empirically, no verifiable relation exists between the expert judgement and the *actual* clarity of cues as visible in mediated political communication. Use of media data in effect studies would therefore be more advisable.

space". Independently from the substantive position parties took on EU reform, they were ranked depending on their communication profile.

2. The finding of the great heterogeneity of patterns of party political communication is interesting as it sheds new light on the debate regarding the "centrality of parties" vs. "parties in decline": while some parties successfully compete for visibility in the public sphere others get lost in the marketplace of published opinion. However, a loud voice, that is strong visibility, does not necessarily equal a successful message. Only when parties can send strongly visible, clear cues can we speak of highly successful mediated communication. And only when parties' messages are weak and diffuse at the same time must their communication be regarded as completely failed. Yet, this was a minority with the French Parti Socialiste as an illustrative example of worst practice.

3. Regarding the determinants of success and failure, the present analysis suggests that highly successful parties (with strong and clear messages) are likely to be mainstream parties with governmental aspirations: those in the pro-camp are incumbent; those in the no-camp are the largest opposition parties in their respective domestic systems. Strong but diffuse messages, be they in favour of or against the Treaty, seem to be a common characteristic of opposition parties, among them especially social democratic parties as well as Christian democrats, that is parties said to generally belong to a pro-European core. These often large mainstream parties might find it difficult to reach a consensus on European integration issues within their own ranks.

4. Regarding the theoretical implications of these findings, the observation of national political parties as ignorant gatekeepers must be revised in some respects. National parties did engage with European reform politics when the reform process "hit home". They did so with varying success in regard to the three criteria that were defined to make a "good cue", that is a party message that supports citizens' opinion formation processes (whether by positive or negative stances). Notwithstanding national parties' performance in EU communication, one has to acknowledge that parties are the largest group of collective actors in European public debates. In this sense, national parties undoubtedly remain gatekeepers, but not necessarily ignorant ones.

5. Considering those parties that did not manage to be clear about their respective position on Treaty reform, it is notable that these more often than not were parties supportive of Treaty reform. It is reportedly more difficult to spin a positive message than a negative one. The reasons for this can be found in the distinction between challengers defending the status quo and reformers arguing for Treaty reform with its various alternatives (Kriesi et al. 2007a: 37). Furthermore, Snow and Benford (1988) argue that frames need to resonate with the public's expectation in regard to empirical credibility, experience and narrative fidelity. Hence, complex arguments at a more abstract level, removed from a daily frame of reference, are more difficult to comprehend. Simple, populist frames are more appealing. In conclusion, parties supportive of EU reform have to make an additional effort in communication, which, however, they do not always bother to make.

What conclusions can be drawn from this summary regarding the political consequences for party political communication in the ongoing (and future) processes of EU Treaty reform? The following are but a few tentative considerations.

Most importantly, the analysis shows that national political parties are key agents in the Europeanisation of national public spheres. This confirms not only the necessity to incorporate national political parties in EU research. It also supports the European Commission's aim to involve national political parties as "partners" in European political communication. While this study draws the overall conclusion that national parties matter in European political communication, we also saw that especially the British and Estonian pro-European parties (in a rather Eurosceptic environment) were quite reluctant to make their position clearly heard in domestic public discourse. A number of generally supportive parties did not even make an appearance in the media, for example the British regional parties Plaid Cymru and the SNP or the Czech European Democrats (SNK-ED). Taking into account that it is more difficult to present a constructive than a populist attitude, these parties – at a contentious stage of European political development – did not conform to expectations that parties should provide citizens with communicative linkages or venues for participation in European politics.

Moreover, qualitative evidence shows that the ambiguity of party messages on the EU is largely due to internal quarrels, that is party actors contradicting each other as more or less (un)friendly dissenters. Gabel and Scheve (2007) have confirmed that internal dissent is arguably harmful to the electoral prospects of political parties. The fact that the overall supportive French Parti Socialiste could not mobilise its followers for a yes-vote in the Constitutional referendum in 2005 speaks for itself.

Parties positively inclined towards European integration arguably do not put enough effort into spinning clear messages as compared to the Eurosceptic parties. A supportive attitude seems to be more difficult to present than mere opposition. Examples of best practice are those parties which, though not large parties, managed to send visible and clear cues, such as the liberal parties in Estonia, the United Kingdom and France – the Reform Party, the LibDems and the UDF, as well as the German Greens. Among the most successful incumbent parties were the Social-democrats in Germany and Poland.

An important precondition for fostering clear supportive messages is hence to overcome internal opposition, which will inevitably become visible in public debate. Clearly, parties can choose between two ways of calming down intra-party dissent: one is to "suppress" it, the other is to deal with it and finally resolve the conflict in one way or another. The latter, however, has unpredictable consequences for party politics on the EU, including the possibility of party splits. This is, for example, rather likely in the short to the middle run for the French Parti Socialiste. If the present trend of increased Euroscepticism within the CSU continues, the prospects for CDU/CSU electoral Union in Germany are also rather poor.

This has implications not only for parties' electoral performance but also for European integration overall, in particular in two respects.

First, as Blumer and Kavanagh note, "the populist currents open chances to revisit long-standing disputes in democratic theory, especially between those who mistrusted and those who advocated a more active mass participation in politics (1999: 64)". In this respect, are referendums on EU reforms advisable or not? In the case of the TCE, the pro- and anti-reform camps among national political parties were of about the same size. This implies that, while EU Treaty reform has now repeatedly encountered the problem of "critical states", which could veto further European integration, a Europe-wide referendum could reveal a real European cleavage between supporters and opponents of further European integration.

The existence of two camps could, of course, also foster public debates aimed at clarifying party positions, thus contributing to the overall legitimacy of whatever course the European Union is to take. If these positions are again not clearly communicated, they can, quite the contrary, also enhance public perceptions of the EU as a rather elitist entity beyond the scope of democratic debate. Party political supporters of any future Treaty reform would therefore be well advised to demonstrate their support for European integration more clearly.

The problem with European party communication is neither that there is no debate, nor that the debate is overtly de- or over-politicised. The key issue is intra-party dissent that coins much of the debate. This devalues the potentially positive impact of party competition on public opinion formation on European issues.

References

Binzer Hobolt, S. 2006. How parties affect vote choice in European integration referendums. *Party Politics*, 12(5), 623–647.

Blumler, J.G. and Kavanagh, D. 1999. The third age of political communication: influences and features. *Political Communication*, 16(3), 209–230.

Blyth, M. and Katz, R.S. 2005. From catch-all politics to cartelisation: the political economy of the cartel party. *West European Politics*, 28(1), 33–60.

Budge, I. 2001. Theory and measurement of party policy positions, in *Mapping Policy Preferences. Estimates for parties, Electors, and Governments 1945–1998*, edited by R. Bellamy, D. Castiglione and J. Shaw. Oxford: Oxford University Press, 75–90.

Budge, I., Klingemann, H.-D., Volkens, A., Bara J., Tanenbaum E. 2001. *Mapping Policy Preferences. Estimates for Parties, Electors, and Governments 1945–1989*. Oxford: Oxford University Press.

Converse, P. 1964. The nature of belief systems in mass publics, in *Ideology and Discontent*, edited by D. Apter. New York: Free Press, 206–61.

Crum, B. 2007. Party stances in the referendums on the EU constitution. Causes and consequences of competition and collusion. *European Union Politics*, 8(1), 61–82.

Day, S. and Shaw, J. 2006. Transnational political parties, in *Making European Citizens. Civic Inclusion in a Transnational Context*, edited by R. Bellamy, D. Castiglione, J. Shaw. Palgrave Macmillan, 99–117.

Deschouwer, K. 2003. Political parties in multi-layered systems. *European Urban and Regional Studies*, 10(3), 213–226.

Deschouwer, K. 2006. Political parties as multi-level organization, in *Handbook of Party Politics*, edited by Katz, R.S. and Crotty W.J. London: Sage, 291–300.

De Vreese, C.H. 2006. Political parties in dire straits? Consequences of national referendums for political parties. *Party Politics*, 12(5), 581–598.

De Vreese, C.H. 2007. A spiral of euroscepticism: The media's fault? *Special Issue: Understanding Euroscepticism. Acta Politica*, 42(2/3), 271–86.

European Commission 2001. *European Governance. A White Paper*. Brussels, 25.07.2001, COM(2001) 428 final.

European Commission 2006. *White Paper on a European Communication Policy*. Brussels, 01.02. 2006, Com(2006) 35 final.

Gabel, M. and Hix, S. 2004. Defining the EU political spaces: an empirical study of the European election manifestos, 1979–1999, in *European Integration and Political Conflict*, edited by G. Marks and M.R. Steenbergen. Cambridge University Press, 93–119.

Gabel, M. and Scheve, K. 2007. Mixed messages: party dissent and mass opinion on European integration. *European Union Politics. Special Issue: What Drives Euroscepticism?* 8(1), 37–60.

Goertz, G. and Starr, H. 2003. *Necessary Conditions. Theory, Methodology, and Applications*. Boulder: Rowman & Littlefield.

Hanley, D. 2006. Keeping it in the family? National parties and the transnational experience. *European View*, 3, 35–43.

Hix, S. and Lord, C. 1997. *Political Parties in the European Union*. New York: St. Martin's Press.

Hooghe, L. and Marks, G. 2007. Special issue: understanding euroscepticism. *Acta Politica*, 42(2/3), 119–354.

Hooghe, L., Marks, G. and Wilson, C.J. 2004. Does left/right structure party positions on European integration? in *European Integration and Political Conflict*, edited by G. Marks and M.R. Steenbergen. Cambridge: Cambridge University Press, 120–140.

Hug, S. and Sciarini, P. 2000. Referendums on European integration. *Comparative Political Studies*, 33(1), 3–36.

Kriesi, H. 2004. Strategic political communication. Mobilizing public opinion in "audience democracies", in *Comparing Political Communication. Theories, Cases, and Challenges*, edited by F. Esser and B. Pfetsch. Cambridge: Cambridge University Press, 184–212.

Kriesi, H. 2007. The role of European integration in national election campaigns. *European Union Politics (EUP)*, 8(1), 83–108.

Kriesi, H., Bernhard, L. and Hänggli, R. 2007. Political strategies in direct-democratic campaigns. National Centre of Competence in Research (NCCR). Challenges to democracy in the 21st century. Working Paper No. 8. Available at http://www.nccr-democracy.uzh.ch/publikationen/workingpaper/political-strategies-in-direct-democratic-campaigns (accessed July 22nd, 2012).

Ladrech, R. 1999. Political parties and the problem of legitimacy in the European Union, in *Legitimacy and the European Union: The Contested Polity*, edited by T. Banchoff and N. Smith. London/New York: Routledge, 93–112.

Ladrech, R. 2002. Europeanisation and political parties: towards a framework for analysis. *Party Politics*, 8(4), 389–403.

Ladrech, R. 2006a. The European Union and political parties, in *The Handbook of Political Parties*, edited by R.S. Katz and W.J. Crotty. London: Sage, 492–498.

Ladrech, R. 2006b. The promise and reality of euro-parties. *European View*, 3 (Spring), 73–79.

Liebert, U. 2007. Europe in contention: debating the constitutional treaty. *Perspectives on European Politics and Society*, Special Issue, 8(3), 235–261.

Lindberg, L. and Scheingold, S. 1970. *Europe's Would-Be Polity: Patterns of Change in the European Community*. Englewood Cliffs: Prentice-Hall.

Mair, P. 2000. The limited impact of Europe on national party systems. *West European Politics*, Special Issue, 23(4), 27–51.

Mair, P. 2006. Political and party systems, in *Europeanization: New Research Agendas*, edited by T. Banchoff and M. Smith. Basingstoke: Palgrave Macmillan, 154–165.

Marks, G., Hooghe, L., Steenbergen, M.R. and Bakker, R. 2007. Crossvalidating data on party positioning on European integration. *Electoral Studies*, 26(1), 23–38.

McNair, B. 2007. *An Introduction to Political Communication*. Fourth Edition. London/New York: Routledge.

Norris, P. 2000. A virtuous circle. Political communications in postindustrial societies. Cambridge: Cambridge University Press.

Packham, K. 2007. From the contentious constitution to the awkward other … social model: the constitutional debate in the British print media. *Perspectives on European Politics and Society*, 8(3), 281–313.

Poguntke, Th., Aylott, N., Carter, E., Ladrech, R. and Luther, K.R. 2007. *The Europeanization of National Political Parties. Power and organizational adaptation*. London/New York: Routledge.

Ragin, C. 1987. The comparative method: moving beyond qualitative and quantitative strategies. Berkeley: University of California Press.

Ragin, C. 2000. *Fuzzy Set Social Science*. Chicago: University of Chicago Press.

Ragin, C. and Sonnet, J. 2004. Between complexity and parsimony: limited diversity, counterfactual cases, and comparative analysis, in *Vergleichen in der Politikwissenschaft*, edited by S. Kropp and M. Minckenberg. Wiesbaden: VS Verlag für Sozialwissenschaften.

Ray, L. 2003a. When parties matter: the conditional influence of party positions on voter opinions about European integration. *Journal of Politics*, 65(4), 978–94.

Ray, L. 2003b. Reconsidering the link between incumbent support and pro-EU opinion. *European Union Politics*, 4(3), 259–279.

Ray, L. 2007. Public opinion, socialization and political communication, in *Handbook of European Union Politics*, edited by K.E. Jørgensen, M. Pollack and B. Rosamond. London: Sage, 263–281.

Reif, K. and Schmitt, H. 1980. Nine second-order elections: a conceptual framework for the analysis of European election results. *European Journal of Political Research*, 8, 3–44.

Risse, T. 2010. *A community of Europeans? Transnational Identities and Public Spheres*. Cornell University Press.

Sartori, G. 1976. *Parties and Party Systems*. Cambridge: Cambridge University Press.

Schmitt, H. 2003. The eurobarometers. Their evolution, obvious merits, and ways to add value to them. *European Union Politics*, 4(2), 243–51.

Schneider, C. and Wagemann, C. 2007a. Qualitative comparative analysis and Fuzzy Sets. Ein Lehrbuch für Anwender und jene, die es werden wollen. Opladen and Farmington Hills: Verlag Barbara Budrich.

Schneider, C. and Wagemann, C. 2007b. *Standards of Good Practice in Qualitative Comparative Analysis (QCA) and Fuzzy-Sets*. COMPASSS Working Papers, WP2007-51 Available at: http://www.compasss.org/WagemannSchneider2007.pdf [accessed: 2 December 2008].

Snow, D.A. and Benford, R.D. 1988. Ideology, frame resonance, and participant mobilization. *International Social Movement Research*, 1, 197–217.

Statham, P. 2008. *Political Party Contestation over Europe in Public Discourses: Emergent Euroscepticism?* Arena Working Paper Series 08/2008, Available at: http://www.arena.uio.no/publications/working-papers2008/papers/wp08_08.xml, [accessed: 16 July 2008].

Steenbergen, M. and Scott, D.J. 2004. The salience of European integration, in *European Integration and Political Conflict*, edited by G. Marks and M.R. Steenbergen. Cambridge: Cambridge University Press, 165–92.

Steenbergen, M., Edwards, E. and de Vries, C. 2007. Who's cueing whom? Mass-elite linkages and the future of European integration. *EUP*, 8(1), 13–36.

Treaty of Lisbon, complete edition, OJ 2010/C 83/01, http://eur-lex.europa.eu/LexUriserv/LexUriserv.do?uri=OJ:C:2010:083:FULL:EN:PDF.

Tsebelis, G. 2005. Assessing the contributions of the DOSEI project. *EUP*, 6(3), 377–390.

Volkens, A. 2007. Strengths and weaknesses of approaches to measuring policy positions of parties. *Electoral Studies*, 26(1), 108–120.

Von Gehlen, A. 2006. Two steps to European party democracy. *European View*, 3(Spring), 161–171.

Wolff, J. 2008. Verhandeln im Schatten der Politikverflechtung. Die deutschen Länder im Europäischen Konventprozess. Wien/ Zürich/Berlin: LIT.

Zaller, J.R. 1992. *The Nature and Origins of Mass Opinion*. Cambridge: Cambridge University Press.

Annex

Table 4.1   List of political parties included in the analysis

Case id	Party abbr.	Original party name	English party name
1	CSSD	Ceska strana socialne demokraticka	Czech Social Democratic Party
2	KDU-CSL	Krest'anska a demokraticka unie – Ceskoslovenska strana lidova	Christian Democratic Union – People's Party
3	ODS	Obcanska demokraticka strana	Civic Democratic Party
4	SNK ED	SNK Evropsti demokrate	SNK European Democrats
5	US-DEU	Unie Svobody-Democraticka Unie	Freedom Union – Democratic Union
6	KSCM	Komunisticka strana Cech a Moravy	Communist Party of Bohemia and Moravia
7	CDU	Christlich-Demokratische Union	Christian-Democratic Union
8	SPD	Sozialdemokratische Partei Deutschlands	Social Democratic Party of Germany
9	FDP	Freie Demokratische Partei	Free Democratic Party
10	CSU	Christlich Soziale Union in Bayern	Christian Social Union in Bavaria
11	Grünen	Bündnis 90/Die Grünen	Alliance 90/The Greens
12	LINKE	Die Linke	The Left (former PDS)
13	REP	Die Republikaner	The Republicans
14	ER	Eesti Reformierakond	Reform Party
15	KESK	Eesti Keskerakond	Centre Party
16	SDE	Sotsiaaldemokraatilik Erakond	Social Democratic Party
17	ResP/Isamaa	Isamaa ja Res Publica Liit or Erakond Isamaaliit	Union of Pro Patria and Res Publica (ex RPU)
18	Rahvaliit	Eestimaa Rahvaliit	People's Union of Estonia
19	UDF	Union pour la Democratie Francaise	Union for the French Democracy
20	PS	Parti Socialiste	Socialist Party
21	VERTS	Les Verts	The Greens
22	UMP	Union pour un Mouvement Populaire	Union for a Popular Movement (former RPR)
23	MPF	Mouvement pour la France	Movement for France
24	FN	Front National	National Front
25	PCF	Parti Communiste Francais	French Communist Party
26	PRG	Parti Radical de Gauche	Left Radical Party
27	SLD	Sojusz Lewicy Demokratycznej	Alliance of Democratic Left
28	PSL	Polskie Stronnictwo Ludowe	Polish Peasants' Party
29	PO	Platforma Obywatelska	Civic Platform
30	S	Samoobrona Rzeczypospolitej Polskiej	Self Defense of the Polish Republic
31	PiS	Prawo i Sprawieliwosc	Law and Justice
32	LPR	Liga Polskich Rodzin	League of Polish Families
33	Lab	Labour Party	Labour Party
34	LibDem	Liberal Democrats	Liberal Democrats
35	SNP	Scottish National Party	Scottish National Party
36	Cymru	Plaid Cymru	Party of Wales
37	Greens	Green Party	Green Party
38	Cons	Conservative Party	Conservative Party
39	UKIP	United Kingdom Independence Party	United Kingdom Independence Party

Table 4.2 ConstEPS media data set (26.10.2004–30.10.2005)

Country	Selected newspapers	Quantitative Sample (no. of articles)
Czech Republic	Blesk, MFDnes, Právo, Reflex, Respekt, Tyden (6)	973
Estonia	Postimees, Päevaleht, Molodezh Estonii (3)	367
France	Le Figaro, Le Monde, L'Express, Le Nouvel Observateur, Le Point (5)	4071
Germany	Bild, Frankfurter Allgemeine Zeitung, Focus, Spiegel, Süddeutsche Zeitung, Die Welt, Die Zeit (7)	1451
UK	The Times, The Guardian, The Sun, The Daily Mirror, The Economist, The Observer (6)	943
Poland	Gazeta Wyborcza, Rzeczpospolita, Nasz Dziennik; Wprost, Newsweek Polska, Tygodnik Powszechny; Super Express, Europa (Fakt) (8)	699
Total	35 domestic print media outlets	8842

Source: ConstEPS, compiled by the author.

Table 4.3 Empirical operationalisation of causal factors

Explanatory dimension	Explanatory variable	Indicator	Matrix abbr.	Name of set	fsQCA membership values and definitions	Data source
Ideological inter-party competition.	Party Family Position on EU Integration.	Stances towards European Integration in general but particularly political integration as it proposed by TCE.	Core	Set of parties belonging to the core of pro-European core party families.	» 1 = party belongs to strong pro-integrationist core, that is social democrats, Christian democrats and liberals; » 0.7 = party belongs politically in general to pro-integrationist green party family; » 03 = party belongs to conservative party family; » 0 = party belongs to radical left or populist right, strongly opposed to further European integration;	Euromanifestos (EMP) the Chapel Hill Expert Judgements, Lewis/Mansfeldova 2006.
	Party Position on EU Constitution.	Official Position on the issue of an EU constitution.	Constitution	Set of parties with a declared positive stance on a European Constitution.	» 1 = party is in favour of EU constitution; » 0 = party is against EU constitution or has not formulated a position on EU constitution.	Euromanifestos (EMP) ConstEPS. Intermediaries Survey EPIN 2004.
Strategic inter-party powerplay.	Strategic Party Competition.	Closeness/distance to power centre in domestic party political arena, that is to government.	Power	Set of parties in governmental power.	» 1 = incumbent party, senior coalition partner; » 0.7 = incumbent party, junior coalition partner; » 0.3 = parliamentary opposition party; » 0 = not in national parliament (= protest party);	Own compilation, homepages of national parliaments, governments, Statistical offices.
	Party Participation in Constitutional Convention.	Closeness/distance to power in European political reform arena, that is Constitutional Convention.	Convent	Set of parties participating in the Constitutional Convention.	» 1 = Party representatives were full members; » 0.7 = Party representatives were candidate/ alternate members; » 0.4 = No party representatives were full/ alternate members; » 0 = No party representatives were candidate members.	Own compilation, use of Convention Archive at <http://european-convention.eu.int/bienvenue.asp?lang=EN>.

Explanatory dimension	Explanatory variable	Indicator	Matrix abbr.	Name of set	fsQCA membership values and definitions	Data source
Ideological and strategic intra-party argument.	Salience of EU Integration for Party.	Degree of salience a party attaches to EU integration issues.	Salience	Set of parties for which EI is an important issue.	» 1 = EI of great importance; » 0.7 = EI of some importance; » 0.3 = EI of little importance; » 0 = EI of no importance at all;	Euromanifestos (EMP) Chapel Hill Expert Judgements.
	Party Unity on EU Integration.	Degree of internal consent and dissent in party leadership.	Unity	Set of parties with a solid agreement on EI within the leadership.	» 1 = a party is completely united; » 0.7 = the party is mostly united; minor dissent; » 0.3 = significant internal dissent; » 0 = strong internal dissent, strongly divided.	Chapel Hill Expert Judgements ConstEPS Intermediaries Survey Sikk (in Lewis/ Mansfeldowa 2006).
Strategic party behaviour/practice.	Party Media Management.	Self-assessment of political party actors in respect to organising/ participating in public events, public protest and media relations.	MediaPR	Set of parties actively communicating on the TCE.	» 1 = high effort to communicate; » 0.7 = rather actively communicating; » 0.3 = somewhat active; » 0 = no to low effort.	ConstEPS Intermediaries Survey on Constitutionalisation.
Context conditions.	Public Participation in Treaty Reform.	Mode of TCE ratification.	Referendum	Set of parties in a context of high public participation in Treaty ratification.	» 1 = referendum has taken place; » 0.7 = referendum planned – postponed/ cancelled; » 0.3 = parliamentary ratification carried out; » 0 = parliamentary ratification planned – postponed/cancelled;	Own compilation.
	Diffuse Public Opinion on EU Integration.	Standard Eurobarometer measure "Support to the membership" 2003–2005.	Support_for_EU	Set of parties in a context of public opinion in favour of EI.	» 1 Strongly Pro-European; » 0.8 Pro-European; » 0.6 moderately Pro-European; » 0.4 moderately Eurosceptic; » 0.2 Eurosceptic; » 0 strongly Eurosceptic.	Eurobarometer.

Table 4.4 fsQCA data matrix of outcome and causal variables

Party abbr.	Positive	Clear	Success	Core	Constitution	Salience	Unity	Power	Media pr.	Convent	Referendum	Support for eu.
CSSD	1	0.3	0.3	1	1	1	0.7	1	0.7	0.7	0.7	0.2
KDU-CSL	1	0.7	1	1	1	0.7	0.7	0.7	0.7	0.7	0.7	0.2
ODS	0	0.7	1	0.3	0	0.7	0.3	0.3	1	0.7	0.7	0.2
SNK ED	0	0		0.3	1	0.7	1	0	0.7	0	0.7	0.2
US-DEU	0	0		0.3	1	1	1	0.7		0	0.7	0.2
KSCM	0	0.3	0.3	0	0	0.7	0.3	0.3	0.3	0	0.7	0.2
CDU	1	0.3	0.3	1	1		0.7	0.3	0.7	1	0.3	0.8
SPD	1	1	1	1	1	0.7	1	1	0.7	1	0.3	0.8
FDP	1	0.3	0	1	1	0.7	1	0.3	0.7	0.4	0.3	0.8
CSU	0	0	0.3	1	1	0.7	0.7	0.3	0.7	0.4	0.3	0.8
Grünen	1	1	0.7		1	1	0.7	0.7	0.7	1	0.3	0.8
LINKE	0	07	0.7	0	1	0.7	0.7	0.3	0.7	0.4	0.3	0.8
REP	0	0		0	0	0.7	1	0		0.4	0.3	0.8
ER	1	0.7	0.7	1	1	0.3	0.7	0.7		0.7	0	0.2
KESK	1	0.3	0.3		1	0.7	0	0.3		0	0	0.2
SDE	0	0		1	0	0.7	0.7	0.3	0	0.7	0	0.2
ResP/Isamaa	1	0.7	1	0.3	1	0.7		1	0	0.7	0	0.2
Rahvaliit	0	0		0.3	0		0.3	0.7	0.3	0	0	0.2
UDF	1	1	0.7		1	1	0.7	0.3	0.7	0.4	1	0.4
PS	1	0	0.3	1	1	1	0.3	0.3	1	0.7	1	0.4
VERTS	1	0.3	0	0.7	1	0.7	0.3	0.3	07	0.4	1	0.4
UMP	1	0.7	1	0.3	1	1	0	1	0.7	1	1	04
MPF	0	1	0.7	0.3	1	0.3	1	0		0.4	1	0.4
FN	0	0.7	0.7	0	0	0.3	0.3	0	1	0.4	1	0.4
PCF	0	1	0.7	0	0	1	1	0.3	0.7	0.4	1	0.4
PRG	0	0		0	1	1	0.3	0.3	0.7	0.4	1	0.4
SLD	1	1	1	1	1	0.7	0.7	1		0.7	0.7	0.4
PSL	0	0.7	0.7	0.3	0	0.3	0.3	0.7	0.3	0	0.7	0.4

Party abbr.	Positive	Clear	Success	Core	Constitution	Salience	Unity	Power	Media pr.	Convent	Referendum	Support for eu.
PO	0	0.3	0.3	0.3	1	0.7	1	0.3	0.7	0.7	0.7	0.4
S	0	0.7	0.7	0.3	0	0.3	0.7	0.3	0.3	0	0.7	0.4
PiS	0	1	1	0	0	0.3	0.3	0.3	0.7	0	0.7	0.4
LPR	0	1	0.7	0	0	0.3	1	0.3	1	0	0.7	0.4
Lab	1	0.3	0.3	1	1	0.3	0.3	1		1	0.7	0
LibDem	1	0.7	0.7	1	1	0.7	1	0.3		0.7	0.7	0
SNP	0	0		0.7	1	0.3	0.7	0.3	0	0.4	0.7	0
Cymru	0	0		0.7	1	0.3	0.7	0.3	0.7	0.4	0.7	0
Greens	0	0.7	0.7	0.7	0	0.3	0.3	0		0.4	0.7	0
Cons	0	0.7	1	0.3	0	0.7	0	0.3		1	0.7	0
UKIP	0	0.7	0.7	0	0	0	0.7	0	0.7	0.4	0.7	0

Chapter 5
Watch-dogs that Cannot Bite? New National Parliamentary Control Mechanisms under the Lisbon Treaty

Aleksandra Maatsch

Introduction

The Treaty of Lisbon opened up new possibilities for involvement of national parliaments in EU politics. Firstly, the Treaty expanded traditional national parliamentary competences regarding control and oversight of the executive and, secondly, created new patterns for parliamentary involvement in EU politics. In contrast to the traditional oversight role, these new possibilities (such as a possibility to address the Court of Justice of the European Union directly or engaging in cooperation with other national parliaments on European security issues) allow parliaments to act more independently and, in addition, to exercise influence at an early stage of decision-making.

The empirical analysis presented in this chapter focuses on reception and evaluation by MPs of the reforms concerning national parliaments. The states under study were: the Czech Republic, France, Germany, the United Kingdom, Hungary and Poland. By analyzing plenary parliamentary debates on ratification of the Lisbon Treaty this chapter targets the following research questions: which particular reforms concerning national parliaments received MPs' attention? How were they evaluated? What functions of national parliaments in EU politics did MPs prioritise?

By concentrating on MPs we can establish how important or feasible the new competences are from the perspective of the institutional actors who are supposed to use them. In particular, national parliaments – as all institutions – have their internal and external constraints, interests, priorities and goals. For that reason they are the most reliable actor to tell whether, how and why they are going to make use of their new competences.

Secondly, by analyzing how MPs receive their new competences in EU politics, we can also establish what functions of national parliaments are particularly important for them. This information is particularly valuable because it allows the assumption that parliaments would demonstrate more activity in areas which have a higher significance for them.

The empirical analysis presented in this chapter demonstrates that national parliaments clearly prioritised the control function and did not devote much attention to the provisions of the Lisbon Treaty that were not related to oversight. According to MPs, the major role of national parliaments in the EU is to control governments and to act as guardians of the subsidiarity principle. Evaluation of the new control functions was mixed: those MPs who evaluated the reforms positively either argued that national parliaments' power of oversight had increased or claimed that democratic control in the EU (as such) has improved. The skeptics followed just one line of argumentation: in their view the new competences of national parliaments are nothing but an illusion of power. The self-portrait of national parliaments that emerges from the empirical analysis recalls a watch-dog that wants to bite, but cannot. MPs in the states analyzed agreed that national parliaments should have a stronger position in the EU, but many of them remained skeptical whether the Lisbon Treaty grants them de facto more power.

Regarding structure, this chapter begins with a presentation of the literature on the role of national parliaments in the European Union, the process of de-parliamentarization and gradual re-parliamentarization. In the next step the chapter outlines the provisions of the Lisbon Treaty applying to national parliaments, followed by a presentation of the methodology, empirical findings and finally discussion.

National Parliaments in the European Integration Process

Transfer of competences to the European level has gradually reduced the scope of national parliamentary competences. By now the role of national parliaments in some policy areas is limited to transposition of EU legislation. European integration has also affected the relationship between national parliaments and governments, clearly empowering the latter (Judge 1995, Katz 1999).

According to Norton (1995) national parliaments adapted to European integration in three stages. During the first phase (the 1950s to the mid-1980s) parliaments were involved in EU politics in a very limited way. The dominant mode of decision-making in the EU was intergovernmental, public opinion supported European integration, national MPs had a low interest in EU affairs and national parliaments introduced very few procedural changes in response to the process. The second phase (mid-1980s to the Maastricht Treaty, effective since 1993) was marked by introduction of supranational elements to decision-making procedures in the EU. The workload of national parliaments related to EU affairs increased, most parliaments established specialised European Affairs Committees and national MPs themselves developed a greater interest in EU matters.

In the third phase (from 1993 onwards) EU competences were extended to new areas and application of the QMV increased, whereas public opinion towards EU integration became more negative. The institutional reforms introduced after the Maastricht Treaty were oriented to combating the democratic deficit in the EU. As a response to that challenge, the role of national parliaments in EU politics has been formally recognised in the Treaties. In particular, Declaration 13 of the Maastricht Treaty (1992) envisaged in a non-binding commitment that 'the governments of the Member States will ensure that national parliaments receive Commission proposals for legislation in good time for information or possible examination'.

Nonetheless, the commitment did not prove to be effective. The Amsterdam Treaty (1997) contained a special protocol annexed specifying that legislative proposals in the Council's agenda should be available to member states for at least six weeks so that the government of each member state would have enough time to inform its own national parliament. Furthermore, during the third phase specialised European Affairs Committees became more involved in EU matters (also through transnational inter-parliamentary cooperation) and strengthened their position vis-à-vis the executive.

Researchers of national parliaments have agreed that in the initial phase of European integration national parliaments suffered a significant loss of power. "Losers", "slow-adapters", "latecomers to European integration", "erosion of parliamentary democracy"– these are only selected slogans depicting the position of national parliaments in the European Union in the early years of European integration. Indeed, according to the most popular hypothesis accounting for the state-of-the-art at that time, the so-called de-parliamentarization hypothesis, the process of European integration took place at the expense of national parliaments (Wessels 1989). Loss of power has been attributed to two processes: (1) direct power-transfer from parliaments to EU institutions in selected policy areas and (2) increase of Qualified Majority Voting in the Council of the EU. As a consequence of the latter, national parliaments were no longer in a position to hold their governments accountable for final decisions taken during Council meetings.

However, since the mid-1990s scholars began increasingly to discuss the re-parliamentarization process. It has been acknowledged that national parliaments are beginning to adapt to functioning in a multi-level polity. The change was induced not only by top-down factors such as institutional reform, but also internal bottom-up reforms of national parliamentary administrative and committee work (Raunio 2008). As a consequence, researchers of national parliaments noted that national parliaments "were fighting back" (Raunio 2008, 2009, Hix and Raunio 2000) and responding to the EU integration process (Maurer and Wessels 2001).

National Parliaments: Winners or Losers of European Integration?

The process of adaptation by national parliaments to the challenges related to European integration has generated a very basic question: are national parliaments losers or winners of European integration? Scholarly positions on that issue depend on two factors: a theoretical approach to European integration and hierarchy of the functions of national parliaments. In particular, a group of scholars representing the intergovernmental stance and prioritising the scrutiny-related function either declares national parliaments to be losers in the European integration process or they claim that national legislatures have made significant progress in adjusting institutionally to the European Union but still remain incomparably weaker than the executive. Another group of scholars point to other than scrutiny-related functions and note that in these areas national parliaments have become much stronger.

Intergovernmental scholars drawing on rational choice assumptions have stressed the fact that national parliaments have become weaker vis-à-vis the national executive and the Council (Moravcsik 1994, Wessel and Maurer 2001). According to scholars representing that approach, governments constitute the central actors of European integration. Therefore, since the capacity of national parliaments to constrain their governments has decreased, that tendency implies a loss of power for national parliaments.

Yet another group of scholars (constructivists, sociological or historical institutionalists) argue that European integration is not exclusively controlled by national governments. For instance, bottom-up processes and the impact of norms should not be overlooked (Elo-Schäfer et al 2006, Töller 2008). These scholars point to the fact that whereas our knowledge of scrutiny-related functions is already very rich, we know little about other functions of national parliaments and how these have been affected by European integration (Raunio 2008 and 2011). Furthermore, we still know little of how European integration impacts horizontal cooperation among national parliaments in the member states (Maatsch 2011) or between national parliaments and the European Parliament (Crum and Fossum 2009).

According to Raunio, government-related functions of national parliaments (scrutiny and law-making) have been prioritised in the European integration process – and also in the Lisbon Treaty – over citizen-related functions (information, representation of constituencies and transnational cooperation) (Raunio 2011). In the literature we can identify the following factors that influence the performance of national parliaments in EU politics: (1) constitutional competences of national parliaments (Holzhacker 2005, Karlas 2011) (2) public Euroscepticism (Karlas 2011), (3) party Euroscepticism (Holzhacker 2005, Raunio 2005, Karlas, 2011), (4) frequency of minority governments (Holzhacker 2005, Saalfeld 2005; Karlas 2011), (5) powers of the opposition (Holzhacker 2005) or (6) political culture (Raunio 2005).

A recent study analyzing oral and written questioning in national parliaments (Rozenberg et al 2011) demonstrates that control of government is not necessarily the prior goal of MPs but rather reduction of the information gap between parliaments and government and, secondly, information of citizens. Whereas written questions tend to be used more often in order to obtain a more detailed policy content analysis, oral questions (scheduled during plenary sessions) are oriented to the public. As Rozenberg argues (Rozenberg et al 2011) oral questions play a special role in the accountability process: "They are generally covered by the media whereas other aspects of parliamentary activities remain largely unnoticed – especially concerning the oversight of the government. In France, for instance, between one and two million people watch Question Time on Wednesday afternoon".

A comparative study by Wessels (2005) demonstrates that MPs themselves are divided with respect to the hierarchy of national parliamentary functions:

there is no uniformity on whether national parliaments should perceive citizens or government-related functions as their priority. Depending on the individual hierarchy of functions, MPs tend to raise different legitimacy claims. Those who prioritise representation are in favour of strengthening parliamentary representation in the European Union, whereas those who assign more importance to governance prefer intergovernmentalism.

Regarding the citizen-related functions of national parliaments, both the parliamentary majority and the opposition are important for representing different constituencies, informing and mobilising them. Although the government controls the agenda, in the shape of policy proposals discussed by the parliament, the opposition's role is to make sure that these proposals are debated during plenary sessions and that citizens are adequately informed about them. In order to remain accountable to their constituencies, governments – and the parliamentary majorities that usually represent the same political line – are compelled to enter into public deliberation and respond to opposition criticism.

Do National Parliaments Want to – and Can They – get More Involved in EU Politics?

The other central question addressed by the literature is whether national parliaments can – or want to – get more involved in EU politics. After all, national parliaments are responsible for national politics and they are voted in on national issues by national constituencies. On the other hand, it is increasingly difficult to separate national from EU politics.

The question whether national parliaments 'can' get involved in EU politics depends on their scope of competences at the national and EU level. The power of national parliaments differs from one policy field to the other. What is important is that, even if EU legislation assigns similar powers to national member state parliaments, the extent to which they utilise these powers depends on national legislation. For instance, the Lisbon Treaty granted new competences to national parliaments in the EU security domain. However, since 'national practices' differ regarding involvement by national parliaments in security issues, national parliaments cannot exercise similar powers on the EU level (Anghel et al 2008). In the first group of states national parliaments play no role at all in European security policy (Bulgaria, Greece and Romania); in the second group parliaments are entitled to debate security measures and vote on them, but their decisions are not binding on their governments (Belgium, France, Poland, Portugal and the UK); a third group is composed of states that not only debate ESDP but can also veto deployment of their troops, although voting can only take place after the meeting of the European Council – ex post vote (Austria, Germany, Cyprus, the Czech Republic, Estonia, Ireland, the Netherlands and Spain); finally, a fourth group of states concerns parliaments that can decide on the ESDP mission ex ante, namely, before their governments attend the meeting of the Council (Finland, Luxembourg and Sweden).

Another question is whether national parliaments are indeed interested in getting involved more deeply in EU politics. As already mentioned, it is increasingly difficult to separate national from EU politics. Furthermore, even if constituencies remain nationally defined, voters expect their national parties to take positions on EU matters as well. On the other hand, monitoring European matters usually involves high costs for national parliaments (Johansson and Raunio 2001). The major field of activity of national parliaments is national politics, so that investing time and resources (for example personnel training) in developing expertise on EU issues could lead to neglecting the core fields of their activity, which in turn could lead to defeat in elections.

Against that background, the loss of national parliaments´ powers does not necessarily have to be interpreted as 'deprivation of power'. Rather, as Saalfeld notes (2005), loss of power by national parliaments can be an effect of two different mechanisms, namely "abdication" or "delegation". The first implies that legislators indeed give up their powers to the executive or the Council. However, in the latter case national parliaments voluntarily delegate some of their powers to different institutions because they contribute to that change in one way or the other. For instance, if national parliaments are not capable of developing expertise in one field (due to lack of personnel or if the issue is of a low salience but implies high costs), they delegate these competences to another body.

Finally, the power relation between national parliaments and executives implies a trade-off between democratic control and efficiency. Namely, if national parliaments obtain more control over government action, the democratic control and legitimacy of the process increases. However, parliamentary control of government action also negatively affects the efficiency of the decision-making process, for instance, by extending it or complicating it with additional approval procedures. On the other hand, weak parliamentary control improves the efficiency of the decision-making process but decreases the quality of democratic control. National parliaments and governments can act strategically by increasing control of the executive but also by tying the hands of the government, which reduces its capacity to negotiate in the Council (Benz 2005).

National Parliaments under the Lisbon Treaty

The Convention and later the Treaty of Lisbon placed a stronger emphasis on national parliaments than previous treaties. The major driving force behind that trend was a motivation to decrease the democratic deficit in the European Union (Kiiver 2006, Klein and Wessels 2006).

Previous treaties did not entail many provisions related to national parliaments. The Treaty of the European Union (TEU) stipulated that national parliaments are the guardians of subsidiarity (art. 5) and hold their governments accountable for their actions in the Council (art. 10). They can also contribute to the good functioning of the Union (art. 12) by taking part in evaluation mechanisms for implementation of Union policies in the area of freedom, security and justice (AFSJ), in political monitoring of Europol and evaluating Eurojust's activities, in the revision procedures of the Treaties and in inter-parliamentary cooperation between national Parliaments and the European Parliament (EP). National parliaments are also entitled to be notified of applications for accession to the Union, in accordance with art. 49 TEU.

With the Treaty of Lisbon national parliaments acquired new possibilities to exercise impact on EU politics in general. These new possibilities concern legislative control (that is scrutiny and the Early Warning Mechanism) and non-legislative functions (institutionalization of inter-parliamentary cooperation, particularly in the Common Security and Defence Policy). Whereas the legislative function concerns national parliaments' involvement in the final stage of the decision-making process, inter-parliamentary cooperation grants more influence in the early stage of agenda-setting. Furthermore, inter-parliamentary cooperation in EU matters allows bypassing national governments in the early stage of decision making, which clearly adds a new dimension to national parliaments' functions in general.

Regarding the general role of national parliaments in the EU, Raunio notes (2011) that the Convention – and later the Lisbon Treaty – prioritised the scrutiny functions of national parliaments. During the Convention a working group "The role of national parliaments" was responsible for preparing a proposal on how to accommodate national parliaments in the European polity in order to foster its accountability and legitimacy. The working group dealt with both scrutiny- and citizen-related functions (regarding representation or information) but the latter eventually received less attention in the Convention. Parliamentary representatives (two MPs for each national parliament) presented very divergent positions regarding the role of national parliaments in the EU, with only MPs from the Nordic countries displaying a more or less similar view (Fraga 2005). However, there seemed to be a common desire among national MPs to improve – in one way or another – the scrutiny-related functions of national parliaments (Fraga 2005). Eventually, other possible modes of involvement in EU politics were marginalised.

To begin with legislative functions, the Protocol on the Role of National Parliaments in the European Union stipulates that national parliaments should be forwarded all EU draft legislative acts as well as agendas for and the outcome of meetings of the Council (including the minutes of meetings). The Protocol also introduced the Early Warning Mechanism allowing national parliaments to withhold EU legislative acts that do not comply with the principle of subsidiarity.

In fact, researchers remain rather sceptical regarding the impact of the Early Warning System. Firstly, it has been noted that the system ignores the fact that the parliamentary majority is very unlikely to adopt a different position from the government (Raunio 2009). In the EU member states division into opposition and government is the major cleavage, not division into government and parliamentary majority. For that reason it is rare that a government would have a different position from a parliamentary majority.

Secondly, parliaments can interfere only in cases when the principle of subsidiarity is violated. These cases are rather rare. Furthermore, the short period necessary for building a "coalition" of national parliaments makes it difficult to put the Early Warning Mechanism into practice (Fraga 2005). It can be also expected that states with well-established scrutiny procedures would make more use of their new competences (Fraga 2005).

The Lisbon Treaty granted national parliaments new possibilities to access information generated at the EU level, also including minutes from Council of Ministers' meetings. In comparison, the Amsterdam Treaty stipulated that national parliaments receive legislative initiatives from their governments, whereas according to the Lisbon Treaty national parliaments receive them directly from the Commission. This reform is beneficial for states that were not properly informed by their governments. However, as some scholars noted, the Commission has recently been publishing all legislative proposals on their web-page as soon as they are presented in the Council (Fraga 2005). Access to the minutes from Council meetings constitutes a very important step towards more transparency in decision-making at the European level. However, the Treaty stipulates that only meetings with legislative issues are to be accessible to national parliaments in the form of minutes. This implies that Council meetings devoted to non-legislative issues will not be equally accessible.

Finally, institutionalization of inter-parliamentary cooperation also received mixed evaluations in the literature (Fraga 2005, Raunio 2011). It has been acknowledged that the COSAC network has a potential to foster inter-parliamentary exchange and transnational debates on topical EU issues. As some comparative studies have already demonstrated, national MPs have in general more intensive contacts with parliamentarians in other states than with representatives of EU institutions (Wessels 2005). Institutionalised inter-parliamentary cooperation offers an incentive for MPs to engage in the early stages of policy-making such as agenda-setting. This, in turn, could strengthen the citizen-related function of national parliaments because MPs could inform their constituencies about the perception of a certain issue in other national parliaments. On the other hand, more skeptically oriented scholars (Šabič 2008) have noted that whereas institutionalised inter-parliamentary cooperation may indeed foster access to and exchange of information, it will not help national parliaments to act and to be perceived as one body.

The Treaty of Lisbon also gives national parliaments an incentive to engage in European security policy. The area of foreign policy is a very complex system: European Common Foreign and Security Policy is embedded in a broad range of policies, such as trade or development policy. The Common Security and Defence Policy is part of the CFSP (Art. 28 A, Lisbon Treaty). However, in contrast to trade-related measures, the CSDP is not listed under exclusive EU competences. In fact, the CSDP belongs neither to shared nor supporting competences but is located between the two. Although the Lisbon Treaty granted the EU a 'legal personality' in security policy (the long-awaited 'face and voice'), the EU is not authorised to act beyond its competences. In the CSDP adoption of legislative acts is not foreseen, only adoption of general guidelines or decisions regarding cooperation measures between member states. The dominant decision-making procedure under that policy in the European Council is unanimity. As a consequence, the term "common" is somewhat misleading in a policy guided, in principle, by intergovernmental rules.

In the institutional set-up of the CSDP national parliaments can get involved in two different ways: as individual actors and collectively. Regarding the latter, the Treaty of Lisbon (Protocol on National Parliaments, Art. 10) stipulates that national parliaments may organise conferences, in particular in order to debate the CSDP, within the framework of the Conference of Parliamentary Committees for Union Affairs (COSAC) that twice a year brings together the Chairs of Defence Committees. Apart from COSAC, national parliaments may also use the framework of the Conference of Foreign Affairs Chairs (COFAC) that functions in a similar manner to COSAC. Both of these institutional bodies may be used by national parliaments in order to exchange information and to exercise an impact on European institutions, for instance, by formulating recommendations.

As this section demonstrates, the reforms introduced by the Lisbon Treaty have not dramatically increased the role of national parliaments in the European Union but nonetheless have created new possibilities for parliamentary involvement in EU politics. Whether national parliaments are to make use of these new functions depends, to a large extent, on MPs themselves. How do they evaluate the new provisions? Are they interested in making use of them? The following paragraphs provide some answers to these questions.

Methodological Approach of this Study

This study focuses on national plenary parliamentary debates which play an important role both in national and EU politics (Norton 1996). During plenary sessions MPs not only pass the law (legislative function) but they also scrutinise their governments and, due to the fact that plenary sessions are well reported in the media, inform citizens about legislative decisions (Auel and Benz 2005). Although the government controls the agenda, which consists of policy proposals discussed by the parliament, the opposition's role is to make sure that these proposals are debated during plenary sessions and that citizens are adequately informed about them. In order to remain accountable to their constituencies, governments – and the parliamentary majorities that usually represent the same political line – are compelled to enter into public deliberation and respond to opposition criticism.

For these reasons parliamentary plenary sessions play a particular role both in domestic and European politics. As Auel (2007: 498) noted: "Parliaments provide a major space for public debate and are thus the ideal forums for the deliberation of important European issues and their domestic implications. By holding their governments accountable, by inducing them to explain European issues and decisions, to clarify European negotiation situations and to justify their negotiation position and behaviour, national parliaments can effectively contribute to making policy processes more transparent and, thus, more accessible for their national public".

The empirical analysis presented in this chapter constitutes part of a larger research project analysing ratification of the Constitutional and the Lisbon Treaty (Liebert 2007; Maatsch 2010; Evas et al 2012; Liebert 2012). The empirical enquiry of the research draws on plenary parliamentary debates devoted to ratification of the Lisbon Treaty in the following countries: France, Germany, the United Kingdom, Poland, Hungary and the Czech Republic. The debates took place from 2007 to 2008 (see Table 5.1). The states under study have different parliamentary systems, namely, either bi-cameral or unicameral. Therefore, in order to analyse the whole legislative process in each state, the analysis covers debates in both lower and upper chambers.

Table 5.1 List of analyzed plenary debates on the ratification of the Lisbon Treaty

Country	Date	Chamber	Reading
Germany	13.03.2008	Lower chamber	1st
	24.04.2008	Lower chamber	2nd
	23.05.2008	Upper chamber	1st
UK	17.12.2007	Lower chamber	1st
	21.01.2008	Lower chamber	2nd
	11.03.2008	Lower chamber	3rd
	12.03.2008	Higher chamber	1st
	01.04.2008	Higher chamber	2nd
	18.06.2008	Higher chamber	3rd
Hungary	17.12.2007	Uni-cameral	1st
Czech Republic	19.03–01.04.2008	Lower chamber	1st
	24.04.2008	Senate	1st
	09.12.2008–18.02.2009	Lower chamber	2nd
	06.05.2009	Higher chamber	2nd
Poland	27–28.02.2008	Lower chamber	1st
	12–13.03.2008	Lower chamber	2nd
	01.04.2008	Lower chamber	3rd
	02.04.2008	Higher chamber	1st
	09.11.2008	Lower chamber	2nd
France	07.02.2008	Lower chamber	1st
	08.02.2008	Upper chamber	2nd

Source: Own.

The methodological approach of this study is based on comparative, qualitative and quantitative discourse analysis. The major goal of this research is to establish how national parliamentarians evaluate their new competences as defined in the Lisbon Treaty.

In the empirical dimension this study identified four major elements of parliamentary discourse: (A) actors, being the authors of statements (classified according to their political affiliation), (B) the subject of the statement (here: Treaty provisions related to national parliaments), (C) the direction of the statement (in favour or against) and (D) justifications (how the decision was justified). This analytical structure was used in order to develop a code-book, an analytical tool allowing conduct of empirical analysis in different states according to the same procedure. The code-book was constructed both in a deductive and an inductive manner. Whereas categories A, B and C were established prior to empirical analysis, category D (justifications) was inductively created (during the analysis).

In the first step, selected plenary debates were analysed (coded) qualitatively with help from Atlas.ti software. In that process the deductively established categories were assigned to speech acts. In the second step, when the coding process was finished, data from all countries analysed was merged and analysed quantitatively. In the course of the qualitative analysis a statement was coded only if it concerned the Treaty provisions related to national parliaments.

Plenary Debates on Ratification of the Lisbon Treaty

The Lisbon Treaty could be ratified if all the national parliaments of the EU member states voted in favour (except where a national constitution requires a referendum). Furthermore, usually more than a simple majority is required in order to ratify any EU treaty. For that reason parliamentary majorities not only had to convince their inter-party or inter-coalition sceptics to vote in favour but they also had to seek support of opposition parties.

Although the new competences of national parliaments were widely contested in MPs' plenary speeches, none of the parliamentary parties rejected the Lisbon Treaty due to dissatisfaction with the legal provisions related to national parliaments. For instance, many MPs who were very skeptical about the Early Warning Mechanism would still vote in favour of the Lisbon Treaty.

Plenary debates offer two different possibilities to contest a legal act: through voting and through discourse (Maatsch 2012). Examination of these two patterns of contestation is guided by different research questions: in the first case we aim to establish the reasons that stood behind MPs´ decision to support or reject a legal act. In the second case, we concentrate on the content of evaluations. In particular, in the case of treaty provisions referring to national parliaments we target the following questions: were MPs´ evaluations positive or negative? Did MPs claim they would use their new competences? What problems or obstacles did they identify? What remedies or improvements did they suggest?

These two patterns of contestation are guided by different logics. Empirical research on national parliaments demonstrated that the major cleavage structuring politics is between the government and the opposition (Raunio 2009). The parliamentary majority usually represents the same stance as the government. However, since the Treaty is a multi-issue legal package, it is fairly unlikely that all MPs in the governing party have the same position on each and every issue. Nonetheless, the parliamentary majority would very unlikely turn against the government because the costs of this decision would be too high. However, parliamentary majorities can still voice their discontent in plenary discourses and vote in line with the government's position.

As other empirical studies have demonstrated (Maatsch 2012), the opposition and governing parties displayed different contestation patterns during ratification of the Lisbon Treaty. Governing parties opted for one of the following two patterns: (1) approval of Treaty reforms in parliamentary debates (positive discourse) and vote in favour of the Lisbon Treaty; (2) disapproval of selected Treaty reforms (critical discourse) in parliamentary debates but nonetheless vote in favour of the Lisbon Treaty. Opposition parties follow different patterns: (1) contestation of Treaty reforms in parliamentary debates (critical discourse) and vote against the Lisbon Treaty; (2) approval of Treaty reforms in parliamentary debates (positive discourse) and vote in favour of the Lisbon Treaty.

With the exception of Hungary, national parliaments' competences received considerable attention: they belonged to the top ten debated Lisbon Treaty provisions in each state under study (for more details see Maatsch 2012). In Germany and in the UK the number of MPs' statements referring to national parliaments' competences was very high (122 in Germany and 97 in the UK), in Poland there were 59 statements, in France 37, in the Czech Republic 27 and in Hungary only 4. Clearly, the very number of MPs' statements – as a proxy for parliaments' attention devoted to the issue – has to be approached carefully. This is due to the fact that plenary sessions may differ in length or internal procedures which can influence the intensity of debated topics. In the sample Hungary is an outlier (only 4 statements devoted to national parliaments). This is due to the fact that the whole ratification debate concentrated on minority rights' provisions which have had a high domestic importance. All other reforms were marginalised.

Which provisions referring to national parliaments received most attention and how were they evaluated? In all the states under study (also including the outlier case of Hungary) competences related to legal control were mostly debated. According to MPs, control of the government constitutes the major function of national parliaments. Legal control is also a yardstick measuring national legislators' power. In the view of MPs, the stronger the legal control exercised by national parliaments the more powerful national parliaments will be. Non-legislative functions, despite their novelty and potential for opening new modes of involvement in EU politics, were not broadly debated by MPs. The Common Security and Defence Policy, which national parliaments are also envisaged to contribute to, was not debated in the context of national parliaments. As one

German MP put it, the new areas of activity do not change the hierarchy of national parliaments' functions:

> The Treaty of Lisbon opens new ways for national parliaments regarding responsibilities and influence. It remains, however, that the central task of the German parliament is to control the government.[1]

Another interesting observation is that evaluations by MPs were very mixed. All MPs stressed the importance of empowering national parliaments but at the same time many were concerned whether the reforms introduced can indeed foster national parliamentary powers in the EU.

Eventually, MPs who positively evaluated the new competences of national parliaments were either pointing to the fact that the mechanisms of legal control were improved or that democratic control in the EU has been strengthened. The first justification was interest-based. MPs were arguing that the Lisbon Treaty improved subsidiarity control predominantly by means of the Early Warning Mechanism. From this perspective national parliaments' role as government 'watchdogs' has been fostered and national parliaments, as an institution, have gained more power in EU politics. The second type of justification, enhancement of democratic control in the EU, was principle-based. MPs were arguing that by strengthening the role of national parliaments, democratic control within the EU improves significantly. By the same token, in their opinion, the democratic deficit is also being reduced. Interestingly, the justification referring to democratic control was present only in three countries: Germany, France and Poland. MPs in the other states referred only to subsidiarity control.

As already mentioned, many MPs approached the new national parliamentary competences with a high level of skepticism. In their view, the reforms created only an 'illusion of power'. This argument was the only theme among critics.

> Our Parliament and other national Parliaments are not being given more real powers; we are simply being given more information. We are being given a mechanism that, as any Committee that has considered it or anyone who really thinks about it will know, is completely and utterly ineffective. This mechanism requires two thirds of a national Parliament to arrive at a view opposing that of their own Government. However, this House, for example, has no tradition of being given a mechanism for arriving at a view opposing the Government. The Government can always whip anything through.[2]

---

1 Der Vertrag von Lissabon eröffnet den nationalen Parlamenten neue Chancen der Mitver- antwortung und der Mitwirkung. Es bleibt aber dabei: Die zentrale Aufgabe des Deutschen Bundestages ist es, Regierungshandeln innerstaatlich zu kontrollieren., Bundestag, plenary session from 13.03.2008, http://www.spdfraktion.de/cnt/rs/rs_datei/0,,9548,00.pdf.

2 House of Commons, 21.01.2008, http://services.parliament.uk/bills/2007-08/europeanunionamendment/stages.html.

Critics were arguing that national parliaments are not going to be able to make much use of their new competences because of their internal, institutional constraints, difficulties in developing cooperation with other parliaments but also time-constraints:

> Again, it does not take much political analysis to work out that the chances of that mechanism being employed on any regular basis are vanishingly small. It could be used only if 14 different national Parliaments, nearly all of which have a Government majority, defeated an EU proposal, and did so within an eight-week period.[3]

> It has always been postulated to grant national parliaments a stronger role. Now we are granted a right to object if the subsidiarity principle is violated. We should gather the required inter-parliamentary majority within eight weeks. Although the deadline is now a third longer than originally planned, you know as well as I do how time-consuming parliamentary procedures are and therefore how difficult it will be to gather that majority in such a short time.[4]

Furthermore, they would point to the fact that the EWM is limited to violations of subsidiarity, which constitute very rare cases. As one British MP also noted, the EWM is not a 'red light' in that national parliaments can only plead for reconsideration of a bill but they do not have power to reject it.

Apparently, the level of discursive contestation among opposition parties was not higher than among governing parties. There were also no significant differences between new and old EU member states. Even though the majority parties were more likely to vote in favour of the Lisbon Treaty than the opposition, they still took the opportunity to voice critical remarks. It can be assumed that this discrepancy was due to the fact that critics would not condemn the very idea of strengthening parliamentary control functions but rather the implementation requirements and mechanisms.

Critics would also make numerous suggestions on how Treaty provisions concerning national parliaments could be improved. These recommendations can be divided into three groups: (a) expansion of the scope of national parliaments' activities, (b) implementation improvements and (c) internal adaptation. Regarding

---

3 House of Commons, 21.01.2008, http://services.parliament.uk/bills/2007-08/europeanunionamendment/stages.html.

4 'Es wird immer postuliert, dass die nationalen Parlamente eine stärkere Rolle bekommen sollen. Wir bekommen nun das Recht der Subsidiaritätsrüge. Wir sollen innerhalb von acht Wochen eine Mehrheit innerhalb des Parlaments herstellen. Obwohl die Frist nun um ein Drittel länger ist als ursprünglich vorgesehen, wissen Sie genauso gut wie ich, wie lang parlamentarische Wege sind und dass es daher außerordentlich schwierig sein wird, so schnell eine Mehrheit herzustellen.' Deutscher Bundestag, 13.03.2008, http://dip21.bundestag.de/dip21/btp/16/16151.pdf.

the first type of recommendations, MPs were arguing that parliamentary control would become stronger and more democratic if parliamentary competences went beyond subsidiarity-related cases.

> I believe that this is one of those decisions that can in the future lead to the fact that the role of this Parliament as well as the importance of you, the 200 elected deputies, will be smaller and smaller. We can already see it today as we only accept laws already adopted elsewhere and our duty is merely to implement them into our legal system. I fear that once the Lisbon Treaty has been adopted, the amount of laws that we have to adopt by default without discussion will be constantly growing. Some of you might not like the fact that your political responsibility will be diminishing, but I am not like that. I believe that I was elected by the citizens of this republic, to whom I have the primary responsibility, and I am ready to act upon this responsibility.[5]

Furthermore, many MPs were postulating introduction of a red-light mechanism which would allow national parliaments to reject a specific legal proposal. The second group of recommendations concentrated on implementation aspects, such as extension of the time-period in the EWM. The third group of recommendations concerned various internal adaptation mechanisms and procedures which national parliaments have to introduce internally in order to use their new competences effectively. One of these proposals concerned strengthening contacts with other national parliaments in the European Union.

> (The Lisbon Treaty) introduces, as already mentioned, new roles for national parliaments. (...) If all these legal documents which we receive are subject to the subsidiarity test, the role of our parliament is going to be radically re-defined. We ourselves have to prepare to undertake it.[6]

---

5   Domnívám, že jedním z těch rozhodnutí, které může do budoucna směřovat k tomu, že význam tohoto parlamentu a vás, 200 zvolených poslanců, bude v čase menší a menší a stále menší. Už dnes to vidíme na tom, kolik zákonů tady pouze přijímáme, protože byly již předtím přijaty někde jinde a my máme pouze povinnost je implementovat do našeho právního řádu. Obávám se, že po schválení Lisabonské smlouvy se objem zákonů, které budou přijímány jinde a někým jiným, bude neustále zvyšovat. Možná se někomu z vás může líbit, že jeho politická odpovědnost se bude tím pádem zmenšovat, ale já takový nejsem. Domnívám se, že byl-li jsem zvolen občany této republiky, mám primární odpovědnost vůči nim a jsem připraven se z této odpovědnosti vůči nim zodpovídat. Poslanecká sněmovna Parlamentu České republiky, 03.02.2009, http://www.psp.cz/eknih/2006ps/stenprot/046schuz/s046034.htm.

6   Ustanawia również inną rolę, o czym już mówiono, dla parlamentów narodowych. (...) Jeżeli teraz wszystkie dokumenty prawne, które będą do nas wpływały, będą podlegały takiemu testowi subsydiarności, to przecież rola naszego parlamentu będzie zupełnie inaczej zdefiniowana. My musimy przygotować się również do tej nowej roli. Sejm, 27.02.2008, http://orka2.sejm.gov.pl/Debata6.nsf/main/2D34814C#077.

Conclusions

The process of European integration has posed challenges to national parliaments. Not only did they lose power vis-à-vis the executive, but they also had to undergo a complex process of institutional adaptation. Despite these difficulties, national parliaments remained keen to be involved in EU politics. As one of the overarching goals of the Lisbon Treaty was to diminish the democratic deficit, national parliaments strengthened their position in EU politics. The new provisions reinforced their existing competences regarding oversight but also introduced new elements of political participation allowing national parliaments to become more active in the early stages of decision-making (agenda-setting).

The empirical analysis presented in this chapter has focused on the question how national parliaments have perceived and evaluated their new competences during ratification of the Lisbon Treaty. The analysis demonstrates that MPs clearly prioritised one of the parliamentary functions, namely control. In their view, national parliaments' primary goal in EU politics is to control the executive and to be the guardians of the subsidiarity principle. For that reason, plenary debates have focused on those provisions of the Lisbon Treaty that related to control. Evaluations of these provisions by MPs were mixed: some MPs welcomed the reforms arguing that control mechanisms were improved or that the general principle of democratic control in the EU has been reinforced. On the other hand, a relatively large group of skeptics has pointed to the fact that the Lisbon Treaty created only an illusion of power for national parliaments. As they noted, the Early Warning System is difficult to implement given, for instance, the time constraints for gathering the required majority in national parliaments, and so on. Furthermore, as many MPs pointed out, national parliaments do not gain that much power: their intervention cannot turn down the law and they cannot intervene on other than subsidiarity-related cases, which are rare.

The empirical analysis presented in this chapter demonstrates that national parliaments are interested in strengthening their role in EU politics. However, in the view of MPs, the new tools provided by the Lisbon Treaty are not very likely to enhance national legislators' position in the EU. As a consequence, there are no strong incentives to assume that parliamentary activity in EU politics would significantly increase after entry into force of the Lisbon Treaty.

References

Anghel, S., Born, H., Dowling, A. and Fuior, T. 2008. National parliamentary oversight of ESDP missions, in *The Parliamentary Control of European Security Policy*, edited by Lord, C., Peters, D., Wagner, W. and Deitelhoff, N. Arena report No 7/08.

Auel, K. 2007 Democratic accountability and national parliaments – redefining the impact of parliamentary scrutiny. *European Law Journal*, 13(4), 487–504.

Auel, K. and Benz, A. 2005. The politics of adaptation: the Europeanisation of national parliamentary systems. *The Journal of Legislative Studies*, 11(3–4), 372–393.

Benz, A. 2005. Conclusion: linking research on europeanisation and national parliaments. *The Journal of Legislative Studies*, 11(3–4), 508–521.

Crum, B. and Fossum, J.E. 2009. The multilevel parliamentary field: a framework for theorizing representative democracy in the EU. *European Political Science Review*, 1, 249–271.

Elo-Schäfer, J., Grimm, S. and Töller, A.S. 2006. European impulses in the Bundestag's legislation from 1983 to 2005, in evaluation based on GESTA [German Bundestag, Federal Legislation Update], set of data, Helmut Schmidt University/University of the Federal Armed Forces, Hamburg.

Evas, T., Liebert, U. and Lord, C. (eds) 2012. Multilayered representation in the European Union: parliaments, courts and the public sphere, ZERP Schriftenreihe No. 64, Baden-Baden: Nomos.

Fraga, A. 2005. After the convention: the future role of national parliaments in the European Union (and the day after ... nothing will happen). *The Journal of Legislative Studies*, 11(3–4), 490–507.

Holzhacker, R. 2005. The power of opposition parliamentary party groups in European scrutiny. *The Journal of Legislative Studies*, 11(3–4), 428–445.

Johansson, K.M. and Raunio, T. 2001. Partisan responses to Europe. Comparing Finnish and Swedish political parties. *European Journal of Political Research*, 39(2), 85–101.

Judge, D. 1995. The failure of national parliaments? *West European Politics*, 18(3), 79–97.

Karlas, J. 2011. Parliamentary control of EU affairs in central and eastern Europe: explaining the variation. *Journal of European Public Policy*, 18(2), 258–273.

Katz, R.S. 1999. *The European Parliament, the National Parliaments, and European Integration*. Oxford: Oxford University Press.

Kiiver, P. 2006. *The National Parliaments in the European Union: A Critical View on EU Constitution-building*. London: Kluwer Law International.

Klein, N. and Wessels, W. 2006. A 'saut constitutionnel' out of an intergovernmental trap? The provisions of the constitutional treaty for the common foreign, security and defence policy, in *EU Constitutionalisation: From the Convention to the Constitutional Treaty 2002–2005. Anatomy, Analysis, Assessment*, edited by L. Rovná and W. Wessels. Prague: Europeum Institute for European Policy. S. 197–233.

Liebert, U. (ed.) 2007. Europe in contention: debating the constitutional treaty, in *Perspectives on European Politics and Society*, 8(3), 235–413.

Liebert, U. 2012. Rethinking the "no European demos' thesis: transnational discursive representation as a prerequisite of EU democracy, in T. Evas, U. Liebert and C. Lord (eds) 2012. *Multilayered Representation in the European Union: Parliaments, Courts and the Public Sphere*, ZERP Schriftenreihe No. 64, Baden-Baden: Nomos, 233–254.

Maatsch, A. 2010. Between an intergovernmental and a polycentric European Union: national parliamentary discourses on democracy in the EU ratification process. RECON online papers, 2010/18, Available at: http://www.reconproject.eu/main.php/RECON_wp_1018.pdf?fileitem=5456416 [accessed: 20 May 2012].

Maatsch, A. 2011. *Ethnic Citizenship Regimes. Europeanisation, Post-War Migration and Redressing Past Wrongs*. Basingstoke: Palgrave Macmillan.

Maatsch, A. 2012. National parliamentary ratification of EU treaty reforms: the interplay of voting and discursive contestation, in *Multilayered Representation in the European Union. Parliaments, Courts and the Public Sphere*, edited by T. Evas, U. Liebert and C. Lord. Baden-Baden: NOMOS.

Maurer, A. and Wessels, W. (eds) 2001. *National Parliaments on their Ways to Europe: Losers or Latecomers?* Baden-Baden: Nomos Verlagsgesellschaft.

Moravcsik, A. 1994. *Why the European Community Strengthens the State: Domestic Politics and International Institutions*. Center for European Studies Working Paper Series 52 (Cambridge: Harvard University).

Norton, P. (ed.) 1996. *National Parliaments and the European Union*. London: Frank Cass.

Raunio, T. 2005. Holding governments accountable in European affairs: explaining cross-national variation. *The Journal of Legislative Studies*, 11(3–4), 319–342.

Raunio, T. 2008. *National parliaments and European integration: what we know and what we should know*. ARENA Working Paper. Oslo: University of Oslo.

Raunio, T. 2009 National parliaments and European integration: what we know and agenda for future research. *The Journal of Legislative Studies*, 15(4), 317–334.

Raunio, T. 2011. The gatekeepers of European integration? The functions of national parliaments in the EU political system. *Journal of European Integration*, 33(3), 303–321.

Raunio, T. and Hix, S. 2000. Backbenchers learn to fight back: European integration and parliamentary government. *West European Politics*, 23(4), 142–168.

Rozenberg, O. et al. 2011. Not only a battleground: parliamentary oral questions concerning defence policies in four western democracies. *The Journal of Legislative Studies*, 17(3), 340–353.

Saalfeld, T. 2005. Deliberate delegation or abdication? Government backbenchers, ministers and European union legislation. *The Journal of Legislative Studies*, 11(3–4), 343–371.

Šabič, Z. 2008. Building democratic and responsible global governance: the role of international parliamentary institutions. *Parliamentary Affairs*, 61(2), 255–271.

Töller, A.E. 2008. Mythen und Methoden. Zur Messung der Europäisierung der Gesetzgebung des Deutschen Bundestages jenseits des 80er-Mythos. *Zeitschrift für Parlamentsfragen*, 39(1), 3–17.

Wessels, B. 1989. *The Community at the Crossroads*. Bruges: College of Europe.

Wessels, B. 2005. Roles and orientations of members of parliament in the EU context: Congruence or difference? Europeanisation or not? *The Journal of Legislative Studies*, 11(3–4), 446–465.

Chapter 6
A Panacea for Democratic Legitimation? Assessing the Engagement of Civil Society with EU Treaty Reform Politics

Petra Guasti

Introduction

Political and scholarly debates abound as regards the nature and conditions of legitimacy of European governance.[1] Assuming that civil society "is a space in which the citizens can be empowered and take on the role of political subjects, as well as a forum testing the legitimacy of political power as regards 'the will of the people'" (Eriksen and Fossum 2012: xiii), the "new politics of European civil society' has been explored in terms of conceptual, normative and empirical issues.[2] As a contribution to unravelling the key puzzle of how civil society relates to the legitimacy and contributes to the legitimation of the European Union (EU), the present chapter explores three questions:

1. What role do social theories and political discourses attribute to civil society in the making of a European polity?
2. More specifically, to what extent does civil society acknowledge the legitimacy of European integration in general and of the EU's Constitutional Reform Treaty, in particular? How do patterns of support vary, depending on national contexts and organisational categories?
3. Which are the conditions which enable civil society to contribute to the legitimation of the emerging EU polity?

In line with the focus of this book – to provide comparative assessments of how the European Union's evolving order interacts with the transformation of democracy in the EU's new and old member states – the main aim of this chapter is to determine the potential of civil society to contribute to the democratic legitimation of the EU.

---

1 For example Lord and Beetham 2001, Craig 1999, Erne 2008, Føllesdal 2004, Héritier 1999, Magnette 2003, Kohler-Koch et al. 2008a, 2008b, Kohler-Koch and Rittberger 2007, Kohler-Koch and Quittkat 2013, Paolini 2007, Smith 2002, Liebert 2011.

2 See the conceptual, normative theoretical and empirical contributions in Liebert and Trenz 2010.

While building on the state of the art research literature, the objective of this chapter is to assess the gaps between theoretical propositions, political discourses, and civil society practices regarding the legitimation of the European polity.

The chapter is organised in three parts – theory, methodology and empirical analysis. The first part reviews the state of the art of the literature on EU legitimacy and civil society, develops the theoretical model – a three-dimensional conception of legitimacy – and the analytical framework. The second part describes the operationalisation of this framework and the research methodology. In the third section, the findings from qualitative and quantitative empirical research are presented. This is structured in five sections: As a caveat against overly optimistic expectations regarding civil society as a source of EU legitimacy, the analysis of CSO's empirical diffuse and specific support patterns in the first section reveals complex constellations with large variations within and across old and new Member States. Sections two, three, four and five assess civil society practices of engaging with the TCE in the light of four criteria on which the procedural legitimation of the EU rests (for more on procedural legitimation of the EU see Lord 1998). These criteria are transparency, inclusion, balance of interests, and representation; their requisite conditions include visibility in public spheres; vertical and horizontal cooperation networks; as well as channels and resources for European political communication with citizens. The concluding part reviews the puzzle regarding the preconditions for civil society to overcome the current deficits and contribute to providing the emerging EU polity with democratic legitimation.

EU Legitimacy and Civil Society: Theoretical Model and Analytical Framework

In the EU research literature the understanding of democratic legitimacy is rooted in different assumptions about the EU as an international organisation vs. an emerging political entity.[3] On the one hand, intergovernmental approaches and conceptions of the EU as an international organisation or regulatory regime hold that its authority derives from indirect sources of democratic legitimacy, or that national governments are held accountable for EU level decision-making. These approaches identify the European Council and the Council of Ministers as the pillars on which the EU's legitimation ultimately rests.[4] On the other

---

   3   In recent years, the literature on legitimacy, and on EU legitimacy in particular, has flourished (Beetham and Lord 1998, Bellamy 2001, Bellamy and Castiglione 1998 , Duff 2003, Føllesdal 2004, Kohler-Koch and Rittberger 2007, Lord and Harris 2006, Meny 2003, Schmitter 2001a, 2001b, 2002, 2003 and 2007, Walker 2003).

   4   Early functionalists, such as Ernst Haas, have conceptualised the European Community as an international organization, whose legitimacy was linked to two pillars: 1. open and prolific participation of voluntary interest groups in decision making; and 2. effective performance of functions perceived crucial by its units (Haas 1964: 195–196). This focus on participation has been revitalised by Philippe Schmitter's proposal to view the EU

hand, federalists conceptualise the EU as a polity evolving into the direction of a multinational supranational state where an ever-increasing share of political and administrative competencies once held by the nation state are being transferred to the EU level. Thus, EU institutions need their own, direct sources of democratic legitimacy.

According to the federalists, the fact that these standards are currently not met by EU decision making has led to legitimacy deficits (Lord and Beetham 2001). As a result, federalist theorists are critical of the current construction of the EU polity, and propose possible solutions such as increasing the competences of the European parliament, to directly elect the Commission President, or participatory policy-networks. The latter, in particular, facilitate the incorporation of organised interests and of stake holders (Héritier 1999). According to Banchoff and Smith, these "new modes of governance" of the EU add to the traditional channels of vertical democratic accountability, but they do not replace them. Rather, they can strengthen out-put legitimacy in addition to indirect legitimacy "borrowed" from the national level (1999: 15).

The Concept of EU Legitimacy

Legitimacy is a central category for analysing why citizens have trust in the authority of institutions they believe to normatively deserve their obedience and, thus, also trust the future compliance of their fellow citizens. Four basic meanings of the concept of legitimacy have been distinguished: legitimacy as legality; legitimacy as justifiability; legitimacy as compliance; and legitimacy as problem solving. Each of these depends on different mechanisms – or institutional arrangements, for instance rule of law or democratic rule; participation or actual consent; policy-output; and accountability procedures. These correspond to three basic types of legitimacy: 1. regime legitimacy, or the extent to which justice is achieved within the polity's institutions vis-à-vis representation, the protection of the individual and minority interests, etcetera; 2. polity legitimacy – the overall support for, and the stability of, the polity as a "self-standing political community"; and 3. performance (output) legitimacy, or the capacity of a given polity to deliver public goods effectively and efficiently (Beetham and Lord 1998). In the political process, all three types may be interlinked; here, they are differentiated for analytical purposes only. Moreover, Christopher Lord and Paul Magnette have identified four vectors of EU legitimation, understood as ideal and not real type processes: 1. *indirect* or derivative legitimation of the Union and its institutions, depending on the legitimacy of the Union's component states, the Union's respect for sovereignty, and on its ability to serve its purpose; 2. *parliamentary* legitimation where EU policies and institutions are legitimated by a combination of elected parliamentary bodies and member states, thus serving the purpose of a series of people and of a citizenry divided along the lines of cultural identity; 3. *technocratic* legitimation

---

as a system of inclusion of aggregated interests, and European governance arrangements as policy "sites" where stake-holders and knowledge-holders would negotiate the definition of policies under the supervision of the EU institutions (Schmitter 2001b).

where EU institutions are legitimated by their ability to offer solutions to problems; 4. *procedural* legitimation which requires the observance of certain procedures, namely transparency, balance of interests, proportionality, legal certainty, consultation or inclusion of stake holders (2004: 184–189). The present analysis focuses on the fourth type defined by procedural criteria making legitimation dependent on three key criteria: transparency, inclusion, balance of interests, and representation.

European Civil Society

Following the theoretical literature, the term civil society has evolved over many centuries, if not millennia,[5] going through multiple conceptual and connotative changes, which have been widely discussed,[6] and which have eventually led to political dispute (Green 1997).[7] According to Jean Cohen, modern civil society is formed and reproduced through varying forms of collective activities, and institutionalised on the basis of law and subjective rules, in particular, which play an important role in stabilising social differentiation (Cohen, in Arato and Cohen 1990: 37).

In this chapter the term civil society delineates the area between the sphere of private interests and the state. It is an area of voluntary association outside the spheres of market, state and private lives in which people realise how interrelated their world is. From the theoretical and historical literature on civil society it can be concluded that the emergence of civil society is the result of democratic politics based on the direct participation of citizens aiming to influence public affairs. While the term "civil society" is rather abstract and used today mainly in theoretical and conceptual contexts, empirical research related to civic society uses the empirical term "non-governmental organisations" (NGOs), conceived as an institutionalised part of civil society. NGO's in general refer to the non-profit sector and its synonyms – the civil sector or third sector.[8]

In current citizenship research authors such as Waltzer (1998) and Meehan (2000) have acknowledged civil society as a useful frame for active (European or global) citizenship. Richard Delanty and Charles Rumford conceive of European civil society as predominantly rooted in national civil societies. In their view,

---

5 Theoretical literature places the origins of the term "civil society" – *societas civilis* – in antiquity (Arato and Cohen 1990: 84–86).

6 The concept is a subject to avid academic discussions, for example between Christoph Bryant and Krishan Kumar in *The British Journal of Sociology* (Bryant 1993, Kumar 1993 and 1994, Neocleous 1995), also Alexander 1997, Habermas 2003, 2011, Keane 1988, Seligman 1992, Waltzer 1998).

7 The substance of the dispute is about the definition of the relationship between the state and the civil society, which especially in post-communist countries is considered to be essentially inconsistent. Based on historical experience, civil society is regarded as the opposition to state power (Arato and Cohen 1988 [Kumar 1993])

8 The Italian political scientist Amitai Etzioni introduced the notion of the third sector (the sector between the state and the economic spheres) in the 1970s, referring to a set of private organisations providing public services sponsored by the state (Etzioni 1973).

national civil society serves as protection against economic globalisation by establishing a basis for maintaining the integrity of the nation state (Delanty and Rumford 2005). Critical authors, such as Meehan, state that it is the supranational, rather than the domestic, arena that provides for a European citizenship. However, in her view European citizenship is currently struggling between market citizenship, which defines citizens predominantly as producers and consumers, and a liberal (or libertarian) notion of privatised citizenship (Meehan 2000).

According to Obradovic, the aim of European governance is to establish institutional opportunities for the participation of stake holders in the decision making process via civil dialogue. From her examination of the civil and social dialogue in European Governance, she concludes that economic dialogue prevails over civil and social dialogue.[9] Moreover, even though the Commission supports the involvement of civic groups in European governance[10] for increasing its efficiency, the boundaries between social and civil dialogue in Europe are blurred. As civil society organisations unlike the social partners are perceived as diffuse, unstable partners, their contribution is limited (Obradovic 2005, Obradovic and Vizcaino 2006). Confirming her findings, Carlo Ruzza has called for sector umbrella organisations as credible (and more efficient) partners for European governance (Ruzza 2006). Hence, in the context of European Governance the involvement of civil society is seen less a reality and more a normative project aimed at improving both governance (efficiency) and democracy (legitimacy).

The Public Sphere as an Arena of Civil Society Engagement with the EU

The public sphere (PS) is the place where the civil society is linked to the power structure of the state Eriksen (2005: 32, see also Eriksen and Fossum 2004). As an arena where equal citizens assemble in public and set their own agenda through open communication, PS enables civil society and social movements to bring up new questions, problems and issues. To the extent to which the PS entitles everybody to speak without any limitations on themes, participation, questions, time or resources, it counterbalances the state as a precondition for the realisation of popular sovereignty. More specifically, PS provides that sort of deliberative arrangements that are required by discourse theory, according to which a norm can be legitimate only, when all affected parties have accepted it in free and rational debate.

The link between PS and civil society is established through active citizenship, defining the public sphere as a space where active citizenship is realised through active

---

9 Although, as Obradovic points out, the idea of civic dialogue was launched to counterbalance the involvement of the sphere of production in European governance, the currently prevailing notion of civil dialogue is that it is complementary rather than contradictory to social dialogue (Obradovic 2005: 322).

10 There are numerous organizations (over 160), and around 1500 interest groups, involved in regular consultations with the Commission, but this is mainly in the phase of pre-drafting legislation (Obradovic 2005, see also Greenwood 2003).

civic and political engagement. Following Marc Morje Howard's conception of civil society, PS rests on legal institutions and organising principles, which not only make the essential core of any modern democratic system but are a key requirement for the notion of active citizenship and the concrete organisations that shape and define the particular character of the democratic system (Howard 2003: 34–35).

Analytical Model and Research Hypotheses

As a framework for analysing the role of civil society for the democratic legitimation of the EU an analytical model of viable civic participation in the EU's multilevel polity is proposed (Figure 6.1). Although national and European levels are differentiated, the figure suggests that processes as well as actors interact across both levels, as their operations often have implications for both, national and European arenas. Here, processes are understood to include (a) relations of representation; (b) networks of communication, interaction and cooperation among civil society organisations; and (c) access to public opinion and political will formation, through mass-mediated public spheres or through inclusion in institutional decision-making. As for the actors, Figure 6.1 distinguishes between citizens on the one hand and EU-level institutions on the other hand, with civil society as intermediary organisations that encompass both, economic actors such as employer associations and trade unions, as well as civil society actors at the national level and EU-level civil society organisations, the so-called "umbrella organisations" (for example ETUC).

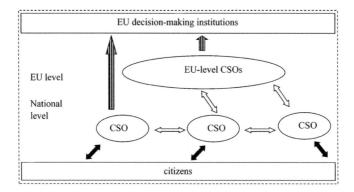

Figure 6.1   Model of viable civic participation in the EU's multilevel polity
Source: Author.

Note: CSO = civil society organisations; (a) black arrows between citizens and civil society organisations = representation; (b) white arrows among civil society organisations on national level and between CSO on national and EU level = cooperation networks and access to national public spheres; (c) black and white arrows between CSO on national and EU level and EU decision-making institutions = inclusion in EU decision-making.

This analytical model helps systematise the hypotheses that have been derived from the research literature for structuring the empirical analysis. In particular, one assumption and four research hypotheses are proposed:

- H1 Assumption on "CSO legitimation of EU":Depending on their diffuse support for European integration in general, and their specific attitudes towards the Treaty establishing a Constitution for Europe (TCE) in particular, CSOs will contribute positively or negatively to the democratic legitimation of the emerging EU polity.
- H2 "CSO's public visibility": Depending on their access to and visibility in national public spheres – or European political discourses – CSOs contribute to the EU's democratic legitimation by promoting information on, communication about and transparency of the EU vis-à-vis the general public.
- H3 "CSO cooperation networks": Depending on the extent to which they are included in vertical networks with EU decision-making institutions, national CSO's will enhance the EU's democratic legitimation.
- H4 "Balanced CSO inclusion": Depending whether the inclusion of civic compared to economic organisations in EU institutional decision-making ensures balance of interests, CSO's contribute to EU democratic legitimation. By contrast, if the inclusion of one type of organisations prevails over that of the other, the EU's democratic legitimacy will be hampered.[11]
- H5 "CSOs as representation agents": Provided their inclusion in EU institutions, CSOs contribute to the EU's democratic legitimation depending on their propensity as agents for representing European citizens vis-à-vis EU decision-making institutions.[12]

Depending on the extent to which these hypotheses H1–H4 are supported by empirical evidence, we will be able to establish the potential of civil society to contribute to the EU's legitimation or, in the negative case, to identify specific gaps in the democratic legitimation of the emerging EU polity.

Data and Methodology

The analytical framework developed above rests on two key concepts – democratic legitimation and civil society. For the purpose of the present empirical analysis,

---

11   Empirically, balanced inclusion will be measured by comparing how the two types of CSO's rank the frequency of their interactions with EU institutions relative to each other.

12   Empirically, active European citizenship in relation to EU polity building will be measured by the extent to which citizens expect civil society organisations to perform as an agent in the EU's constitutive treaty reform processes.

civil society is operationalised in terms of organised as well as individual, forms of civic and political participation, that is comprises civil society organisations and civic forms of individual political participation.[13] A combination of two different data sets from the ConstEPS research project[14] will be used for developing theoretically structured and empirically grounded arguments regarding the potentials of civil society for enhancing the democratic legitimation of the European polity. These data sets include (1) the ConstEPS media data set (2004–5) and (2) the ConstEPS civil society data set (2007). The analysis of the media data set provides empirical evidence regarding the second research hypotheses H2 (see above) on CSO access and transparency – or the visibility of civil society actors in Europeanising national public spheres. The data set on civil society organisations is used for mapping CSO positions on the TCE and Europe (H1); for testing H3 (CSO inclusion), H4 (CSO balance of interests) and H5 (representation).

(1) The ConstEPS media data set covers the TCE ratification period during October 2004 to October 2005 across six EU member states. The data set has been constructed from 8.540 articles selected from 36 printed media; from these, a sample of 185 articles was drawn for a qualitative analysis of European political discourses in the Czech Republic, Estonia and Poland (as new Member States) and France, Germany and the UK (as old Member States; for more detailed information, see Annex 6.A1). The selection of a representative sample of print media articles for qualitative political discourse analysis was based on the following criteria: (1.) the overall coverage by month, (2.) the share of the periodicals over time, and (3.) the coverage of key events in the ratification debate. Based on this qualitative media sample, a comparative political discourse analysis[15] was conducted based on the computer package Atlas.ti (Maatsch/Gattig 2008). For this purpose, a coding scheme was developed by the ConstEPS research team, aimed at identifying and comparing distinctive elements in national political discourses on the EU polity, including actors; topics; argumentative strategies; justifications; interaction and relation; as well as relevant issues from domestic contexts.

(2) The "ConstEPS CSO data set" was constructed from interviews that ConstEPS team members and collaborators conducted with national CSO's in the six ConstEPS countries between February and June 2007. In each country,

---

13   The basic definition of civil society organization is that of an institutionalised form of civil society, the type of organizations included in this definition varies between countries, but in this research it includes various interest and advocacy groups with institutionalised stucture.

14   The ConstEPS research project "Citizenship and Constitutionalization: Transforming the Public Sphere in East-West European Integration" was based at the Jean Monnet Centre for European Studies of the University of Bremen, was directed by Prof. Ulrike Liebert and funded by Volkswagen Foundation (2005–8).

15   Within the ConstEPS Research, "[p]olitical discourse analysis determines how political elites and mass media construct public opinion – and, hence, potentially, how the social constituencies of the emerging European polity conceptualize the EU, its legitimacy, and the roles and competences of member governments, citizens and civil society" (Liebert 2006: 2–3).

approximately 24 semi-structured interviews were held with NGOs, political parties and economic organisations. In addition to comprising CSO's present in the ConstEPS media sample, the sampling included national level organisations with links to EU-level umbrella organisations, and/or represented in the European Social and Economic Council (top-down principle), as well as organisations influential in TCE politics at the national level (bottom-up principle). The data set used in the present analysis includes 95 interviews with both European and national-level CSOs (NGOs and economic organisations such as trade unions and employers associations) from both new and old Member States (Czech Republic, Estonia, France, Germany, Poland and the UK). The analysis was based on both qualitative and quantitative methods, including statistical and network analysis.

Empirical Findings

The presentation of empirical findings is structured in five parts: First, the ConstEPS media data set is analysed for establishing whether and to what extent, in the TCE ratification process, CSO have gained access to the print media for providing information on CSO's positions to the general public. Second, based on the ConstEPS CSO interview data set, the linkages among actors and institutions are scrutinised. Here, a network analysis is conducted for identifying the patterns of civil society organisations' linkages to EU institutions and political parties on the one hand, and to citizens and other CSOs on the other. In the third and last part, using the ConstEPS interview data supplemented by macro data, the three types of democratic legitimacy are evaluated in order to delineate the kind of legitimation that organised civil society appears most likely to provide to the EU polity.

Contributing to EU Legitimation? CSO's Complex Support Patterns

This section first establishes a framework for analysing complex positions on Europe, and then moves to a comparative analysis of the ConstEPS data, including an in-depth look into CSO's by Member States. Drawing from the literature on Euro-scepticism, a two-dimensional model of attitudes toward the Constitutional Treaty is adopted.[16] Here, the horizontal (x) axis represents positions towards European Integration, and the vertical (y) axis refers to orientations towards the TCE, both reaching from negative through a neutral to positive values. Four patterns of complex attitudes combing diffuse support for/rejection for Europe and specific support/rejection towards the TCE can be discerned, accordingly: (1)

---

16 Following Kopecky and Mudde's (2002) examination of Euro-scepticism, we define support for Europe as a multi-layered concept in relational rather than absolute terms, thus distinguishing between diffuse and specific support for Europe. For the purpose of this chapter, diffuse support refers to general support for Europe, and specific support relates to the position on the Constitution/Constitutional Treaty.

specific support for the TCE combined with a refusal of European integration; (2) support for both, European Integration and the TCE; (3) refusal of both, European Integration and the TCE; (4) support for European Integration, but rejection of the TCE (see Table 6.1).

Table 6.1   Complex patterns of support towards the EU

Positions on Europe (diffuse support)	Positions on TCE (specific support)	
	Negative	Positive
Positive	(1) Euro-critics	(2) pro-Europeans
Negative	(3) Euro-sceptics or anti-Europeans	(4) pragmatic status quo defendants

The data analysis indicates that out of a total of 92 civil society organisations in the sample considered here, 83 indicated a position on both Europe and on the Constitution. Furthermore, only three out of the 83 organisations indicated a neutral position on both axes, and further eight indicated a neutral position on one of the axes. It can, thus, be stated that not only do civil society organisations have a position on Europe, but their positions on Europe are rather polarised. While the majority of CSOs position themselves within the second and fourth cluster (specific and diffuse support and refusal, respectively), there are also organisations located in the mixed first and third quadrants. While the patterns of specific plus diffuse support (or refusal) are rather clear, let us look into the cases with mixed positions:

In the first quadrant, there is only the Liberal Institute of the Friedrich Naumann Foundation (Germany). The Liberal Institute supports the idea of a constitution for the EU, while being simultaneously critical of the centralising tendencies of European integration. This very well illustrates the ambiguous nature of specific vs. diffuse support for/against the TCE/European integration.

Moreover, three CSOs indicate a pattern of weak diffuse support and neutrality regarding the TCE, thus positioning themselves in the fourth field. This position can be labelled "Euro-realist" – respondents are generally supportive of the ideas of European unification, but are simultaneously very critical of the politically compromised reality of the TCE.

By analysing the data by individual Member States, varying patterns of complex support towards the EU can be discerned:

A moderate level of polarisation between plain supporters and wholesale rejecters prevails among CSO's from the Czech Republic, the majority of which is located either in the second or the third quadrant. Here, combined diffuse and specific support is strongest among economic actors. Below, we will therefore scrutinise the networks of economic and civic organisations, to determine whether differential levels of inclusion in EU decision-making to the advantage of economic organisation can be identified, leading to stronger diffuse support for European integration and also foster specifically positive attitudes towards the TCE.

The majority of Estonian CSO respondents populates the second, pro-European integration and pro-TCE camp, with the exception of the Landowners Union. This indicated diffuse support for the EU, but rejection of the Constitution based on the fact that the organisation did not have enough information on the latter. Looking at the reasons given by the respondents for their positions, this position can be defined as passive-pragmatic. It also illustrates the close connection between the Constitutional Treaty and further enlargement and deepening of the Union, as the Constitutional Treaty is viewed as a vehicle of further deepening of the European Union.

In France, all CSO respondents positioned themselves in the fourth, pragmatic-European, camp. Similar to the Czech Republic, also here economic pro-European CSOs tend to indicate both, diffuse and specific patterns of support for the European Union.

Unlike in France, most of the German CSOs are located in the second, pro-European, quadrant. The two outliers are the Liberal Institute and Attac positioned in the first and the fourth camps, respectively. While the position of the Liberal Institute was described above, the position of the Attac indicates diffuse support combined with a specific rejection of the Constitution, and is based on critique and rejection of the current Constitutional Treaty, and not of (the) Constitution per se. Like in the Czech Republic and France, also in Germany economic organisations, offer stronger diffuse and specific support for Europe than NGOs.

Polish CSOs offer a very interesting country specific pattern. While all organisations here exhibit diffuse support for European integration, they vary in their position on the TCE. Thus, all respondents are located in the second and third camps. In particular, two organisations – Stefan Batory Foundation and Agricultural Circles Association – have neutral positions on the Constitution, while at the same time indicating diffuse support for Europe. Located in the fourth quadrant, three CSO's – Adam Smith Center, the Women's Rights Center, and the Consumer association – reject the Constitution, and the remaining organisations indicate more or less diffuse as well as specific support. In Poland, no differences were found regarding support for Europe among economic organisations and NGOs.

British CSOs represent yet another pattern. Here, the organisations are located in the second, pro-European, and the fourth, Euro-sceptical, quadrants, as well as in the third quadrant. However, the majority of organisations indicate a neutral position on the Constitution. Like in the Czech Republic, also here some CSOs are located in the third quadrant, expressing diffuse as well as specific rejection. Also similarly to the Czech Republic, NGOs tend here to be more critical compared to economic organisations towards both, Europe in general and the TCE in particular.

Regarding EU level organisations, a similar pattern like that in Germany can be detected, with all organisations falling into the pro-European camp. The nature of support is rather strong and active, as most organisations indicate direct participation in the drafting of individual articles of the Constitutional Treaty. Furthermore, it is interesting to note that European-level organisations were facing specific challenges in regard to the building this position on the Constitutional Treaty – they had to search for compromises among their diverse membership bases. This is why "European Free Alliance" as well as "Coordination Paysanne Européenne" adopted neutral positions on the Constitutional Treaty.

To summarise, there is no straightforward simple answer to the question whether or not civil society contributes to the EU's democratic legitimation. Not less than three patterns of complex attitudes towards European integration in general and, more specifically, vis-à-vis the TCE have been detected among the CSO's from six Member States under study here: (1). A strong pro-European pattern – with dominant diffuse support for Europe, combined with rather strong specific support for the Constitution/Constitutional treaty, prevailing among the civil society organisations from France, Germany (with Attac and Liberal Institute being crucial out-layers) and at the EU level; (2). A pattern of strong diffuse support for Europe with ambiguities – both specific support as well as specific rejection towards the TCE – in Estonia and Poland; (3). A Euro-critical pattern, with more or less polarised attitudes and a majority of CSOs located in the second and third camps, albeit out-layers in the fourth quadrant; this pattern can be found in the Czech Republic and the UK.

The next question addressed is about the enabling conditions and the constraining factors that shape CSO's contribution to EU legitimation. The following four sections present empirical findings for illustrating four kinds of conditions that enhance the role of CSOs: access to and visibility in the mass media (2); inclusion in vertical and horizontal cooperation networks (3); European political communication (4) and predispositions to act as agents of citizens' representation (4).

CSO Visibility in the Mass Media

By shedding light on the EU's politics of treaty reform, public debates are a mechanism and precondition for engendering EU transparency vis-à-vis the general public. Empirically, the visibility of CSOs in the public sphere has been measured by an analysis of print media coverage of TCE ratification, based on comparative political discourse analysis, assessing the relative visibility of CSO's positions (vis-à-vis those of state and EU actors) on key issues of EU polity building (established by the TCE).

The comparative print media based European political discourse analysis helps identify similarities and differences in the patterns of how organised civil society has gained access to national public spheres and, thus, has rendered visible EU treaty reform in general and its own position, in particular.

From the comparative analysis of CSO visibility in the British, Czech, Estonian, French, German, Latvian, and the Polish TCE debates, three clusters of cases emerge, each defined by a differing level of active involvement on the part of organised civil society:

The first cluster includes countries with highly involved CSO's – in our case, only France falls into this category so far. In France, the dominant organised civil society organisations were lobby groups, when measuring primarily the extent of their visibility. However, if both the visibility and number of articles in which CSO's were mentioned are taken into the consideration, then trade unions appear to be important as well.[17] Present in French debates were also advocacy groups and social movements, such as ATTAC, and critics of globalisation, as well as various NGOs.

The second cluster – the most highly populated one – includes countries with medium visibility of the organised civil society. Here, in terms of numbers of occurrences, Polish and UK based CSO's lead this second group, followed by Germans and Estonians. However, if we take into account also the number of articles referring to CSO's, German and Czech ones appear to dominate the group (see Table 6.2 overleaf). In Germany, the most visible type of organised civil society were think-tanks, followed by "general CSOs" and social movements. In Germany and the UK, the visibility of organised civil society can be mainly attributed to think-tanks, followed by employers associations and social movements. While the think-tanks were also the most visible category in Estonia, the second largest category here were trans-national NGO's such as Estonia Open Foundation. Trade unions only appeared once in our data for Estonia. The lack of visibility of trade unions is an interesting finding also from the Polish case. Here, the church clearly dominated other civil society organisations in the ratification debate (table 6.2).

The third cluster of civil society organisations who gained access to and became visible in national ratification debates is constituted by those from the Czech Republic, with a rather limited involvement of organised civil society actors in the debate, with the exception of think-tanks. The analysis of the Czech media sample helped identify domestic think-tanks, such as the Institute for International Relations (UMV), the Association for International Issues (AMO), and the Center for Economy and Politics (CEP). Their members contributed to the media both actively (writing articles) and passively (being cited by the media). In terms of foreign think-tanks, the Heritage Foundation – a conservative US think-tank – was also visible (Rakušanová 2006).

---

17   In the course of the analysis, the number of times the particular type of organised civil society appeared in the media, as well as the number of articles, in which the organised civil society was mentioned were measured. The number of articles was used to provide a certain corrective of the differences in terms of style.

Table 6.2 CSO visibility in national media coverage of EU treaty ratification, by member states

Category of Organisations	CzechRep	Estonia	France	Germany	Poland	UK
Trade unions		1 (1)	7 (5)			
Lobby			14 (2)			
Employers' associations	2 (2)		1 (1)	1 (1)		1 (1)
Civil society (general)		5 (1)	1 (1)	4 (1)		
Foundations					1 (1)	
Churches					13 (2)	
Charities						
Advocacy groups			3 (3)			
Social movements			2 (2)	2 (1)		1 (1)
Think-tanks	5 (4)	7 (2)		6 (6)		11 (2)
Professional associations						
Other NGOs			1 (1)			
Total	**7 (6)**	**13 (4)**	**29 (15)**	**13 (9)**	**14 (3)**	**14 (4)**

Source: ConstEPS media data set (Oct 2004–Oct 2005).

Note: Numbers refer to total amount of occurrences of CSO category, numbers in parentheses to number of print articles with at least one occurrence of CSO category.

Comparing East and West, the overall visibility of organised civil society in national ratification debate was lower in the new Member States (NMS) than in the old ones, both in terms of the number of times civil society organisations were mentioned in the media, and the number of articles which made references to organised civil society (Table 6.3). The dominant type of CSO in one of the new Member States – Poland – was the Church, think-tanks were more visible than other types of CSO's in both Estonia and the Czech Republic. To a much lesser degree, trade unions and employers' associations gained visibility in the media as participants in the ratification debates in the NMS.

National think-tanks were the most visible type of organised civil society in the ratification debate not only in NMS but also EU-wide, both in terms of the number of times they appeared in the media, and the number of articles that included a reference to them. The second most visible category was lobby groups. In the OMS, the social partners – both trade unions and employers associations – were also more present in the ratification debates than their counterparts in the NMS's (see Table 6.3).

Table 6.3   CSO visibility in media ratification debates, by old and new Member States

Category of CSOs	NMS (No. of articles)	OMS (No. of articles)
Interest organisations	0	0
Trade unions	1 (1)	7 (5)
Lobby		14 (2)
Employers' associations	2 (2)	3 (3)
Civil society (general)	5 (1)	5 (2)
Foundations	1 (1)	0
Churches	13 (2)	0
Charities	0	0
Community groups	0	0
Advocacy groups	0	3 (3)
Social movements	0	5 (4)
Watchdog organisations	0	0
Think-tanks	12 (6)	17 (8)
Umbrella organisations	0	0
Professional associations	0	0
Other NGOs	0	1 (1)
Total (articles mentioned)	**34 (13)**	**56 (28)**
Total (articles analysed)	88	97

Source: ConstEPS data set (Oct 2004–Oct 2005).

Note: Numbers refer to total amount of occurrences of CSO category, numbers in parentheses to number of print articles with at least one occurrence of CSO category.

There are different ways of interpreting the low level of visibility of CSOs in the mass media. The above findings might support Delanty and Rumford's (2005) argument that European civil society remains predominantly rooted in national civil societies which serves as a protection against economic globalisation rather than a catalyst of Europeanisation.

However, the limited access of civil society to European political discourses in national public spheres might also be a result of other factors. On the one hand, the prevalence of top-down Europeanisation processes might reduce national civil society to a rather limited role (Della Porta and Caiani 2006). In line with this argument, Maurer et al. (2005: 4–22) have implied that the role of civil society organisations in the European constitutional process was not to inform citizens about their positions vis-à-vis the TCE, but rather to mobilise them for participating in referenda, as well as to establish supportive channels of communication, participation and influence for state and EU institutions. On the other hand, assuming that the establishment of European civil society proceeds along functional lines, ad-hoc coalitions for key issues of shared concern would emerge from transnational networks and umbrella organisations aimed at bridging pre-existing national civil societies. Such expectations would be consonant with research findings from the project "Organized Civil Society and the European Governance" (CIVGOV), as building advocacy coalitions for environmental or antiracist concerns appears a valuable and effective civil society strategy vis-à-vis the EU (Ruzza 2005, 2006). This strategic orientation would explain the relatively limited attempts of national NGOs to get access to general public spheres, or to become visible in the national print media: national CSO's might simply use the more effective, informal channels of communication about EU issues of shared concern, via face to face communication, telephone or internet.

After having explored CSO public visibility as a mechanism for enhancing transparency – defined above as the first criterion for procedural legitimation – the next section turns to the second defining preconditions for EU procedural legitimation: CSO inclusion through cooperation networks that engage with EU treaty reform politics.

CSO Inclusion in Vertical and Horizontal Cooperation Networks[18]

Having selected "inclusion" and "balance of interests" as two more defining criteria on which legitimation through democratic procedures rests (see above), this section presents findings from vertical and horizontal network analysis. CSOs may develop vertical networks with EU institutions and actors on the one hand and horizontal networks among themselves, on the other hand. The question is whether and how these networks balance a) the social interests of NGOs (including think-tanks) with the interests of economic organisations (trade unions and employers' organisations), and b) the interests of CSOs from old and new MSs.

The empirical network analysis shows that the new Member States vary considerably:

- In the Czech Republic only two NGO's out of 10 have been found that are well-connected to EU institutions, one think-tank (AMO) and one foundation responsible for distributing EU funds to CSO's. By contrast, all other NGO's have only weak connections to the EU. Interestingly, three NGOs don't have any connections to EU level NGO's, either. As for Czech economic organisations, they are generally better connected than NGOs and think tanks. Trade unions tend to maintain relationships with their EU-level counterparts and other organisations, while employers' organisations are

---

18 I would like to thank Ewelina Pawlak for her help with creating the network analysis matrixes as well as the graphs. On NGO networks in multilevel governance comp. Pleines 2008.

- equipped with numerous linkages connecting them to both their European counterparts and to EU-level political actors. Czech Employers tend to have stronger political links than Czech NGOs and think-tanks.
- Polish NGOs' networks with the EU appear to be better developed than those of their Czech counterparts. However, Polish economic organisations are less well-connected than Czech trade unions and employers organisations and exhibit fewer links to EU-level political actors. In Estonia, as in the Czech Republic, economic organisations have stronger links at the EU level than the other organisation types.
- Comparing the density of vertical networks of the Czech Republic, Estonia and Poland, respectively, stronger links between national and EU-level organisations can be found in Poland and in the Czech Republic than in Estonia. Also, Estonian organisations show a stronger tendency toward bilateral, rather than multilateral, networks.
- Turning the focus now on the old Member States, the findings are varied, as well:
- Germany exhibits a similar pattern to that observed in the Czech Republic. With regard to NGO networks with the EU, our sample includes only two well-connected NGOs and several weakly connected ones. However, German economic organisations do not seem entertain stronger networks than their NGO counterparts.
- In the UK both NGOs and economic actors have established multilateral networks. In contrast with the other OMSs under study, British NGOs, and especially think-tanks, tend to be very well-connected with political actors from the EU level. As for economic organisations, both trade unions and employers have established comparatively rather strong multilateral networks of cooperation. Significantly, British economic organisations seem to be less in touch with political party groupings in the European Parliament than their counterparts in other Member States.
- Similarly to the case of the UK, the network analysis of French and German NGOs and economic organisations shows that both have developed multilateral domestic as well as transnational networks. In general, in OMSs, we find a larger differentiation of such networks. In France, for instance, economic organisations as well as civil society actors concentrate on the relationship with European political parties and transnational civil society and economic actors. In Germany, both economic and civil society actors tend to prefer institutional partners. German economic organisations developed the strongest links to EU-level institutions – both the European Commission and the European Parliament.

While German civil society actors prefer domestic institutions, such as the German Government and Bundestag. In the UK, economic organisations as well as civil society organisations have strong transnational civil society links and links to transnational economic actors. Civil society actors in the UK also engaged in relationships with European party groups.

The second hypothesis outlined above suggests that CSO inclusion in vertical networks with EU institutions is a favourable condition for EU legitimation, while the third hypotheses underscored the balance of interests. Empirically, CSO's inclusion has been measured by vertical interactions with EU institutions relative to national institutions and organisations The findings from the network analysis of CSOs can be summarised as follows: (1) economic organisations are generally better connected to the EU than NGOs; (2) both employers' organisations and trade unions are often also part of multilateral transnational networks; (3) moreover, economic organisations often have horizontal links to European political parties, too; and (4) looking in more detail at the NGOs, it can be stated that think-tanks tend to be better connected than other NGOs.

Given the rich evidence it seems reasonable to conclude that CSO's are by no means excluded from EU decision-making institutions and organisations. Inclusion as the second condition for EU legitimacy is present, at least partially. Across all MS's, organised civil society actors (NGOs, think-tanks, and economic organisations) did develop bilateral as well as multilateral links to EU-level organisations and party groupings in the European Parliament. Yet, network analysis exhibits a complex and highly asymmetric pattern of inclusion, to the advantage of economic organisations, where NGOs appear to lag behind, especially from the NMSs.

The question is whether and how CSOs – whether more or less included in vertical or horizontal networks of cooperation – make selective use of the channels of European political communication – conceived here as a condition for reaching out to and mobilising mass publics for engaging in EU constitutional politics.

CSOs in European Political Communication

Turning to the fourth step of the empirical analysis, evidence is presented regarding the multiple channels of European political communication that CSO's have used for engaging with the drafting and ratification of the TCE. The analysis is based on respondents' evaluation of the effectiveness of alternative modes of communication in EU constitutional politics. As in the previous section, NGOs and economic organisations are differentiated in country-wise analysis. Generally speaking, it can be said that the ConstEPS data show that CSOs have not only gained access to the mass media but have used a variety of other channels of European political communication, as well: from the Internet over informal campaigns to Social Partnership dialogue and EU political consultations, both, at the national and European levels.

Among the NMSs, Czech NGOs indicated that they participated mainly in public debates, followed by direct communication to citizens, and thirdly via political consultations. Economic organisations, on the other hand, favoured social dialogue, political consultations at the national and European levels, and activities directed against (Euro-sceptical) political parties. In Estonia, civil society actors utilised institutional debates (Convention), political consultations and transnational communication, including participation in the European Economic and Social Committee. In Poland, more pro-active forms of communication were used by civil society, such as Internet based communication, petitions, conferences at the European level, and the media. As to the OMSs, UK based organisations also ranked the mass media and media-related campaigns highest in their domestic engagement with EU treaty ratification. German actors were more oriented towards political communication within EU institutions, such as the Convention or the European Economic and Social Committee on the one hand and towards developing transnational links, on the other.

The empirical findings show that due to the high level of politicisation of mass media debates dominated by political parties (for example in France and the Czech Republic), civil society organisations (CSOs) engage with channels of access and communication other than the printed mass media, including internet campaigns, informal campaigns, social partnership dialogue or political consultations at the national and European levels. Thus, rather than limiting themselves to the intermediary communicative role of the print media, CSOs also used more informal but direct communication channels towards both decision makers and citizens. Furthermore, the data confirm the fact that CSOs preferred activities aimed directly towards national and European institutions, rather than communicating to the public via media.

To sum up, for engaging with EU constitutional reforms, CSOs use multiple channels of European political communication that combine intermediaries such as the print media with forms of direct communication with both decision makers and citizens. Thus, the third hypothesis, can be partially confirmed.

CSOs as Agents of Citizen Representation vis-à-vis EU Institutions

The fourth condition for EU procedural legitimation examined here is "representation". As the data demonstrate, civil society organisations utilise various channels of communication with citizens and the public at large. They engage a range of activities directed towards citizens, not only national and EU institutions. The aim is to comparatively explore whether CSOs prefer to communicate with the public via the mass media or through alternative communication channels, and how CSOs from the OMSs and NMSs compare to each other.

As Graph 6.1 shows, two different patterns can be detected: In countries like Estonia, Germany, Poland, the UK, and at the EU level, economic organisations were more often involved in citizen-related communication than NGOs. By comparison, in the Czech Republic and in France, NGOs were more engaged in this respect. CSO engagement with citizens also varies as regards its intensity: While in Estonia and at the EU level, on average over 80 percent of CSOs claim to be involved in citizen-related activities, in the UK and the Czech Republic, the number is just over 40 percent, and in Germany and Poland little more than 30 percent.

CSO engagement with citizens took two main forms, direct and indirect ones (through umbrella organisations and transnational structures). When passive CSOs were asked for the reasons for their non-involvement in this field, answers can be classified in the following four categories: (1) lack of interest, was not part of the organisation's priorities (for example producer organisations, employer organisations and some NGOs); (2) opposition to such activities, for instance, by some Euro-sceptical groups; (3) lack of invitation to participate, for instance on the part of some Euro-critical and Euro-sceptical[19] groups and trade unions); 4) missing domestic debate or discontinuation of domestic debate after the ratification failure (some economic organisations).

Comparing citizen-related activities to those directed towards institutions (Graph 6.2 and Graph 6.3), it can be seen that NGOs in the old Member States, at the EU level, and in Poland, were more active in addressing institutions, while Czech and Estonian NGOs were not very active at all. This finding can be attributed to the different styles of national TCE debates, which were legally formalistic in Estonia and politically polarised in the Czech Republic.

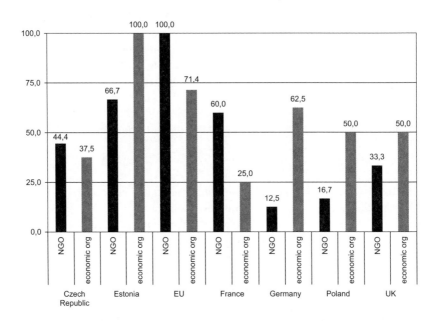

Graph 6.1 Involvement in activities engaging the public, civil society and citizens

Source: ConstEPS Interviews (N=76).

---

19 The difference is made between Euro-critical organizations, which are vocal critics of specific aspects of the emerging European polity and Euro-sceptical groups which are critics of the enlargement process as such.

A Panacea for Democratic Legitimation? 155

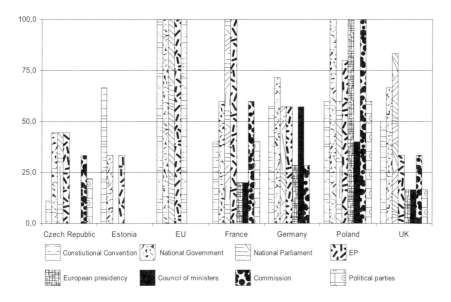

Graph 6.2   Institutions addressed by NGOs regarding the TCE
Source: ConstEPS Interviews (N=68).

As for the national vs. European institutions being addressed, there is no clear pattern accruing among the countries under study. The EU-level CSOs addressed all institutions at the EU and national levels, with the exception of political parties, which were contacted to a much smaller degree. French organisations tended to speak mainly to their national and to the European parliamentarians. Polish NGOs communicated mainly with the national government, the EU Presidency and the Commission. In the UK, the national Government and Parliament were the main addressees. NGOs in all countries, with the exception of the Czech Republic, put great emphasis (over 50 percent) on addressing the Constitutional Convention. Among NGOs in all countries, least attention was paid to political parties.

As for the economic organisations, these were very active at the EU level, in the UK, in Poland and in Germany, less active in France and in the Czech Republic, and passive in Estonia. Similarly as regarding the activities of the NGOs, in this area no clear pattern has emerged. The EU-level economic organisations addressed all institutions, with the exception of political parties. Polish, as well as British, and to a lesser extent also German economic organisations talked to national governments and parliaments. French and Czech economic organisations were much less active, but they communicated with the Constitutional Convention, national governments, the national and the European Parliaments, and the Commission. Moreover, economic interest organisations stated that they addressed the Constitutional Convention to a much smaller degree than NGOs.

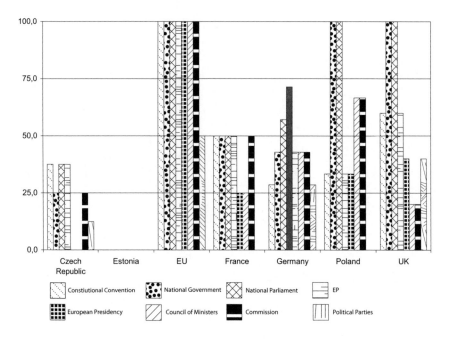

Graph 6.3 Institutions addressed by economic organisations regarding the TCE

Source: ConstEPS Interview (N=68).

The data presented here support the claim that civil society organisations combine media communication with direct channels of communication to both citizens and to national and European-level institutions. Yet, the communication towards institutions seems to be relatively stronger than that towards citizens.

Summary of Findings

The empirical results presented here confirm the relatively low visibility of organised civil society during the constitutional reform process as it was reflected by the mass media. Yet, this supports the findings of Della Porta and Caiani (2006) regarding the marginalisation of civil society in processes of top-down Europeanisation. Albeit to the lesser degree, they also support the argument developed by Maurer et al. (2005).

The analysis demonstrates that most civil society organisations held a position on the Constitution/Constitutional Treaty. Thus, the first hypothesis could be falsified by ConstEPS data analysis revealing three different patterns of complex attitudes towards Europe.

Moreover, as the cross-national comparative analysis of organised civil society shows, national civil society organisations tend to have both, bilateral and multilateral links to EU-level organisations and party groupings in the European Parliament. Nevertheless, economic organisations are generally better connected than NGOs; both employers' organisations and trade unions are often part of multilateral transnational networks; economic organisations more often than not have developed horizontal links to European political partiers; and finally, looking in more detail into different types of NGOs, it is revealed that think-tanks tend to be better connected than most other kinds of NGOs.

The analysis has also showed that civil society organisations use multiple channels of communication, combining the intermediary role of printed media with more direct channels of communication, directed towards both, decision makers and citizens.

Looking at the fourth vector of legitimation outlined in the theoretical part above, large differences could be detected between the civil society and economic actors with respect to the four procedural conditions (or criteria), "transparency", "inclusion", "balance of interests" and "representation". Out of the 94 CSOs under study, no less than 27 are represented in the European Economic and Social Committee (EESC), among which the overwhelming majority are economic actors. Those CSOs that were included tended to exhibit positive positions on European integration and the TCE. On the other hand, Euro-sceptical groups tended to be excluded from the same vertical networks.

The correlation analysis of the four conditions for EU procedural legitimation (transparency, inclusion, balanced interests, representation) and CSO attitudes on the EU and the TCE shows that both are correlated among both civil society and economic actors (Guasti 2009). Furthermore, a positive correlation can be found between the openness of civil society organisations and their position on the Constitution, and a negative correlation between the networks of economic organisations and their position on the Constitution. This means, then, that pro-European and Euro-sceptical groups tend to avoid interaction with each other.

Conclusions

The aim of this chapter was to explore the potential of civil society to contribute to the legitimation of the emerging European polity. Therefore, while building on the state of the art of the EU literature, the chapter aimed at identifying existing gaps between theoretical perspectives, discourses and practices. Developing a five step empirical analysis, the chapter has adopted four criteria on which procedural legitimation through civil society depends – transparency, inclusion, balance of interests, and representation.

This brings us back to the three questions posed in the introduction. Regarding the dominant discourses about the role of civil society in legitimating Europe, the findings from our research further confirmed the arguments reported by the Civil Society Contact Group (CSCG, Fazi and Smith 2006), namely that the main aim of civil society organisations at the EU level appeared to be networking and lobbying. The academic as well as the official discourse on civil society's role in the establishment of the new European democratic order is incoherent and fluid both in institutional and temporal terms; that is there is no unitary discourse on civil society, but rather multiple discourses by different institutions and at different time periods. By contrast, the self-description by civil society on the European level is clearly utilitarian, pointing to its goal is to reach the level of impact and efficiency that the partners of the social dialogue already have. Therefore, we find inconsistency between the official roles attributed to organised civil society by EU institutions and EU elites, and their practical expectations.

As regards the second question, our analysis reveals found complex patterns of civil society attitudes towards the issues of the EU and TCE – ranging from unfettered support over mixed attitudes to rejection.

Finally, concerning the conditions for civil society to contribute to the legitimation of European constitutionalisation, empirical evidence is mixed, pointing to half-filled as well as partially empty glasses. Regarding the deficits, the main findings about civil society engagement with EU constitutional politics can be summarised in three arguments concerning key impediments to EU legitimation:

Firstly, the condition of *transparency* is weakened, on the one hand, by top-down processes of Europeanisation that constrains the access of bottom-up civil society to national public spheres. On the other hand, it is also undermined by lack of norms or procedures for checking the democratic credentials of actors who do have access to or even control means of mass communication with biased discourses about the EU.

Secondly, the condition of *balanced inclusion* is undermined by differential access to EU decision-making processes by civil society, to the disadvantage of NGOs compared to the advantages of economic organisations. It is also undermined due to qualitative differentiation in the status and nature of civil and social dialogue regarding the formal inclusion of civil society in the TCE and in EU governance;[20]

Thirdly, the condition of *representation* through CSO's is weakened by the relative marginalisation of citizens in civil society's vertical communication and cooperation networks, compared to the centrality of EU decision making institutions in vertical interactions.

These impediments, arguably, originate in the process of top-down Europeanisation. This faces civil society organisations with a dilemma: Given their limited resources, the organisations under study choose to concentrate predominantly on EU or national level institutions and parliamentary party groups, rather than citizens. For maximising their influence on European constitutionalisation, they unwillingly contribute to widening the gap between civil society and citizens. While close contact to the citizens is one of the goals the emerging European civil society sets for itself, it is in contradiction to the demands of bureaucratical

---

20 Erne 2008, Fazi and Smith 2006, Kohler-Koch et al. 2008a, 2008b, Kohler-Koch and Quittkat 2013, Obradovic 2005.

structures of European institutions. It is paradoxical that by contrast, the so called "Euro-sceptic" organisations remain closer in touch with the citizens, while their access to European level institutions remains limited. Conversely, the impact of these groups on the public opinion is not negligible. As Ulrike Liebert points out, the European civil society is caught in its dual nature as loyal (and dependent) partner of the EU institutions and its original role of challenging and contentious agent in the process of EU polity formation (2011: 119).

To summarise, civil society is found to be an active player in the politics of EU constitutional treaty reform, however, an actor with generally speaking limited access and impact. Another effect of the constitutionalisation process is the emerging transnationalisation of civil society – growing communication and cooperation among civil society organisations across national boundaries. Horizontal interaction takes place along ideological lines and the interaction among pro-European and Euro-critical organisations remains virtually non-existent. Key factor in the emerging transnationalisation is the access to decision-making processes as well as the intention to maximise policy impact by joining efforts. Nonetheless, in terms of transnationalisation, we still witness struggles to overcome the East-West divide. Civil society organisations from the old and the new member states are still in the process of learning to communicate with each other, to define a shared ground as well as a common agenda. This has been highlighted by the contentions about the TCE, especially the failure of the French referendum that put the spotlight on the political conflict about European integration and the politicisation of national public spheres.

In this current constellation, civil society does not offer a panacea for resolving the democratic legitimation deficit of the European Union. Democracy in the enlarged EU remains severely handicapped by lack of strong commitment to change the current practices of citizens' and civil society's involvement in European governance. It is constrained by a lack of political will to implement deep changes of the existing structures, namely channels of communications, and patterns of conduct. To answer the third question posed in the introduction – these are some of the conditions required by the emerging transnational European civil society to contribute to enhancing the democratic order of the European polity.

References

Alexander, J. 1997. The paradoxes of civil society. *International Sociology*, 12(2), 115–133.

Arato, A. and Cohen, J.L. 1990. *Civil Society and Political Theory*. Cambridge and London: MIT.

Banchoff, T. and Smith, P.M. (eds) 1999. *Legitimacy and the European Union: The Contested Polity*. London: Routledge.

Beetham, D. and Lord, Ch. 1998. *Legitimacy and the European Union*. London/New York: Longman.

Bellamy, R. and Castiglione, D. 1998. Between cosmopolis and community: three models of rights and democracy within the European Union, in D. Archibugi, D. Held and M. Kolher (eds), *Reimagining Political Community*. Oxford: Polity Press, pp. 152–178.

Bellamy, R. 2001. The "right to have rights": citizenship practice and the political constitution of the EU, in *Citizenship and Governance in the European Union*, R. Bellamy and A. Warleigh (eds). London: Continuum, 41–70.

Bellamy, R. and Warleigh, A. (eds) 2001. *Citizenship and Governance in the European Union*. London: Continuum.

Bryant, Ch.G.A. 1993. Social self-organisation, civility and sociology: a comment on Kumar's "Civil Society". *The British Journal of Sociology*, 44(3), 397–401.

Bryant, Ch.G.A. 1993. Social self-organisation, civility and sociology: a comment on Kumar's "civil society", in *The British Journal of Sociology*, vol. 44, no. 3, pp. 397–401.

Craig, P. 2003. What constitution does Europe need: the house that Giscard built: constitutional room with a view. London: The Federal Trust.

Delanty, G. and Rumford, C. 2005. Rethinking European society. The global civil society context, in G. Delanty and C. Rumford. *Rethinking Europe. Social Theory and the Implications of Europeanization*. London and New York: Routledge, 168–183.

Della Porta, D. and Caiani, M. 2006. The Europeanization of public discourse in Italy: a top-down process. *European Union Politics*, 7(1), 77–112.

Duff, A. 2003. A liberal reaction to the European convention and the intergovernmental conference, *Federal Trust Papers*, July (London: Federal Trust).

Eriksen, E.O. 2005. An emerging European public Sphere, *European Journal of Social Theory*, 8(3), 341–363.

Eriksen, E.O. and Fossum, J.E. 2004. Europe in search of its legitimacy: the strategies of legitimation assessed. *International Political Science Review*, 25(4), 435–459.

Eriksen, E.O. and Fossum, J.E. 2012. *Rethinking Democracy and the European Union*. London: Routledge.

Erne, R. 2008. *European Unions: Labors' Quest for Transnational Democracy*. Ithaca: Cornell University Press.

Etzioni, A. 1973. The third sector and domestic missions. *Public Administration Review*, 33(4), 314–323.

Fazi, E. and Smith, J. 2006. *Civil Dialogue: Making it Work Better*. Brussels: CSCG.

Føllesdal, A. 2004. The seven habits of highly legitimate new models of governance. NEWGOV Paper. Available at: http://www.follesdal.net/ms/Follesdal-2005-Leg-nmg-NEWGOV.pdf [accessed: 18.10.2010].

Green, A.T. 1997. Občanská společnost, ideje a utváření politiky. *Sociologický časopis*, 33(3), 309–320.

Greenwood, J. 2003. *Interest Representation in the European Union*. Houndmills: Palgrave Macmillan.

Guasti, P. 2009. European civil society and the legitimacy of the European polity. Paper in the panel, Civil Society and the Public Sphere in the Reconstruction of Democracy in Europe, 21. IPSA World Congress (Santiago de Chile, Chile).

Haas, E.B. 1964. *Beyond the Nation State. Functionalism and International Organizations*. Stanford: Stanford University Press.

Habermas, J. 2003. *The Future of Human Nature*. Oxford: Polity Press.

Habermas, J. 2011. *Zur Verfassung Europas. Ein Essay*. Frankfurt: Suhrkamp.

Héretier, A. 1999. Elements of democratic legitimation in Europe: an alternative perspective. *Journal of European Public Policy*, 6(2), 269–282.

Howard, M.M. 2003. *The Weakness of Civil Society in Post-Communist Europe*. Cambridge: Cambridge University Press.

Keane, J. 1988. *Democracy and Civil Society*. London: Verso.

Kohler-Koch, B. and Rittberger, B. (eds) 2007. *Debating the Democratic Legitimacy of the European Union*. Lanham: Rowman & Littlefield Publishers.

Kohler-Koch, B. and Larat, F. 2008a. *Efficient and Democratic Governance in the European Union*. CONNEX Report Series Vol. 9. Mannheim: MZES.

Kohler-Koch, B., De Biévre, D. and Maloney, W. 2008b. *Opening EU Governance to Civil Society – Gains and Challenges*, CONNEX Report Series, vol 5. Mannheim: MZES.

Kohler-Koch, B. and Buth, V. 2013. The balancing act of European civil society: between professionalism and grass roots, in B. Kohler-Koch and C. Quittkat, *De-Mystification of Participatory Democracy. EU Governance and Civil Society*. Oxford: Oxford University Press, 195–224.

Kopecky, P. and Mudde, C. 2002. Two sides of Euroscepticism: party positions on European integration in east central Europe. *European Union Politics*, 3(3), 297–326.

Kumar, K. 1993. Civil society: an inquiry into the usefulness of an historical term. *The British Journal of Sociology*, 44(3), 375–395.

Kumar, K. 1994. Civil society again: a reply to Christopher Bryant's "social self-organisation, civility and sociology". *The British Journal of Sociology*, 45(1), 127–131.

Liebert, U. 2006. Structuring political conflict about Europe: media, parliaments and constitutional treaty ratification. ConstEPS internal Material No. IV. Outline for country case studies. Bremen: CEuS.

Liebert, U. 2011. Exit, voice or loyalty: the new politics of European civil society, in *The New Politics of European Civil Society*, U. Liebert and H.J. Trenz (eds). London: Routledge.

Liebert, U. and Trenz, H.-J. 2010. *The New Politics of European Civil Society*. London and New York: Routledge.

Lord, Ch. 1998. *Democracy in the European Union*. Sheffield: Sheffield Academic Press.

Lord, C. and Beetham, D. 2001. Legitimizing the EU: is there a 'post-parliamentary basis' for its legitimation? *Journal of Common Market Studies*, 39(3), 443–462.

Lord, C. and Magnette, P. 2004. E Pluribus Unum? Creative disagreement about legitimacy in the EU. *Journal of Common Market Studies*, 42(1), 183–202.

Lord, Ch. and Harris, E. 2006. *Democracy in the New Europe*. London: Palgrave Macmillan.

Maatsch, S. and Gattig, A. 2008. Technical coding guidelines for comparative print media/text analysis using ATLAS.ti computer software. RECON Working Paper, Jean Monnet Centre for European Studies, University of Bremen; online available at http://www.monnet-centre.uni- bremen.de/pdf/wp/MaatschGattig_RECONWP5_ManualATLAS.ti_2008.pdf.

Magnette, P. 2003. Will the EU be more legitimate after the convention, in Shaw, J., Magnette, P., Hoffman, L and Verges Bausili, A. 2003. *The Convention on the Future of Europe Working Towards and EU Constitution*. London: The Federal Trust.

Maurer, A., Devrim, D., Lang, K.-O., Stengel, A. 2005. Ratifikationsverfahren zum EU-Verfassungsvertrag. *Diskussionspapier der FG 1*, 2005/5 Berlin.

Meehan, E. 2000. Europeanization and citizenship of European Union. *Yearbook of European Studies*, 14(1), 157–177.

Meny, Y. 2003. Della Demokratie en Europe: old concepts and new challanges. *Journal of Common Market Studies*, 41(1), 1–13.

Neocleous, M. 1995. From civil society to the social. *The British Journal of Sociology*, 46(3), 395–408.

Obradovic, D. 2005. Civil society and the social dialogue in European governance. *Yearbook on European Law*, 24(1), 261–328.

Obradovic, D. and Alonso Vizcaino, J.M. 2006. Good governance requirements for the participation of interest groups in EU consultation, in *Participation of Civil Society in New Modes of Governance. The Case of the New EU Member States. Part 3: Involvement at the EU Level*, H. Pleines (ed.), Arbeitspapiere und Materialien, No. 76–9/2006, Universität Bremen: Forschungsstelle Osteuropa, 19–44.

Paolini, G. 2007. *The Legitimacy Deficit of the European Union and the Role of National Parliaments*. Fiesole: EUI Dissertation.

Pleines, H. (ed.) 2006. Participation of civil society in new modes of governance. The case of the new EU member states. Part 3: involvement at the EU level, in *Arbeitspapiere und Materialien*. No. 76–9/2006. Universität Bremen: Forschungsstelle Osteuropa, pp. 19–44.

Pleines, H. 2008. Czech environmental NGOs: actors or agents in EU multi-level governance? *NewGov Policy Brief* No. 20, 2008.

Rakušanová, P. 2006. The constitutional debate – a one man show? Václav Klaus and the constitutional discourse in the Czech media. ConstEPS Working Paper No. 2006/6. Bremen: Bremen University.

Ruzza, C. 2005. *Organized Civil Society and the EU*. Paper presented at the 3rd ECPR general Conference in Budapest.

Ruzza, C. 2006. European institutions and the policy discourse of organised civil society, in S. Smismans (ed.) *Civil society and legitimate European governance*. London: Elgar, pp. 169–195.

Schmitter, P. 2001a. What is there to legitimize in the European Union and how this might be accomplished? Mimeo: EUI.

Schmitter, P. 2001b. *How to Democratize the EU ... and Why Bother?* Oxford: Rowman & Littlefield Publishers.

Schmitter, P. 2002. Organized labor between the practice of democracy and the prospect of democratization of Europe, in *Europe – One Labour Market?* L. Magnusson and J. Ottosson (eds). Bruxelles: Peter Lang.

Schmitter, P. 2003. Democracy in Europe and Europe's democratization. *Journal of Democracy*, 14(4), 71–85.

Schmitter, P. 2007. Political accountability in "real-existing" democracies: meaning and mechanisms. Firenze: Instituto Universario Europeo.

Seligman, A.B. 1992. *The Idea of Civil Society*. New York: Free Press.

Smith, M. 2002. Civil society: interest groups and social movements, in R. Dyck (ed.) *Studying Politics: An Introduction to Political Science*. Scarborough: Nelson, pp. 290–310.

Walker, N. 2003. Constitutionalising enlargement, enlarging constitutionalism. *European Law Journal*, 9(3), 365–385.

Waltzer, M. 1998. *Towards a Global Civil Society*. Providence: Berghahn Books.

Chapter 7

Still "Second Order?" Re-examining Citizens' Voting Behaviour in European and National Elections 1999–2009

Alexander Gattig, Ewelina Riekens and Ulrike Liebert

Introduction

Since the first direct elections to the European Parliament (EP) in 1979, its powers in European Union (EU) decision-making have expanded significantly. The year 2009 marked the seventh European elections being held in 27 EU member states, inviting citizens to elect an EP that had grown from an initial 410 to 736 Members of the European Parliament (MEPs). Yet, to date, citizen participation in European elections has steadily decreased, from 61.99% in 1979 to 42.97% in 2009. How can this paradox be explained?

Theoretically, participation in elections to the EP or in European referendums has been conceived as a measure for the democratisation of the EU and thus the legitimacy of European political decision-making: "The higher the turnout, the deeper and more widespread becomes the conviction of the citizens that political decision-making is justified and democratically justified. The higher the turnout, the higher is the expected level of democratic legitimacy" (Agné 1999: 119). In terms of democratic practices, the previous chapters of this book have demonstrated that "democratization of the EU from below" is not just an empty word but an evolving process promoted by social practices in fields where citizens are involved in building Europe's order, from the construction of Union citizenship (see Evas and Liebert, above) and voting in EU treaty ratification referendums (see Gattig and Blings, above) to political party communication about EU treaty politics (see Packham, above), national parliamentary debates (see Maatsch, above) as well as civil society participation in EU reform (see Guasti, above). Along with referendums, European elections provide the most important opportunity for European citizens to engage with EU politics. Hence, what exactly are the conditions that motivate citizens to participate in EP elections and what circumstances discourage them?

An expanding literature is dedicated to European political participation and electoral research, with an impressive range of propositions aimed at answering these questions (see, among others, Reif and Schmitt 1980; van der Eijk and Franklin 1996; Marsh 1998; Sinnott 1999; Schmitter 2000; Rose 2004; Schmitt

2005; Hix and Marsh 2007; Wessels 2005; Manow 2006; Wessels 2007; de Vreese et al. 2007; Franklin 2007; Marsh et al. 2007; Rohrschneider and Clark 2007; Hix 2008; Hobolt et al. 2008; van der Eijk and Schmitt 2008; Hix and Marsh 2011; Söderlund et al. 2011; Bhatti and Hansen 2012; Walczak et al. 2012). The aim of the present chapter is to contribute to this developing research field by exploring the patterns, motives and conditions that explain citizen voting in European Parliament elections (EE). For this purpose, a triple comparative perspective is adopted: first, we compare EE turnout to national electoral participation patterns, thus mapping for the EU-27 cross-national variation of turnout gaps. Second, we establish trends over time, by comparing European and national electoral turnout patterns from 1999 to 2009, that is, before and after Eastern enlargement. Third, we compare the motives and conditions for electoral turnout of citizens from old member states to those from the new member states, from a macro-, meso-, and micro-level perspective.

We highlight in particular the impact of political parties which have up to now received very little attention in relation to citizen electoral participation. This is especially striking since developments in party strategies, electoral outcomes, and party-voter alignments both in old member states as well as in post-communist societies have received much attention in the literature (see for example, Evans and Whitefield 2000; Walczak et al. 2012). By linking these three elements we supplement a recent study by Hix and Marsh (2011) who similarly focus on political parties and party families but neither link them to individual voting behaviour, that is the micro-level, nor explore differences between old and new member states, that is the macro-level.

Anticipating our argument in a nutshell, we expect that over the decade 1999-2009 EE turnout has been shaped by contradictory influences from the macro-, meso- and micro-level: First, at the macro-level, Eastern enlargement has brought ten new member states into the EU, among them eight post-communist, still unconsolidated democratic regimes characterised by weak popular predispositions to participate in national elections; thus, enlargement could be expected to negatively impact EE turnout. Then, at the meso-level, through the introduction of the Euro and subsequently European treaty reform, contestations against deepening European integration have helped politicise the EU, affecting the national mass media, political parties and citizens; this should have positive effects for EE participation. Finally, at the micro-level, processes of generational change and social and cultural modernisation have also impacted citizens' cognitive predispositions, values and subjective identity constructions, enhancing de-alignment from conventional mass membership parties (thus decreasing electoral turnout), but also promoting "new citizens" politics' by voter mobilisation and realignment through new and smaller parties.

As a result, overall European election turnout has dropped, even though European elections arguably have become less "second-order national elections" and more genuine elections, as we will demonstrate. Moreover, gaps between national and European levels of electoral participation have diminished, while convergence between old and new member states has increased. Our most important finding is that albeit electoral outcomes and party programs are still more in flux in the new than in the old member states they are slowly converging towards party family alliances, with shared characteristics.

The chapter is structured as follows: Section two reviews the state of the art on European integration in general and EE in particular with the aim of identifying propositions that explain citizen participation, or lack of it, in European elections. In section three, we present the data and methods on which we base our comparative, including statistical, analyses of macro-, meso- and micro-level data, with a focus on the meso-level. The fourth section presents our empirical findings, then interprets and discusses them, followed by the conclusions.

Explaining Citizen Turnout in European Elections

We start with the classic proposition that citizens conceive of European elections as second-order national elections, and, then, in the second step, address arguments for the claim that citizens perceive of EE as genuine elections in their own right. In the third step, empirical hypotheses about the conditions for each of these contrasting preconceptions are developed, distinguishing micro-, meso- and meso-level explanatory factors, with a particular focus on the latter, namely, political parties.

European Elections as "Second-order National Elections"

In all EU member states, electoral participation in EE is historically lower than in national parliamentary elections (van der Eijk and Franklin 1996: 149). Many researchers interpret this fact as a consequence of the "second-order nature" of European elections where allegedly less is at stake than in (primary) national elections (Reif and Schmitt 1980; Schmitt 2005; Axt 2006). In this terminology, EE are second-order because they are subordinate (or secondary) to national elections, in several respects: a) In EE, allegedly, there is "less at stake", for instance the EP has not enough powers to effectively influence EU decision-making, or its role is perceived to be weak (Schmitt 2005); b) EE constitute a new, cross-national "specific arena" with a complicated system of party coalitions, on which the level of information is low, making it difficult for the voter to choose between parties and assess the impact – or effectiveness – of their vote; c) electoral procedures differ between national elections and EE, adding to the difficulty of choices among parties and the perception of consequences of the vote; d) while media communication about EE is weaker, party campaigns are crucial, but their effects short-lived; e) political changes in the European arena are perceived by voters as less important than national, that is "main arena political changes"; and f) as a consequence of social and cultural changes trends towards de-alignment weaken party political affiliations at the European more than at the national level (Reif and Schmitt 1980; Schmitt 2005).

Van der Eijk and Franklin drew a sceptical conclusion, as regards the empirical validity of the "second-order model" of EE: "In general it can be said that our attempts to understand turnout in European elections on the basis of our prior understanding of turnout in national elections has not yielded very much. The question should be turned around: what European elections can teach us about the determinants of turnout?" (van der Eijk and Franklin 1996: 153) Before we turn to these determinants, we will briefly review arguments supporting the preconception of EE as genuine elections in their own right that citizens perceive as distinct from national ones.

Genuine European Elections

In a comparative perspective (Rittberger 2006), variation in turnout rates has increased; a fact that is partly due to the enlargement(s) from the EU-15 to the new EU-27. This increase holds even after controlling for those member states with compulsory voting, such as Belgium and Luxemburg. Average turnout rates have varied considerably over time and across EU member states (see Annex Table 7.1). Moreover, electoral participation in European elections is lower than in first-order national elections (parliament elections). Despite these relatively well-known facts not very much is known about the exact patterns of variations and dynamics.

Changes in electoral choice among different elections are described as vote switching (Marsh 2007). These shifts can be due to shifts in the policy arena from the national level to the EU. Moreover, they can be motivated by two reasons. On the one hand, in line with the second-order thesis, vote switches may be provoked by national concerns, for example, the intention to punish a national government. On the other hand, citizens may also switch their vote depending on genuine European considerations, that is, if they base their decision on party policy positions on European matters (Marsh 2007; Carruba and Timpone 2005).

Both elections belong to one political system and are connected to each other, voting behaviour in one arena can influence (affect) decisions in other elections; the first-order arena affects electoral behaviour in second-order national elections. Among the main explanations for the relatively lower turnout in EE was that European issues had lesser resonance with nationally minded publics to whom the consequences of election results for policy-making in the EC/EU were hard to discern (van der Eijk and Franklin 1996).

However, even within this general tendency of lower turnout in EE it is unlikely that the same tendency will similarly apply to partisans of all political parties: some parties may be more successful in mobilising their supporters than others, for example because they better explain the importance of the EU or because they are able to convince their supporters that (further or less) European integration is beneficial. Likewise, some parties may more efficiently address and channel national protest and dissatisfaction with either the national government or European integration or both. As a consequence some parties will generally improve their vote share in EE compared to national elections while others will lose votes.

In sum, to explain citizens' voting behaviour – differentiated by electoral participation rates and electoral choices – two main theoretical conceptions can be distinguished in empirical election studies. These theoretical accounts of electoral participation can be further differentiated depending on the level which they emphasise: macro-level electoral or institutional system characteristics; meso-level agents such as political parties and the mass media; or micro level conditions for individual citizen choice. The following paragraphs describe these three levels of analysis in more detail. The aim is to develop testable research hypotheses on the conditions that explain which of the two – "second-order national" or "genuine European" elections – models citizens and intermediary agents adopt when engaging with EE, either in relation to the macro-level (old vs. new member states), the meso-level (parties or party families), or to micro-level individual attitudes.

Hypothesising Macro-level Effects on Citizen EE Turnout

To explain why citizens turn out and how they vote in EE, the macro-institutional context certainly matters: since citizens do not live in a vacuum and their political choices are not singular acts, their casting of a vote or failure to do can be explained to a certain extent by macro level factors that are specific to member states. More specifically, we may expect that across EU member states, electoral turnout will vary and lead to different patterns of voting behaviour, depending on a range of legal, institutional, and cultural characteristics, including length of membership in the EU. We hypothesise that citizens from older member states will be more knowledgeable about advantages and disadvantages of European integration and thus will be more likely to view EE as genuine elections than citizens from the newer member states. Citizens from more recent member states will lack these experience(s) and knowledge resources and therefore will be more likely to treat EE as second-order national elections. However over time they will catch up with their southern and western counterparts, which will likely result in a convergence of turnout gaps between old and new member states.

Hypothesising Meso-level Effects on Citizen EE Turnout

For present purposes we treat political parties as the most relevant actors on the meso-level that will be covered extensively in the following analyses. However, previous research also demonstrated the relevance of other actors on this level, for example, the mass communication media. For example, in a comparative analysis de Vreese and his colleagues demonstrated that during the European elections in 1999 and 2004 European issues were salient in the media, with differences between old and new member states regarding whether and to what extent the EU gained face and voice during EE campaigns (de Vreese et al. 2005; de Vreese et al. 2007). The mass media stimulate complex learning processes in which political preferences are framed for articulation on the day of the election. Conventionally, citizens' attitudes towards the EU and EE have been shaped by mass media based information and communication along national lines. Accordingly, a longitudinal study of the transnationalisation and Europeanisation of public spheres covering the period 1982–2005 has confirmed for five European countries – Austria, Denmark, France, Germany and the United Kingdom – the nationally segmented character of Europeanisation in the media (Wessler et al. 2008). Yet, contentious national debates about Constitutional Treaty ratification in France and The Netherlands have fostered transnational discursive interactions among the mass media of old and new member states, indicating the emergence of shared models of political conflict on European integration (Liebert et al. 2007: 243ff).

In this chapter we will not further elaborate on the effects of the mass media on European elections but focus on political parties instead. Political parties are very important agents in the intermediate spheres between citizens, national and European level elections. They have been objects of European comparative elections studies, for example, by van der Brug and van der Eijk (2005) comparing party strategies, programmes and communication. Bernhard Wessels showed that political parties, their candidates and European officials were responsible for the low turnout at the last European elections, because they did not effectively mobilise citizens to actively participate (Wessels 2007). Additionally, Hix concluded: "European Parliament elections are also not really about EU office holders or EU policy issues, because national parties and national media treat these elections as mid-term contest in the national electoral cycle" (Hix 2008: 70).

An important division in the analysis of electoral studies, public opinion, and political parties is their location along a left-right axis. Firstly, voter preferences with respect to the operation of market forces differ, with some voters being strongly in favour of (massive) economic redistribution by the state while others strictly oppose state redistribution and prefer to leave the distribution of economic resources to market forces alone. In addition, national party systems can likewise be organised along this axis with socialist parties on the left hand who favour economic redistribution by the state and conservative parties on the right hand opposing this (Lipset and Rokkan 1967). Since the party identification of voters and their political left-right identification correlate with party ideologies it is therefore possible to position voter attitudes along the same axis.

Consequently, placement on the left-right axis serves as a common distinction in both theoretical and empirical comparative electoral studies. For example, Marsh, Mikhaylov and Schmitt (2007: 7) conclude "that there is a sizeable effect of left-right orientations on EP vote choices, particularly in party systems with low effective threshold for new parties to enter; where the left-right and the pro-/anti-integration dimension of party competition are correlated; and where there is high perceptual agreement in the electorate on where the parties stand in terms of left and right". In addition to the classic left-right division, the "GAL/TAN axis" was included (Hooghe et al. 2004: 121 ff) in order to properly place political parties according to their ideological predispositions regarding political integration in the EU. This new dimension is conceived as ranging from "GAL", that is green/alternative/libertarian, to "TAN", or traditional/authoritarian/nationalist. It "is an ideological axis that displays a simple, linear relationship in support for EU integration" (Crum 2007).Thus, attitudes of voters and parties are displayed in a two-dimensional space, sometimes called the "Hooghe-Marks model" of regulated capitalism vs. neoliberalism (Marks and Steenbergen 2004: 5ff.), as well as a "new politics dimension". In the present analysis, we use party positions on the two important dimensions mentioned above, the left-right placement and placement on the GAL-TAN axis, to infer voter positions.

Hypothesising Micro-level Effects on Citizen EE Turnout

Empirically testable explanatory approaches to citizen electoral participation and choice on the micro-level include classic theories such as rational choice theory, the sociological approach, and the socio-psychological model (Aldrich 1993). Regarding multilayered systems of representation, Rohrschneider and Clark argue that individual motivations can be explained by the "transfer hypothesis". This means that individuals apply their evaluations of national-level phenomena to the EU level when voting in EE (Rohrschneider and Clark 2008: 132). Thus, in accordance with the second-order model of EE, citizens will be primarily attached to national politics so that their European attitudes and behaviour depend on evaluations of the political process in the national arena, for instance regarding government and party performance. However, as early as the 1994 EE, Richard Sinnott found evidence against the second-order model: "The problem is that this plausible model receives little or no support when tested against the evidence of voter perceptions, attitude and behaviour" (Sinnott 1999: 66–67). Analysing turnout in the 1994 EE, he found that "attitudes to and perceptions and experiences of Europe and of the European Parliament make a difference to people's participation" (Sinnott 1999: 70). This again underlines the tension between voter perceptions of EE as second-order elections and EE as a political contest *sui generis*.

A large range of micro-level attitudes and perceptions can be singled out as correlates of electoral turnout. For instance the view that EU membership is a good thing or that the process of the EU unification "should be pushed further" indicate individual "diffuse support" for the EU political system; as they concern the entire integration process, they should be positively related to turnout in EE. Individuals who think that they themselves or their country, or both, have benefited from EU membership or from further European integration should also be expected to be more active in the electoral process as a form of taking part in the European polity. We expect these variables to influence turnout positively. Trust in European institutions can be interpreted as an indicator of support for the European political system and likewise should have a positive effect on electoral participation. Political interest helps to explain to what extent voters are involved in political life, and how much attention they give to European political issues. European election campaigns aim at mobilising political interests as a precondition for turnout. "There is indeed strong evidence that political interest is closely associated with turnout. The more interested one is the more likely one is to vote" (Blais 2007: 631). Therefore, political interest in European election campaigns indicates a certain degree of electoral involvement and thus should be expected to positively affect electoral participation.

The variable "European identity" measures another aspect of general support for the European political system and should positively influence individual participation in EE. By comparison, "national identity" should have a positive effect on electoral participation in national elections, as it can be understood as an expression of national identification with the domestic political system, specific policies and political actors. "Satisfaction with democracy" expresses an individual's evaluation of democratic principles, norms and practices in a given system. Since electoral participation is one of the crucial preconditions of democracy, satisfaction with the latter should be positively correlated with electoral turnout.

Case Selection, Data and Methods

Regarding case selection, we include all EU member states in the analysis of EE turnout in the three subsequent elections from 1999, 2004 and 2009. Yet, for establishing turnout gaps between EE and national elections and analysing variations by political parties, we focus on six countries, only – for the old member states France, Germany and the UK, and for the new member states the Czech Republic, Estonia, and Poland – as these six cases have been the focus of most chapters in this book.

In our empirical analyses we will first focus on the macro and meso-level and use the 2009 EES individual data set for testing effects at the micro-level. For space reasons we leave more systematic tests of the interactive effects between these three levels to future research and use the present analysis for testing a limited range of hypotheses about what motivates (or constrains) citizen voting behaviour in EE.

To answer this research question we use aggregate data from official statistics on turnout rates, vote shares of political parties in national and European elections and Chapel Hill expert surveys. We integrate the three approaches to voting behaviour on different levels: First, we investigate the "second vs. first order gap in turnout" and compare participatory rates and their trends for the six countries. Here, we distinguish between old and new member states (macro-level). Second, we compare multilevel turnout gaps and their respective trends, by calculating differences in vote shares between the national and the European level by political parties (meso-level). The third perspective links voter decisions for political parties to their political ideologies along the left-right axis as well as their attitudes to EU integration along the GAL-TAN axis (micro-level). For these ratings we rely on the Chapel Hill expert survey (Steenbergen and Marks 2007; Hooghe et al. 2010).

We analyze EE voting behaviour at these three levels for three years in which EE have been held, that is, 1999, 2004, and 2009. If European elections had become increasingly important in their own right – less "second-order national" effects and more "pan-European political swings" (Hix and Marsh 2011) towards genuine European elections – we expect the following trends indicating consolidation of a pan-European political space: first, less cross-national variation among old and new member states; second, less divergence in vote shares among political parties, and, third, a more clear-cut pattern of political party families' vote shares clustering across European political space, for instance along the left-right or the GAL-TAN axes (Marks and Steenbergen 2004).

For a strict test of the hypothesised effects on the micro-level we use individual level data from the European Parliament Electoral Study 2009 (2009 EES voter study) which were collected at the time of the 2009 European Parliament elections (4 to 7 June 2009) and include 1000 interviews from each EU member state (27096 citizens were interviewed in total).[1] To test our micro-level variables, our dependent variable is turnout (yes/no), while our independent variables are differentiated by socio-demographic and political items. The latter include diffuse "political support for the EU's political system", "trust in EU institutions", "political interest in European campaigns", the existence of a "national" or "European identity", and "satisfaction with democracy" at the national or European level, or both. Support for the EU political system is measured by individual "evaluations of EU membership" and "evaluation of EU-unification progress".

As socio-demographic control variables we include better education, older than 35, and being male as socio-demographic factors which should influence electoral participation positively.

Citizen Voting Patterns and Dynamics 1999–2009: Empirical Findings

We present our findings in three steps, starting with macro-level comparisons among old and new member states, then turning to meso-level variations at the level of party votes and concluding with micro-level analyses of attitudinal factors.

Cross-national Comparison of Turnout Gaps: Macro-level Findings

The last EE revealed "turnout gaps" not only between old and new member states but also within both member state groups, too. Compared to national election turnouts, gaps in European electoral participation varied (Annex Table 7.1.). For instance in Germany and the UK the turnout gap between national and European elections was largest, with about 30% more participation in national elections. The French turnout gap was smaller, but still national turnout was about 19% above the level of European turnout. In the group of new member states, the biggest gap could be observed between national and European turnout in the Czech Republic (about 36%), followed by Poland (29%) and Estonia, with a gap of about 17%.

---

[1] Information on the study can be find on the project website: www.piredeu.eu.

To answer the question concerning turnout gaps between national and European elections and whether and to what extent these diverge between old and new member states, Figures 7.1–7.3 use aggregate national level data for comparing turnout patterns in the EE of 1999, 2004 and 2009 and in national elections.[2] For the new member states (CZ – Czech Republic, EST – Estonia, PL – Poland) the analysis is evidently limited to the two post accession elections of 2004 and 2009. The three spots at the lower bottom in the scatter plot display the national turnout result before Europe's Eastern enlargement (CZ = 74%, EST = 57,7%, PL = 47,9). The diagonal line symbolises identical turnout rates between national and European elections. That is, in case of the absence of a first-order vs. second-order gap for all countries all elections would be placed on the diagonal. On the contrary, the further a turnout result (mapped as spots on the graph) is placed away from the diagonal the bigger the gap between the two electoral levels.

The space under the diagonal thus reflects the extent of the second-order nature of European elections compared to national elections. Likewise, albeit only theoretically,

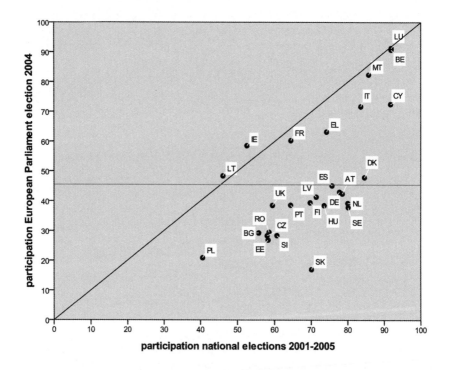

Figure 7.1   European and (preceding) national electoral turnout 2004, EU-27

---

2   For details concerning turnout results compare data in the Annex Table 7.1.

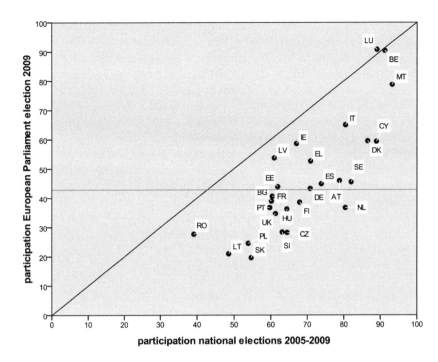

Figure 7.2　European and (preceding) national electoral turnout 2009, EU-27
Source: Official Statistics published by the European Parliament.

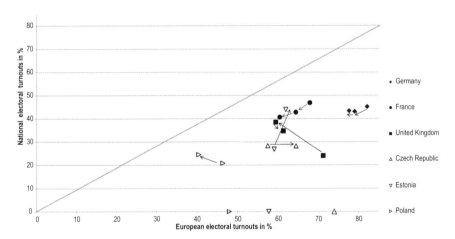

Figure 7.3　Changes in European and national electoral turnouts 1999–2004–2009 (CZ, Estonia, Poland, France, Germany, and UK)

the space above the diagonal indicates the strength of the first-order nature of European elections compared to national elections. Since several elections were held during the time span, several spots per country appear in the diagram. The respective trends for each county are displayed by arrows, that is if the second-order gap for a given country becomes less pronounced an arrow appears in the direction of the diagonal.

The results show that, unsurprisingly, turnout is lower in European elections in all six selected countries, supporting the notion of EE as second-order elections. By looking at the trends (arrows) the main finding is a wide fluctuation: for new member states Poland and Estonia the gap between national and European elections reduces while for the Czech Republic we observe relative stability. In old member states France and the United Kingdom the gap increased while in Germany a slight reduction occurred. Thus, (slightly) opposing trends appear for old and new member states. It should also be noted that these trends imply convergence between old and new member states since the turnout gaps were initially more pronounced for the latter.

Comparing Cross-party Variations: Meso-level Findings

The next question concerns the second vs. first order gap with respect to political parties: do parties lose in European elections, and if so, which? This more detailed analysis shows patterns of voting behaviour for party choices for European and national levels of representation. In total 38 national parties were included but the specific parties varied across elections. Figure 7.4 compares results for national and European level elections for all three points in time. The presentation follows the same logic as in Figures 7.1–7.3, that is, the diagonal represents identical vote shares for a specific party in both types of election, divergence from the diagonal implies either higher shares in EE (positive divergence) or higher shares in national elections (negative divergence). Compared to the figures previously, Figure 7.4 displays several parties located above the diagonal, indicating that these have benefited from European elections.

In the 1999 EE, small parties generally gained in EE compared to national elections, indicating that they more effectively mobilised their supporters. This may be an effect of the protest base of some of these parties which, due to the second-order nature of EE, makes it more likely for their supporters to vote in EE in order to voice their dissatisfaction with national matters or the national government. In the old member states, especially in Germany and the UK, large conservative parties gain similar support in EE and national elections (or fare even better in EE), while for social democratic parties there appear to be (sometimes huge) negative gaps. The only exceptions to this pattern appear to be the French UMP and the French social democrats. For the former there is a consistent huge negative gap, for the latter in the first two elections there is almost no gap and only in 2009 the PS displays the huge negative voting gap which is common for social democratic parties. The French and German Green parties do consistently better in EE than in national elections.

Notably, this result cannot be explained as a government/opposition effect since the German Greens were in office in both 1999 and 2004. The British

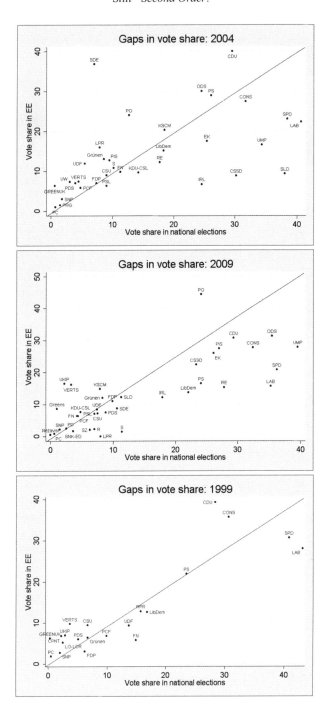

Figure 7.4 European/national gaps in party vote share 1999–2004–2009

regional parties SNP and CYMRU obtained similar results throughout the whole period. The extreme-right wing French Front National shows a clear trend towards normalisation. The second largest cluster includes four parties (UDF, RPR, LibDem), which obtained clearly better electoral results (11%–21%) at national than at European level.

The 2004 EE show clear second-order effects for all bigger parties in the new member states, the only exception being the Czech KSCM and ODS. For the major social-democratic parties SLD, CCSD, there are clear second-order effects. In general the area below the diagonal is more scattered for the second time point. Some parties (IRL, SLD) were still winners on the national level. Parties from the new member states by and large belong to this pattern, which is thus more complex, while the distances between electoral results on the two levels of representation are bigger. The Polish PO and Estonian SDE obtained clearly better results in EE.

The 2009 EE that took place five years after Eastern enlargement showed much lower cross-national and cross-party variation compared to 2004. This indicates convergence in two important aspects: first, between old and new member states, and second, between national and European elections. Moreover, in comparison to 2004, there is relative stability as to the respective party positions. That is, parties by and large occupy the same position in the graph as in 2004. This can be interpreted as a "normalisation": parties and voters to some extent have become accustomed to EU elections as an(other) election, albeit of slightly less importance than national elections. Still smaller parties are generally doing better in EE, indicating that for those parties there is a stable "European bonus". Again, we attribute that bonus to their ability to mobilise their electorate as a form of protest against the respective major parties.

Left-right Axis of Party Positions

We now link the above findings to party positions on the left-right and GAL-TAN axes and begin with the "classical" left-right axis. Figure 7.5 opposite should be read similarly to the previous ones: the horizontal line depicts identical results in national and European elections; the vertical depicts a neutral position on the left-right axis. Central positions in the diagram thus indicate political positions in the middle of the political spectrum and show similar results in national and European elections.

Analysis of Figure 7.5 for 1999 demonstrates that more conservative parties generally fared better in EE than their social-democratic counterparts. Likewise, green parties on average also performed better in EE. One explanation is that both conservative and green parties draw on more highly educated electorates that potentially benefit from European integration. The (French and German) liberal parties fare slightly worse in EE compared to national elections. On the whole, the pattern can best be described by an inverted U-shape where parties in the middle of the left-right axis display (sometimes huge) negative gaps while parties at the end of the axis display parity or even positive gaps. After accession the picture by and large repeats itself: the ends of the left-right continuum parties receive higher vote

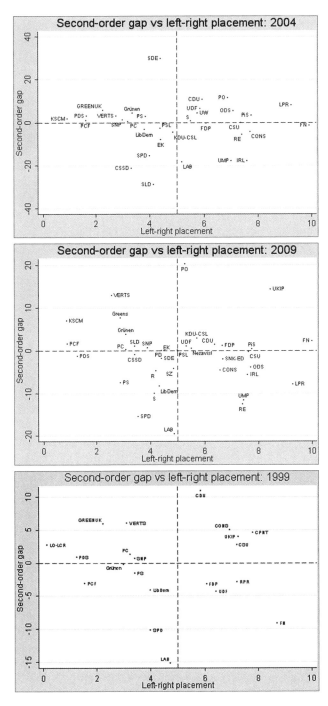

Figure 7.5 European/national vote gaps by parties' left-right placement 1999–2004–2009

shares in EE and (sometimes huge) negative gaps in the middle. Noteworthy in this respect is the swing from the extreme right-wing Front National from the party with the largest negative turnout gap to a party which actually does better in EE.

For the 1999 EE, the first cluster includes four parties with a clear pattern of being right wing and more successful at European than at national level (CONS, CSU, UKIP, CPNT). In contrast, the German CDU is placed more centre-right and obtained its best results in the 1999 EE. The second pattern of centre-left parties with balanced results between national elections and EE characterises three parties (SNP, CYMRU, PDS), while two parties – The Greens in France and the UK – were more successful in EE than in national elections. The French communist party (LO-LCR) is located strongest to the left with fairly good electoral results in EE. The third cluster comprises four parties with a shared pattern, of which three achieved almost equal turnout results (Die Grünen, LibDem, PS). The German SPD and the British LAB belonged to the losers, both of which had a more centrist political ideology. Finally, the fourth cluster includes three parties with a common pattern; with the French FN as an outlier. Summarising the 1999 EE results by party, their placement along the left-right axis of political ideologies shows that all four fields of the matrix are similarly populated.

Compared to 1999, the 2004 EE brought significant changes. Most importantly, a considerable number of parties moved from the margins to the centre, with few outliers (LPR, FN). Notably, the newcomers from the new member states contributed to strengthening the group of parties with more centrist orientation and more positive results in EE than national elections. Clusters two and three comprise the biggest share of parties from new and old member states characterised by relatively better or balanced results in EE and more or less leftist orientations. Cluster three features four EE losers with centrist political stances. Finally, cluster four shows a great deal more fluctuation and diversity among centre-right EE losers in 2004 than in 1999, as none of the parties from the old member states stayed in this pattern; the cluster was newly composed.

The 2009 EE demonstrates continuation of these trends towards centrist positions. Compared to 2004 the left-right positioning of parties – captured through expert interviews in 2006 – shows both concentration and variation. All four fields include political parties with similar features close to the centre, with several outliers also present.

GAL-TAN Variation of Partisan Votes

In a similar fashion, Figure 7.6 displays the patterns and changes of partisan vote shares, although here clustered along the GAL-TAN axis. While the general pattern appears similar to that of the left-right axis – to some extent parties on the left may tend to be more inclined to the GAL position than parties on the political right – with some notable exceptions:

Compared to the left-right spectrum the positioning of the parties along the GAL-TAN axis does not yield much change regarding their performance in

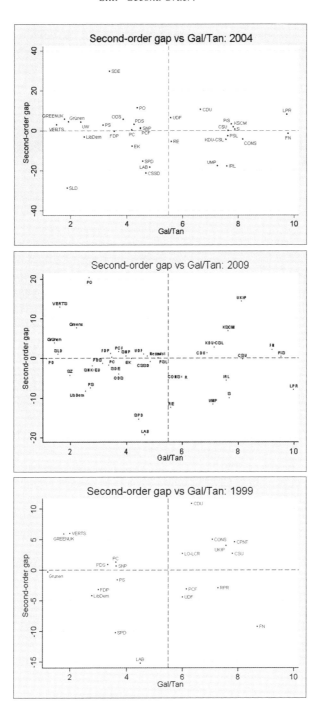

Figure 7.6 European/national vote gaps by parties' GAL-TAN position 1999–2004–2009

national elections and EE. Only a few parties changed their positions (LO-LCR, PDS). Compared to the left-right patterns of Figure 7.5, Figure 7.6 shows more concentrated patterns that are more polarised, too. If plotted along the GAL-TAN axis, parties similarly concentrate on the GAL part of the axis, while their positioning from the centre towards TAN is more varied.

Micro-level Effects: Findings from Micro-level Analyses

The individual-level analysis showed marked differences between the countries. Still, the following empirical analysis can only partly explain this variation, because macro-level variables as political system characteristics such as compulsory voting or the time of the election have a highly relevant impact on turnout but are not taken into account here.

In the following, we present the results of binary logistic regressions both simultaneously for all six countries under study as well as for all countries individually. We find very little evidence for age and gender to affect participation either simultaneous or individual analysis. The only exception was Estonia where turnout decreased with age. Similarly, education only affected turnout in Estonia and Poland, with more highly educated respondents more likely to vote in both cases. With all countries collapsed, higher education similarly (slightly) raised the voting probability. We thus find only weak evidence for socio-demographic variables affecting turnout in EE.

As to attitudinal items, identity item(s) strongly affected turnout: in the complete sample respondents describing themselves as having primarily a national identity were less likely to vote than respondents with a European identity. Thus, feeling "European" is associated with greater involvement in EE. However this result is mainly due to the strong effect of national identity on absenteeism in the UK. In all other countries, respondents with a national identity and a European identity were statistically indistinguishable. This effect is due to the large standard error associated with the respective estimates which resulted in non significant results, despite the quite pronounced positive and negative parameters. Respondents indicating that they either hold a national and European identity or a European and national identity showed similar turnout rates to respondents with a solely European identity. Noteworthy here is Germany where holding a national and European identity as opposed to a solely European identity significantly *raises* the probability of voting. Thus, the main effect of identity appears to be the absence of a primarily national identity. If an individual does not solely identify herself with the respective nation then she is more likely to vote irrespective of what the specific type of European identity is.

For the whole sample, the level of satisfaction with democracy in the respondents' own country did not affect turnout but the level of satisfaction with democracy in the EU did increase turnout. Turning to individual countries, we see that (again) most parameters do not reach significance. Here, the exceptions are France, where satisfaction with French democracy leads to lower turnout in EE, and Estonia, where satisfaction with democracy in the EU raised turnout. On the whole, respondents' satisfaction with democracy on the European level thus is more important for turnout.

Respondents' attitudes to the EU membership of their country were as expected strongly related to turnout. In comparison with those who evaluate EU membership neutrally ("neither good or bad"), in the whole sample those who evaluated their country's membership positively had a higher likelihood of voting in EE. Closer inspection reveals that this effect is mainly due to the strong effects of this variable in Germany and the Czech Republic. Those who evaluated their country's membership in the EU negatively were indistinguishable from those who were neutral. The only exception here was Poland where respondents with a negative attitude towards EU membership had a much *higher* propensity to vote (potentially for euro-sceptic parties). This may indicate that referendums concerning European integration are seen as opportunities to voice dissatisfaction but elections for the EP are not and consequently are more strongly influenced by whether a respondent feels positive about the EU.

Trust in the EU had no effect on turnout either for the whole sample or for individual countries. Contrary to expectations, approving further EU integration was associated with a *lower* likelihood of voting. However, in the analysis of individual countries, this result is significant only for Great Britain. Interest in the election campaign strongly raised the probability of voting in all countries as well as in all countries individually.

Considering both national and European elections to be important resulted in a stronger propensity to vote with slightly stronger effects for the importance of EE. Perhaps the most interesting result here is the discrepancy between the two parameters in France: while (as in many other countries) considering EE to be important is associated with a higher propensity to vote, (unlike other countries) considering national elections to be important is absolutely unrelated to turnout. So, while for the other countries there appears to be an underlying tendency to view national and European elections either as important or unimportant and accordingly either to vote or not to vote, in France the electorate appears to view these two elections as different entities. Finally, the two variables controlling for respondents' perception of national and European parliamentarians' interest in citizens had very little effect on turnout.

Turning to differences between old and new member states, that is, comparing model fit across countries, reveals that the variables chosen appear to be more important for the new than for the old member states (higher levels of explained variance and more parameters were significant). More specifically, socio-demographic variables had a stronger impact in the new member states while attitudinal items had a stronger impact in the old member states. This may indicate that in the new member states turnout is more strongly influenced by the classic lines of conflict while in the old member states these conflicts have to some extent been replaced by new attitudinal divisions.

Summary and Conclusions

The ultimate question whether or not the pattern of citizens' EE politics that we have identified indicates a long-term trend towards "first-order European elections" and, moreover, towards re-alignment of parties and partisan votes in a transnational European political space, requires additional analyses that are beyond the scope of this chapter. With these limitations, the present analysis seeks to shed light on the complex causal pattern behind the paradoxical trend that European election turnout has decreased over time albeit during the same period the European Parliament has steadily enhanced its powers and symbolic centrality in the EU's would-be democratic polity. For that purpose, we qualify the classic account for the turnout gap in European (compared to national) elections – that is, the "second-order election" thesis. We admit that in European more than in domestic votes the structuring effect of long term predictors of the vote (social class, religion, gender, and left-right party identification) has weakened, while short term factors (such as "less at stake" perceptions, lack of information and communication, weak party campaigns, or evaluation of national government performance) have taken centre stage for explaining turnout gaps. Yet, we claim that this account is not sufficient to differentiate the European constituency primarily along national lines – that is by member states. Our findings suggest that Europeans' electoral behaviour is more complex, and that transnational patterns of electoral participation can be identified, where positive turnout can be explained in terms of a "new style of citizen politics" (Dalton 2007) that has emerged in EE.

The major result from the qualitative-quantitative analysis of the conditions for European electoral turnout presented here can be summarised by the following points:

1. The "second-order national election" thesis holds for EE only for explaining turnout at the macro, that is country, level. With analysis of the vote shares for several national parties the picture changed. Different patterns of electoral decision are visible, including parties, mainly smaller ones, that receive higher vote shares in EE. This holds for both old and new member states.
2. The picture of the second vs. first-order gap on the two levels of representation is not constant, but it changes over time and space. Moreover, it indicates a trend towards more stable patterns, thus providing some evidence for a normalisation of European elections with stable patterns. This could be an indication of a process of transformation between the levels. How strongly the national level influences electoral decisions for the European level still remains open and should be investigated in electoral studies based on individual data surveys.
3. Changes are present between the new and old member states; turnout varies between different party groups and depends on their ideological orientation and on attitudes to European integration.

In sum, both election models ("second-order national" and "genuine European elections") only partly fit our empirical evidence. Both capture different combinations of individual, meso- and macro-level characteristics leading to positive or, alternatively, to negative voting behaviour outcomes. To ultimately test these models, we therefore suggest integrating macro-, meso– and micro level analyses of citizen turnout patterns in EE. Here explanations should be based on the lines explored in this book. That is, the individual characteristics should comprise cognitive preconditions, namely political interest, political information about the EU; perceptions of and trust in the EP; political efficacy, and normative democratic expectations towards the EU, controlled by sociodemographic factors. The meso-level should include party and media systems while the macro-institutional conditions should cover length of EU membership.

Annex

Table 7.1   European election turnout in EU-27, 1979–2009

The last column of Table 7.1 lists the percentage differences between the European elections of 2004 (25 member states) and the European elections of 2009 (27 member states), referring to substantial variations in turnout trends.

Country	1979	1981	1984	1987	1989	1994	1995	1996	1999	2004	2007	2009	Diff
GER	65.73		56.76		62.28	60.02			45.19	43.00		43.27	0.27
FR	60.71		56.72		48.80	52.71			46.76	42.76		40.63	-2.13
BE	91.36		92.09		90.73	90.66			91.05	90.81		90.39	-0.42
IT	85.65		82.47		81.07	73.6			69.76	71.72		65.05	-6.67
LUX	88.91		88.79		87.39	88.55			87.27	91.35		90.76	-0.59
NL	88.91		50.88		47.48	35.69			30.02	39.26		36.75	-2.51
UK	32.35		32.57		36.37	36.43			24.00	38.52		34.70	-3.82
IE	63.61		47.56		68.28	43.98			50.21	58.58		58.64	.06
DK	47.82		52.38		46.17	52.92			50.46	47.89		59.54	11.65
EL		81.48	80.59		80.03	73.18			70.25	63.22		52.61	-10.61
ES				68.52	54.71	59.14			63.05	45.14		44.87	-0.27
PT				72.42	51.1	35.54			39.93	38.60		36.77	-1.83
SE							41.63		38.84	37.85		45.53	7.68
AT									49.40	42.43		45.97	3.54
FI								67.73	30.14	39.43		38.60	-0.38
CZ								57.60		28.30		28.22	-.08
EE										26.83		43.90	17.07
CY										72.50		59.40	-13.10
LV										41.34		57.70	12.36
LT										48.38		20.98	-27.40
HU										38.50		36.31	-2.19
MT										82.39		78.79	-3.60
PL										20.87		24.53	3.66
SI										28.35		28.37	0.02
SK										16.97		19.64	2.67
RO											29.47	27.67	-1.80
BG											29.22	38.99	9.77
EU	61.99		58.98		58.41	56.67			49.51	45.47		42.97	-2.5*

Diff displays the difference 2009–2004 or 2007 respectively

Table 7.2 European and national election turnout in six EU member states 1999–2004–2009 (in percentage)

Member States	National election	EU 15/1999	National election	EU 25/2004	National election	EU 27/2009
GER	82.2	45.2	79.1	43.0	77.7	43.2
FR	67.9	46.8	64.4	42.7	60.4	40.6
UK	71.2	24.0	59.4	38.9	61.4	34.7
CZ	74.0		58.0	28.4	64.4	28.2
EST	57.7		58.2	26.8	61.9	43.9
PL	47.9		46.3	20.8	40.5	24.5
Average EU		49.51		45.5		43.0

Source: European Parliament (2009), national election results from the respective national election preceding the respective EE.

Table 7.3 Multivariate analyses of turnout determinants in European elections (logits, main effects, s.e. within brackets)

	All countries		UK		Germany		France		Czech Republic		Poland		Estonia	
Constant	3.54 (.44)	***	4.42 (1.12)	***	3.92 (.99)	***	3.73 (1.26)	**	4.01 (1.77)	*	#		45.8 (13.2)	***
Age	.00 (.00)		-.00 (.00)		-.00 (.000)		-.00 (.00)		-.00 (.001)		-.00 (.00)		-.02 (.01)	**
Age finished education	.03 (.01)	**	.02 (.03)		.04 (.03)		-.02 (.02)		-.003 (.03)		.09 (.04)	*	.13 (.04)	***
Gender (ref. category: males)	-.03 (.07)		-.30 (.17)		-.03 (.19)		.018 (.18)		.09 (.20)		-.23 (.24)		.15 (.21)	
EU membership is good	.36 (.09)	***	-.13 (.23)		.65 (.23)	**	-.15 (.23)		.90 (.25)	***	.49 (.30)		.17 (.26)	
EU membership is bad (ref category: Neither)	.08 (.13)		.05 (.23)		-.006 (.34)		.26 (.32)		-.10 (.31)		1.50 (.55)	**	.24 (.55)	
Trust in the EU	-.05 (.04)		.07 (.09)		-.13 (.11)		-.17 (.10)		-.09 (.14)		-.02 (.15)		-.23 (.15)	
Further EU integration	-.05 (.01)	***	-.07 (.04)	*	-.002 (.04)		.03 (.03)		-.06 (.04)		-.09 (.05)		.03 (.04)	
Little interest in election campaign	-.85 (.05)	***	-.85 (.10)	***	-.83 (.13)	***	-.78 (.11)	***	-1.30 (.14)	***	-1.00 (.05)	***	-.47 (.12)	***
Disagree: parliament interested in EU citizens	.06 (.04)		.01 (.09)		.06 (.11)		.08 (.09)		.26 (.12)	*	-.07 (.15)		.26 (.14)	
Disagree: parliament interested in country citizens	-.001 (.04)		.09 (.07)		-.07 (.10)		-.042 (.79)		.035 (.10)		-.11 (.12)		.28 (.10)	**
Disagree: EU election important	-.25 (.04)	***	-.17 (.07)	*	-.17 (.09)	*	-.24 (.09)	**	-.20 (.11)		-.64 (.14)	***	-.19 (.11)	
Disagree: national election important	-.20 (.04)	***	-.23 (.08)	**	-.12 (.09)		.016 (.08)		-.52 (.10)	***	-.40 (.13)	**	-.24 (.11)	*
Identity:														
National identity	-.52 (.22)	*	-1.73 (.66)	**	.69 (.38)		-.34 (.48)		.52 (.85)		#		-.60 (.76)	
National and European/European and national	-.008 (.22)		-1.14 (.67)		.81 (.36)	*	.37 (.46)		.36 (.85)		#		-.48 (.76)	
Ref: European identity	-.08 (.26)		-1.40 (.79)		.41 (.44)		-.025 (.53)		.65 (.96)		#		.075 (.88)	
Satisfaction with Democracy in country	-.07 (.57)		-.18 (.12)		-.20 (.15)		-.29 (.15)	*	-.001 (.17)		.023 (.21)		.23 (.17)	
Satisfaction with democracy in EU	.12 (.06)	*	.05 (.13)		-.08 (.16)		.29 (.16)		.04 (.19)		.08 (.23)		.46 (.20)	*
Pseudo R² (Nagelkerke)	.286		.298		.256		.219		.430		.528		.243	
G² (17 df)	950.73	***	190.17	***	153.92	***	119.386	***	253.61	***	274.40	***	103.39	***
N	4205		780		812		726		664		616		582	

Note: * p < .05, ** p < .01, *** p < .001, coding: voted 1, did not vote 0; European Election Study 2009, own calculations.

Table 7.4   List of political parties (abbreviations)

Germany (GER)

SPD	Sozialdemokratische Partei Deutschlands (Social Democratic Party)
CDU	Christlich Demoktaische Union Dutschlands (Christian Democratic Union)
CSU	Christlich-Soziale Union in Bayern (Christian Social Union)
FDP	Freie Demokratische Partei (Free Democratic Party)
PDS	Die Linke (Left Party)
Grünen/Bündnis 90/	(Greens)

France (FR)

RPR	Rassemblement pour la République
UDF	Union pour la Démocratie Française (Union for French Democracy)
PS	Parti Socialiste (Socialist Party)
UMP	Union pour la Majorité Présidentielle (Union for the Presidential Majority)
FN	Front National (National Front)
PCF	Parti Communiste Français (French Communist Party), 2009 FDG (Front de Gauche)
Verts	Les Verts (The Greens)

United Kingdom (UK)

Lab	Labour
C	Conservative
L Dem	Liberal Democrat

Czech Republic (CZ)

CSSD	Ceská Strana Sociálne Demokratická (Czech Social Democratic Party)
KDU-CSL	Krestanská a Demokratická Unie – Ceskoslovenská Strana Lidová (Christian and Democratic Union – Czechoslovak People's Party)
KSCM	Komunistická Strana Cech a Moravy (Czech and Moravian Communist Party)
ODS	Obcanska Demokraticka Strana (Civic Democratic Party)
SZ	Strana Zelených (Green Party)
USDEU	Freedom Union–Democratic Union (Czech: Unie Svobody–Demokratická unie, US–DEU)
Democrats	(Czech: SNK Evropští demokraté Suveren)

Estonia (EST)

SDE	Sotsiaaldemokraatlik Erakond (Social Democratic Party)
EK	Eesti Keskerakond (Estonian Centre Party)
EME	Eesti Maarahva Erakond (Estonian Country People's Party; then R)
IL	Isamaaliit (Fatherland Union / Homeland Alliance / Pro Patria Union, than RP)
M	Moodukad (Moderates, than SDE)
RE	Eesti Reformierakond (Estonian Reform Party)
EURP	Eestimaa Uhendatud Rahvapartei (Estonian United People's Party)
KE	Eesti Koonderakond (Estonian Coalition Party)
RP	Erakond Res Publica (Union for the Republic) – Res Publica IRL
Greens	Erakond Eestimaa Rohelised)
R	Rahvaliit (Estonian People's Union)
IRL	Union of Pro Patria and Res Publica (Isamaa ja Res Publica Liit)

Poland (PL)

AWS	Akcja Wyborcza Solidarnosc (Solidarity Election Action – Catholic nationalist)
SLD	Sojusz Lewicy Demokratycznej (Democratic Left Alliance ex-Communist)
UW	Unia Wolnosci (Freedom Union – free-market liberal), 2005: PD Partia Demokratyczna (Democratic Party)
ROP	Ruch Odbudowy Polski (Movement for the Reconstruction of Poland – nationalist)
PSL	Polskie Stronnictwo Ludowe (Polish Peasant Party – anti-reform rural)
UP	Unia Pracy (Labour Union)
PO	Platforma Obywatelska (Citizens' Platform)
PiS	Prawo i Sprawieliwosc (Law and Justice)
SO	SamoObrona (Self-Defence)
LPR	Liga Polskich Rodzin (League of Polish Families)
SdPl	Socjaldemokracja Polska (Social Democracy of Poland)
LiD	Lewica i Demokraci (Left and Democrats) (SLD, UP, PD) until 2008
SLD-UP	Sojusz Lewicy Demokratycznej-Unia Pracy (Democratic Left Alliance-Labor Union)

References

Agné, H. 1999. To share democratic legitimacy between different political levels, in *Citizen Participation in European Politics*, edited by The Swedish Commission on Democracy, Stockholm: Statens Offentliga Utredningar, 117–136.

Aldrich, J.H. 1993. Rational choice in turnout. *American Journal of Political Science*, 37(1), 246–278.

Axt, H.-J. 2006. Wahlen zum Europäischen Parlament: Trotz Europäisierungstendenzen noch immer nationale Sekundärwahlen, in *Wahlsysteme und Wahltypen. Politische Systeme und regionale Kontexte im Vergleich*, edited by C. Derichs and T. Heberer, Wiesbaden: VS Verlag für Sozialwissenschaften.

Bhatti, Y. and Hansen, K. 2012. The effect of generation and age on turnout to the European Parliament – How turnout will continue to decline in the future. *Electoral Studies*, 31(2), 262–272.

Blais, A. 2007. Turnout in elections, in *The Oxford Handbook of Political Behavior*, edited by J. Dalton and H.D. Klingemann, Oxford: Oxford University Press, 621–633.

Blondel, J., Sinnott, R. and Svensson, P. 1998. *People and Parliament in the European Union. Participation, Democracy, and Legitimacy*. Oxford: Clarendon Press.

Blumler, J.G. and Fox, A. 1980. The involvement of voters in the European elections of 1979: its extent and sources. *European Journal of Political Research*, 8(1980), 359–385.

Carrubba, C. and Timpone, R.J. 2005. Explaining vote switching across first- and second-order elections. Evidence from Europe. *Comparative Political Studies*, 38(3), 260–281.

Crum, B. 2007. Party stances in the referendums on the EU constitution: causes and consequences of competition and collusion. *European Union Politics*, 8(1), 61–82.

Dalton, R.J. 2004. *Democratic Challenges Democratic Choices. The Erosion of Political Support in Advanced Industrial Democracies*. New York: Oxford University Press Inc.

Dalton, R.J. and Klingemann, H.-D. 2007. *The Oxford Handbook of Political Behavior*. Oxford University Press.

De Vreese, C.H., Banducci, S.A., Semetko, H.A. and Boomgaarden, H.G. 2007. The news coverage of the 2004 European parliamentary election campaign in 25 countries, in *European Elections after Eastern Enlargement. Preliminary Results from the European Election Study 2004*, edited by M. Marsh, S. Mikhaylov and H. Schmitt. Mannheim: CONNEX Report Series No 01.

European Parliament 2009. *Public Opinion Review. European Elections 1979–2009*. Public Opinion Monitoring Unit, Special Edition.

Evans, G. and Whitefield, S. 2000. Explaining the formation of electoral cleavages in post-communist democracies, in *Elections in Central and Eastern Europe. The First Wave*, edited by H.D. Klingemann, E. Mochmann and K. Newton, Berlin: Edition Sigma, 36–68.

Franklin, M.N. 2007. Turning out or turning off? How the EP elections of 2004 shed light on turnout dynamics, in *European Elections after Eastern Enlargement. Preliminary Results from the European Election Study 2004*, edited by M. Mikhaylov and H. Schmitt, CONNEX Report Series No 01, 53–70.

Hix, S. and Marsh, M. 2007. Punishment or Protest? Understanding European parliament elections. *The Journal of Politics*, 69(2), 495–510.

Hix, S. and Marsh, M. 2011. Second-order effects plus pan-European political swings: an analysis of European Parliament elections across time. *Electoral Studies*, 30(1), 4–15.

Hix, S. 2008. *What's wrong with the European Union and How to Fix It*. Cambridge: Polity Press.

Hobolt, S.B., Spoon, J.-J. and Tilley, J. 2008. A vote against Europe? Explaining defection at the 1999 and 2004 European Parliament elections. *British Journal of Political Science*, 39(1), 93–115.

Hooghe, L., Marks, G. and Wilson, C. 2004. Does left/right structure party positions on European integration? in *European Integration and Political Conflict*, edited by G. Marks and M. Steenbergen, Cambridge: Cambridge University Press.

Hooghe, L., Bakker, R., Brigevich, A., de Vries, C., Edwards, E., Marks, G., Rovny, J. and Steenbergen, M. 2010. Reliability and validity of measuring party positions: the Chapel Hill expert surveys of 2002 and 2006, *European Journal of Political Research*, (4), 684–703.

Liebert, U. 2007. Structuring political conflict about Europe: national media in transnational discourse analysis, in *Europe in Contention: Debating the Constitutional Treaty*. Special Issue, Perspectives on European Politics and Society, 8(3), 235–261.

Lipset, S. and Rokkan, S. 1967. *Party Systems and Voter Alignments*. New York: Free Press.

Manow, P. 2006. Elektorale Effekte negativer Integration? Die Europäische Gemeinschaft und die Europawahlen, 1979 bis 2004, in *Transformationen des Kapitalismus*, edited by J. Beckert, B. Ebbinghaus, A. Hassel and P. Manow, Frankfurt a.M.: Campus.

Marks, G. and Steenbergen, M. 2004. *European Integration and Political Conflict*. Cambridge: University Press.

Marsh, M. 1998. Testing the second-order election model after four European elections. *British Journal of Political Science*, 28(3), 591–607.

Marsh, M. 2007. Vote switching in European Parliament elections: evidence from June 2004, in *European Elections after Eastern Enlargement. Preliminary Results from the European Election Study 2004*, edited by M. Marsh, S. Mikhaylov and H. Schmitt. CONNEX Report Series No 01, 71–95.

Marsh, M., Mikhaylov, S. and Schmitt, H. 2007. *European Elections after Eastern Enlargement. Preliminary Results from the European Election Study 2004*. CONNEX Report Series No 01.

Moravcsik, A. 2002. Defence of the "democratic deficit": reassessing legitimacy in the European Union. *Journal of Common Market Studies*, 40(4), 603–24.

Reif, K. and Schmitt, H. 1980. Nine second-order national elections, a conceptual framework for the analysis of European election results. *European Journal of Political Research*, 8(1), 3–44.

Rohrschneider, R. and Clark, N. 2008. Second-order elections versus first-order thinking: how voters perceive the representation process in a multi-layered system of governance, in *The Multilevel Electoral System of the EU*, edited by C. van der Eijk and H. Schmitt. CONNEX REPORT SERIES, 4, 137–163.

Rose, R. 2004. *Europe Expands, Turnout Falls: the Significance of the 2004 European Parliament Election*. Stockholm: International Institute for Democracy and Electoral Assistance.

Schmitt, H. 2005. The European Parliament elections of June 2004: still second order? *West European Politics*, 28(3), 650–679.

Schmitt, H. and van der Eijk, C. 2005. Non-voting in European Parliament elections and support for European integration, in *European Elections and National Politics. Lessons from the Past and Scenarios for the Future*, edited by W. van der Brug and C. van der Eijk, Southbend: University of Notre Dame Press.

Sinnott, R. 1999. European Parliament elections. Institutions, attitudes and participation, in *Citizen Participation in European Politics*, edited by The Swedish Commission on Democracy, Stockholm: Statens Offentliga Utredningar, 57–74.

Söderlund, P., Wass, H. and Blais, A. 2011. The impact of motivational and contextual factors on turnout in first- and second-order elections. *Electoral Studies*, 30(4), 689–699.

Steenbergen, M. and Marks, G. 2007. Evaluating Expert Surveys. *European Journal of Political Research*, 46(3), 347–366.

TNS Opinion & Social 2008. *Eurobarometer 69: 1.Values of Europeans*. Survey requested and coordinated by the Directorate General Press and Communication (European Commission), Brussels, November 2008. Available at: http://ec.europa.eu/public_opinion/archives/eb/eb69/eb69_values_en.pdf [accessed: 30. 6. 2012].

TNS Opinion & Social 2008. *Standard Eurobarometer 69. Public Opinion in the European Union*. Survey requested and coordinated by the Directorate General Press and Communication (European Commission). Brussels, June 2008 (first results, data annex, national reports). Available at: http://ec.europa.eu/public_opinion/archives/eb/eb69/eb69_en.htm [accessed: 30. 6. 2012].

TNS Opinion & Social 2008. *Special Eurobarometer 299/Wave 69.2: The 2009 European Elections*. Survey requested by the European Parliament, Brussels, September 2008. Available at: http://ec.europa.eu/public_opinion/archives/ebs/ebs_299_en.pdf [accessed: 30. 6. 2012].

Van der Brug, W. and van der Eijk, C. 2005. *European Elections and National Politics. Lessons from the Past and Scenarios for the Future*. Indiana: University of Notre Dame Press.

Van der Eijk, C. 1999. Why some people vote and others do not, in *Citizen Participation in European Politics*, edited by The Swedish Commission on Democracy, Stockholm: Statens Offentliga Utredningar, 13–55.

Van der Eijk, C. and Franklin, M.N. 1996. What voters teach us about Europe-wide elections: what Europe-wide elections teach us about voters. *Electoral Studies*, 15, 149–166.

Walczak, A., van der Brug, W. and de Vries, C. 2012. Long- and short-term determinants of party preferences: inter-generational differences in Western and East Central Europe. *Electoral Studies*, 31(2), 273–284.

Wessels, B. 2005. Europawahlen, Wählermobilisierung und europäische Integration, in *Wahl-Kampf um Europa*, edited by J. Tenscher, Wiesbaden: VS Verlag für Sozialwissenschaften, 86–105.

Wessels, B. 2007. Mobilization and attitudes equals turnout – a simple equation? in *European Elections after Eastern Enlargement. Preliminary Results from the European Election Study 2004*, edited by M. Marsh, S. Mikhaylov and H. Schmitt, CONNEX Report Series No 01, 205–229.

Wessler, H., Peters, B., Brüggemann, M., Kleinen-von-Königslöw, K. and Sifft, S. 2008: *Transnationalization of Public Spheres*. Palgrave.

Index

Amsterdam Treaty 117, 122
Atlas.ti 8, 9, 92, 125, 142
    Atlas.ti based comparative discourse analysis 9
audit democracy 2

balance of interest 136, 138, 141–142, 150–152, 157
bottom-up 33, 88, 98, 117–118, 143, 158
    dynamics 50
    perspective 5, 6, 7
Bundestag 93, 100, 127–128, 151

case law 9, 26, 27, 31, 33–34, 42, 51
    as defining feature of multilevel European polity 25
citizens 1, 2–5, 7–9, 13–19, 23–29, 31–33, 38–40, 46–51, 61–63, 65–67, 69, 71, 75, 77, 83, 84–86, 87, 93, 96, 102–103, 118–119, 123, 129, 135, 139–140, 142–143, 146, 152–154, 156–158, 159, 165–166, 168–170, 183
    cross-border mobile 25
    migrant denizens 25
    non-national Union citizens 25, 31
    residents 26
    third country nationals 26
citizenship 1, 5, 14, 18, 19, 33, 39, 43
    beyond nationality and state territory 4
    equal basic rights 4
    European, *see* European citizenship
    inclusive membership 4
    of the Union, *see* European citizenship
Citizenship Directive 27, 29, 30, 32, 34
citizenship rights, *see* European Citizenship rights
Citizenship of the Union 27, *see also* European Citizenship

civil society 1, 2, 5, 7–8, 9, 13, 14, 16–18, 25, 135–144, 146–150, 152–154, 156–159
    civil society organisations 1, 2, 7, 9, 16 18, 139–159
    civil society practice 16, 136
    engagement with EU treaty reform 16
    European civil society 138–139, 149–150, 159
    formal and informal inclusion in policy-making 16
    mobilisation 7
    participation 5, 7, 165
Civil Society Contact Group 158
Common Security and Defence Policy 121–122, 126
communication, channels of 150, 153, 156–157, 159
Comparative Political Discourse Analysis (ComPDA) 5, 8, 9, 10–11, 142, 146
    for assessing transnational discursive exchanges 11
    combining qualitative and quantitative methods 13
    data sets from 11, 13–14
    four vital elements of 11
    mandating multi-linguistic research design 10, 13
    for mapping comparative meanings across different languages 13
    media as agents of 12
    as method for identifying patterns of political communication 12
    as variable for shaping agency 12
Constitutional Convention (Convention) 87–88, 110, 155
constitutional crisis, choice and change 13, 19
constitutional pluralism 24

Constitutional Treaty, *see* TCE
Constitutional Treaty ratification 6, 16–17, 76, 170
constraining dissensus 2
Convention on the Future of Europe 6
COSAC 122, 123
CSCG, *see* Civil Society Contact Group
cues 15, 62, 75, 78, 84, 86–88, 91–92, 95–103
Czech Republic 13, 22, 29, 34, 84, 91, 101, 115, 119, 124, 126, 142–148, 150–151, 153–155, 173–175

delegating national regulatory powers
  model of 3
deliberative-discursive approach 3
democracy 1, 2, 4, 7, 8, 13–14, 18, 37, 73–75, 81, 85, 117, 135, 139, 159, 172–173, 182–183, 187
  dual track 7
  empirical theory of 8
  federal multinational 2
  reconstitution of 2, 14
  regional-European 2
democratic autonomy 23
  national 23
democratic constitutionalism 3, 4, 9
  beyond the state 3, 2
  different models of 3, 9
  normative theoretical accounts of 4
democratic deficit 16, 18–19, 21, 51, 62, 116, 120, 127, 130
democratic law 25
democratic legitimacy 1, 5, 7, 17, 18, 19, 74, 83, 85, 136, 137, 141, 143, 165
  across and beyond state borders 5
  conditions on which it relies 5
  conventional models of 18
  conventional and unconventional sources of 7
  flawed 18
  new modes of generating 5
democratic linkages 2
democratic mechanisms 19
democratic order 158–159
democratic practices 2, 3, 4, 14, 16, 18, 165
  involved in making the EU's order 3

democratic rule 7, 137
  key elements of 7
democratic theory 1–3, 7, 14, 16, 104
  associational 7
  beyond the state 2–3
  direct 7
  of European constitutionalisation 1, 158
  of European integration 2–3, 14
  liberal 7
  participatory 7
  principal-agent model of 19
democratisation from below 6, 10
discourse analysis 5, 8–13, 92, 125, 142, 146, 191
discursive framing
  of European integration 5
diversity 1, 13, 15, 23–24, 37, 39, 48–49, 51, 85, 91, 93, 96, 180
  reconciling d. with unity 48

Early Warning Mechanism 121, 122, 125, 127
economic interests, *see* Voting, economic
economic reasons, *see* Voting, economic
EESC, *see* European Economic and Social Committee
elites 1, 4–5, 7, 13, 67, 76, 86, 142, 158
elitist 3, 7, 38, 104
  accounts 3
  focus on EU treaty reform 3
  focus of European integration 7
  in two main varieties 3
empirical data sets 8, 13
EU Citizenship Directives 30
  national implementation of 29, 30
EU preliminary reference mechanism 33
Eurobarometer 68–69, 71, 73–74
Europe as a "discursive battleground" 9, 6
European Citizenship 8, 9, 15, 17, 23–32, 34–41, 44, 47–52, 138–140, 142, 165
  case law, dynamics of 34,
  as challenge to the nation state 51
  competing models of 37
  enhancing popular democratic sovereignties 52
  evolving regime of 24

inclusive, multilayered and
multicultural conception of 23
legal provisions from the Rome to the
Lisbon Treaties 26ff.
as mutually inclusive citizenship 15
as necessary but not sufficient for a
democratically legitimate European
order 52
as postnational, cosmopolitan
citizenship 38
as result of litigation practices by
citizens and courts 24
as secondary to nation state citizenship
37
as supranational European Citizenship
38, 44
universal, cosmopolitan, post-national 23
see also Citizenship of the Union 27
European Citizenship cases 35–36
brought to the ECJ, by nationality and
referring court, 36
European Citizenship rights 1, 4, 15,
28–29, 33–34, 48–51, see also
main EU law provisions after the
Lisbon Treaty, Table 2.1, 28
European constitutionalism 1, 5
constitutional development 5
constitutionalisation 15
contentious politics of 5
evolving norms of 1
European Court of Justice (ECJ) 9, 14–15,
24–37, 39–48, 51–52
citizenship provisions (primary and
secondary law), see Table 2.1, 52ff.
support for competing models of
citizenship in a union of states 49
European demos 18
lack of 18
European Economic and Social Committee
153, 157
European elections 7, 9, 17–18, 66,
165–170, 172–174, 176, 178,
183–185, 187
citizens' participation in 17
as genuine elections 17
less "second order national elections" 17
variation among political parties 92
European Election Study (EES) 172–173

European federalists 1
European identity 6, 51, 68, 75–76, 81,
172–173, 182
European integration 1–11, 14–17, 23,
61–68, 75–76, 83–88, 93, 96–99,
101–104, 116–118, 141–146, 159,
166–171, 178, 183–184
European political communication 15
national political parties in 15
European order 3, 18
bottom up approach to 7
construction of 6
as discursive battleground 6
in interaction with democratic practices
18
as a process of constitutionalisation 3
self-constitution of the 3
European Parliament 17–18, 28, 47, 118,
121, 131, 137, 151–152, 155, 157,
165–166, 170–171, 173, 175,
183–184
European Trade Union Confederation
(ETUC) 140
European Union (EU)
as a confederal model of negative self-
regulation 4
constitutional treaty reform 3, 9, 18,
68, 84, 92, 159
constitutionalisation 1, 4, 8
constitutionalism 4, 6
dual nature of 18, 25, 159
as multilevel political community 19
ratification crisis of 3
as Union of states and citizens 3, 18
Europeanisation 1, 48, 50, 68, 83–85, 96, 103
of domestic politics 1
of member state democracies 3
of national democratic processes 4
Eurosceptic 18, 88, 94, 103

federalist aspirations 4
failure of 4
financial and fiscal crisis in the eurozone 4
France 13, 15, 30, 35–37, 39, 61, 63, 65,
67, 69, 71–76, 84, 91, 93, 99, 101,
103, 115, 118–119, 124, 126–127,
142–143, 145–148, 151, 153, 155,
170, 172, 175–176, 180, 182–183

Germany 13, 29–30, 34–37, 41, 44–46, 53–55, 84, 91, 93–94, 100–101, 103, 124, 126–127
globalisation 24, 37, 139, 147, 149
   in relation to citizenship 24

Hungary 29, 30, 35, 115, 124, 126

inclusion 16, 37–39, 50, 64–66, 136–158
individual human and civic rights 24
immigration 24

Laeken summit 1, 13, 18
legitimacy 1–21, 23, 37, 62, 83–85, 104, 119–121, 135–143, 152, 165
legitimation 16, 135–138, 140–146, 150–153, 157–159
liberal intergovernmentalism 3,
Lisbon Treaty, 1, 9, 13, 16–17, 26–29, 115–116, 118–130
   democratic principles of 27,
   non-discrimination 27
Litigation 1, 5, 8, 15, 24–26, 29, 31–34, 45, 48, 51
   as European Citizenship practice 31ff.
   as form of civil engagement 24
   as form of participatory citizenship practice 26
   as key to the dynamics of citizenship change in the EU 26

Maastricht Treaty 23, 26–27, 29, 116–117
   citizenship provision 27
mass media, *see* media
mass public sphere 5,
media 1–2, 5, 7, 9–10, 12–13, 18, 62–63, 76, 84–88, 90–98, 100–103
member states 1–3, 6, 8–9, 13, 15, 17, 19, 21, 24–27, 29, 31–39, 41–48, 50–51, 66–67, 73, 77, 84–86, 89, 91–92, 96, 117–118, 121, 123, 125, 128, 135–137, 142–144, 146, 148–151, 154, 159, 165–167, 169–170, 172–176, 178, 180, 183–184, 185–186
mobilisation 10, 84, 103

National citizenship regimes 29, 37, 39
   acknowledging the primacy of 39
   recognition of 24
National Courts 24, 26, 29–34, 40, 44, 49, 51
   interaction with European Court of Justice 32
national identity
   "Eros" of 23, 37, 172, 182
national parliament 5, 7–9, 16–17, 110, 115–130, 167
new citizen politics 1
new member states, *see* member states

old member states, *see* member states

Parliament, parliamentary 5, 7–9, 16, 22, 87, 97–99, 100, 115–130, 137, 158, 165, 167
   control mechanisms under the Lisbon Treaty 16, 115
   guardians of the subsidiarity principle 16, 116
   representation 7, 119
   scrutiny 130
   watch-dogs of national governments 16
partisan 86, 90, 96–97, 168, 180, 184
permissive consensus 86, 93
plenary debates 125, 130
Poland 13, 22, 30, 34–36, 45, 84, 91, 99, 101, 103, 115, 119, 124, 126–127, 142–143, 145–146, 148, 151, 153–155, 172–176, 182–183
political conflict 2–3, 5–6, 10–11, 159, 170
   across European member publics 6
   structuring of 6
   transforming patterns of 6
political discourse analysis 5, 8–13, 142, 146, *see also* Comparative Political Discourse Analysis (ComPDA)
political elites, *see* elites
political parties, 1–2, 5, 9, 10, 14–19, 62–63, 66–67, 70, 72, 75–76, 84–104, 108, 131, 143, 151–153, 155, 166–173, 176–184
political sociology 2–3, 5, 7–8, 64
   of democratic integration beyond the state 3

of democratisation of the Union 18
  of the EU 2
  of European integration 5, 7–8
politicisation 1, 2, 4, 18, 65, 153, 159
  of domestic EU politics 4
  of EU constitutional reform 2
postfunctional approaches to European
  integration 4
protest politics 5
Protocol on the Role of National
  Parliaments in the European Union
  121, *see also* Parliament
public opinion 7, 13, 17, 19, 78, 84–86, 90,
  96, 98–99, 102, 104, 116, 140, 142,
  159, 170
public sphere 1, 5, 11, 14, 18, 83–85, 91,
  101–103, 136, 139–142, 146,
  149–150, 158–161, 170
public support 5, 18, 67, 87
  for the EU 5

Qualitative Comparative Analysis (QCA)
  8, 9, 15, 89–90, 97, 101, 107

referendum(s) 1, 5, 7–9, 15, 17–18, 61–63,
  68–71, 73, 76–77, 87, 93, 96–101,
  103–104, 125, 159, 165, 183
  national referendum(s) about EU treaty
    reform 15
reflexive integration in the EU 6
representation 4–7, 12, 118–121, 136–146,
  153, 157–158, 171, 176–178, 184

salient EU issues 84, 97, 169
second-order-election 66, 85, 165,
  167–169, 107, 171, 176, 184
social field 6–8, 19
  of citizens' civil society participation
    practices 5, 7, 165
  of EU treaty ratification through
    popular referendums 5, 8
  of European citizens' political practices
    7
  of European (and national) electoral
    participation practices 5

of legal-judicial litigation practices 5,
  8
of making the EU's order 5
of parliamentary EU treaty reform
  ratification practices 5, 8
of political party communication
  practices 5, 8
as preconditions for citizen's agency in
  European politics 8
selection of 8
as socially constructed "field of action"
  7
social movements 5, 10, 31, 139, 147–149
Social Partnership Dialogue 152–153
spillover effects by judicial decisions 25
State sovereignty 23
subsidiarity 16, 116, 120–122, 127–130
supranational unity, principle of 23

TCE (Treaty on the Constitution for
  Europe) 61–63, 65–77, 82, 84, 87,
  89, 91–95, 98, 100–104, 110–111,
  136, 141–159
third-country long-term residents 28, 43,
  see also main EU law provisions
  after the Lisbon Treaty, Table 2.1,
  p. 28
transnationalisation 159, 170
transparency 122, 136–142, 146, 150,
  157–158
Treaty of Lisbon 83, 115, 121–123, 118,
  119, 120, 122, 127
Turnout, electoral 9, 15, 17–18, 64, 69–72,
  165–176, 180, 182–184

Union Citizenship, *see* European
  Citizenship
United Kingdom 29, 34, 53, 84, 94, 98, 99,
  101, 103, 115, 124, 170, 176
Unity 48
  reconciling with diversity 48

Volkswagen Foundation 2n1
Voting, economic 63, 65, 67, 72, 75, 170